I0086248

Double Standards, Single Purpose

Double Standards, Single Purpose

REFORMING HOUSING REGULATIONS TO REDUCE POVERTY

Saad Yahya, Elijah Agevi, Lucky Lowe,
Alex Mugova, Oscar Musandu-Nyamayaro
and Theo Schilderman

Practical
ACTION
PUBLISHING

Practical Action Publishing Ltd
25 Albert Street, Rugby, CV21 2SD, Warwickshire, UK
www.practicalactionpublishing.com

© Intermediate Technology Publications 2001

First published 2001\Digitised 2013

ISBN 10: 1 85339 525 0
ISBN 13 Paperback: 9781853395253
ISBN Library Ebook: 9781780443171
Book DOI: https://doi.org/10.3362/9781780443171

All rights reserved. No part of this publication may be reprinted or reproduced
or utilized in any form or by any electronic, mechanical, or other means, now
known or hereafter invented, including photocopying and recording, or in any
information storage or retrieval system, without the written permission of the
publishers.

A catalogue record for this book is available from the British Library.

The authors, contributors and/or editors have asserted their rights under the
Copyright Designs and Patents Act 1988 to be identified as authors of their
respective contributions.

Since 1974, Practical Action Publishing has published and disseminated books
and information in support of international development work throughout
the world. Practical Action Publishing is a trading name of Practical Action
Publishing Ltd (Company Reg. No. 01159018), the wholly owned publishing
company of Practical Action. Practical Action Publishing trades only in support
of its parent charity objectives and any profits are covenanted back to Practical
Action (Charity Reg. No. 247257, Group VAT Registration No. 880 9924 76).

Reasonable efforts have been made to publish reliable data and information,
but the author and publisher cannot assume responsibility for the validity of all
materials or for the consequences of their use.

The manufacturer's authorised representative in the EU for product safety is
Lightning Source France, 1 Av. Johannes Gutenberg, 78310 Maurepas, France.
compliance@lightningsource.fr

Contents

Illustrations

Boxes

Tables

Foreword

At least six hundred million of our fellow men and women are living in health- and life-threatening conditions. It is therefore important that no effort be spared in the search for relevant solutions. Inadequate shelter has been found to be a major contributory factor to ill health and social stress among poor people especially those living in urban areas, which are becoming increasingly important places of residence, work and economic activity throughout the world. It is estimated that by the year 2015 one person in five will be living in urban agglomerations of more than a million.

The manner in which people house themselves is, however, anything but haphazard. It is guided by a complex web of rules, codes and regulations which in large measure determine not only the quality of housing, but also its cost. Thus a family's ability to access decent shelter is closely linked to the standards in use, but existing codes in many developing countries do not make housing more available or affordable since they originate from a colonial past and are inappropriate to today's conditions. The needs of millions of people living in poverty and in unplanned settlements cannot be met by a regulatory system which relies on outmoded and rigid technical prescriptions that do not take into account what ordinary people think, say and do.

This book presents research work on housing standards in several countries and the methods used to revise codes so as to make them more relevant to the needs of the poor. It focuses on the standards revision process, the methods adopted, the participants and possible outcomes. The research results have highlighted the need for commitment, single-mindedness and creativity. They have also stressed the need for inclusiveness and participation. All these are values which UNCHS (Habitat) has consistently espoused in its pursuit of pragmatic and acceptable solutions to the challenges of human settlements. UNCHS is committed to working, together with its partners, towards achieving substantive reforms in the design and management of building codes, infrastructure standards and planning regulations, especially where they affect the living conditions of low-income households.

These issues were the subject of international debate among governments, non-governmental organizations and private sector representatives in Istanbul at the 1996 Habitat II Conference, where the Habitat Agenda was adopted by 171 governments. Five years after Istanbul, in June 2001, the General Assembly of the United Nations will hold a special session in New York known as Istanbul +5, to review and appraise implementation of the Habitat Agenda worldwide. In assessing progress towards the implementation of the Habitat Agenda commitments and strategies, governments will prepare country reports incorporating the view of all partners. I have no doubt that the ideas developed in this book will enrich that event. Apart from stimulating debate on housing standards, the findings will also promote awareness of the linkages between housing standards and poverty reduction. UNCHS

(Habitat) will for its part support activities in those areas that have been identified as worthy of further attention, such as appropriate institutions for reviewing and enforcing standards and infrastructure guidelines for informal settlements. In this regard, the Global Campaign for Secure Tenure will stress the need for compatible land development standards and enabling regulations. The parallel Campaign for Good Governance also emphasizes the need for efficiency and equity in regulatory efforts.

This book is a commendable example of successful international collaboration between developing country researchers, international non-governmental organizations and donor countries. It is most important that many more such partnerships are created and made to work. I wish to thank both the United Kingdom's Department for International Development and the Intermediate Technology Development Group for their contribution towards realizing the goals of the Habitat Agenda, and the authors for sharing the knowledge that project research and interventions have generated.

Dr Anna Kajumalo Tibaijuka
Executive Director
UNCHS (Habitat)

Acknowledgements

The authors would like to thank everybody who has contributed to this book. Our gratitude goes in the first place to the urban residents of Nakuru in Kenya and Chitungwiza in Zimbabwe, who have given their time, insights and opinions on the issue of housing standards as it affects their livelihoods. Our thanks also go to the excellent field staff – Absolom Masendeke, Peter Tawodzera and Timothy Madziwa in Zimbabwe; Josiah Omotto, Margaret Ng'ayu and Amon Ng'anga as well as Nura Ahmed, Kukuwa Saleh and Milka Langat in Kenya. At the same time, we are grateful to the councillors and professional staff of the municipalities concerned for becoming partners in the project, and jointly moving the standards issue forward at the local level.

Over the four years of research, we have been able to establish a network of shelter specialists with a specific interest in standards, regulations and procedures. Some of them – Khaled Abdelhalim (Egypt), Emmanuel Byaruhanga (Uganda), Osita Okonkwo (Malawi), Mamadou Diagne (Senegal), Pauline McHardy (Jamaica), Li Shirong and Wei Ming (China); Susil Sirivardana (Sri Lanka); Stuti Lall (India); Natan Jere (Zambia), Liz Kraayenbrink (RSA) and Vincent Ragassi (Earth building standards for Africa) – have contributed country or regional case studies, for which we are most grateful.

Many more stakeholders, including representatives of community-based and non-governmental organizations, as well as various authorities, standards bodies and private practices participated in a number of workshops, seminars and conferences organized by the project in Kenya, Zimbabwe and the UK. Our thanks go to all those who provided their time and ideas to those events which helped to shape this book. We are especially grateful to the Institution of Civil Engineers in London for hosting the final international conference, and to members of its Appropriate Development Panel, including Diana Mitlin, Rob Petts, Andy Cotton and Darlene Torey, for organizing the event.

The research for this book would not have been possible without funding from the UK's Department for International Development (DFID). We are also encouraged in our future work by the growing emphasis that DFID is placing on the issue of standards and regulations in its own strategies.

For work behind the scenes, our special thanks go to Sue O'Herlihy and Maristela Coupe for producing the range of case studies and for typing the text (with others in Kenya), and to Kimberly Clarke for editing the book.

The publishers would like to thank the following for giving permission to use their photographs: Lucky Lowe (photos 2, 3, 5, 7, 8 and 10), Morris Keyonzo (photos 6 and 11), Theo Schilderman (photos 1 and 4), and Colin Parker (photo 9). The publishers would also like to thank Ahmed Soliman for permission to use the cover photograph.

Acronyms

AAK	Architectural Association of Kenya
ABT	appropriate building technologies
ALGAK	Association of Local Government Authorities of Kenya
APPEP	Andhra Pradesh Primary Education Project
ARSO	African Regional Standards Organization
ASCEND	Association for Settlement and Commercial Enterprise for National Development
BBC	British Broadcasting Corporation
BSI	British Standards Institute
CBO	community-based organization
CDCs	community development councils
CEB	compressed earth blocks
CECS	China Association of Construction Standardization
CNN	Cable News Network
CODINORM	Organisme Ivoirien de Normalisation et de Certification
CRATerre-EAG	Earth Building Centre, Grenoble School of Architecture
CSC	Commonwealth Science Council
DFID	Department for International Development
DSQMC	Department of Standards and Quotas of the Ministry of Construction
EHSP	Enabling Housing Standards and Procedures
ESCAP	Economic and Social Commission for Asia and the Pacific
FCR	fibre concrete roofing (tiles)
FDI	foreign direct investment
FGD	focused group discussion
FOVI	Mexican Housing Trust Fund
GoK	Government of Kenya
GTZ	German Technical Co-operation Agency
HIOMC	Housing Industrialization Office of the Ministry of Construction
HRDU	Housing Research and Development Unit
ICRC	International Commission of the Red Cross
ILD	Instituto para la Libertad y Democracia – Institute for Freedom and Democracy, Peru
ININVI	Instituto Nacional de Investigación y Normalización de la Vivienda
ISO	International Standards Organization
ITDG	Intermediate Technology Development Group
IUHP	Integrated Urban Housing Project
IULA	International Union of Local Authorities

KWS	Kenya Wildlife Service
LA	local authority
LOCOMAT	Local Materials Organization, Burkina Faso
LSD	local standardization department
MANTAG	minimum agrément norms and technical advisory guide
MCN	Municipal Council of Nakuru
MCR	micro concrete roofing (tiles)
MLGRUD	Ministry of Local Government Rural and Urban Development
MOC	Minstry of Construction, China
MOLA	Ministry of Local Authorities, Kenya
MPCNH	Ministry of Public Construction and National Housing
NACHU	National Cooperative Housing Union
NCC	Nairobi City Commission/Council
NGO	non-governmental organization
NHC	National Housing Corporation
NPA	National Plan of Action
RIBA	Royal Institute of British Architects
RSA	Republic of South Africa
SABS	South African Bureau of Standards
SHHA	Self Help Housing Authority
SSBs	stabilized soil blocks
THA	traditional housing areas
UK	United Kingdom
UNCHS	United Nations Centre for Human Settlements
UNDP	United Nations Development Programme
UNHCR	United Nations High Commission for Refugees
UNICEF	United Nations Children's Fund
USA	United States of America
USAID	United States Agency for International Development
WEDC	Water Engineering and Development Centre
WHO	World Health Organization
WWF	Worldwide Fund for Nature

1
FACETS AND FOUNDATIONS

Introduction

Since 1990 the crisis of poverty in the South has become more concentrated in urban areas, a process influenced by global trends and events. As a result, many development agencies that have traditionally worked in rural areas have found that their skills and resources are increasingly needed in urban areas. The Intermediate Technology Development Group (ITDG) was no exception, and it soon became apparent to the members of its International Shelter Programme that the key to solving the problems of urban shelter in developing countries lay in formulating and applying appropriate standards, regulations and procedures. Working with the urban poor, particularly in Africa, ITDG learned that the existing standards often impair the livelihoods of the poor. This finding was first noticed in projects focusing on income generation in the informal construction sector, where the absence of standards for alternative materials and technologies, such as building with soil, stabilized soil or micro-concrete roofing tiles proved to be a major barrier in preventing the informal sector from increasing its share of the urban shelter market. At the same time, the lack of appropriate building materials denied poor people access to affordable shelter. When the lot of the poor with regard to urban shelter is considered, much larger constraints appear. Less than half of the urban population in developing countries can afford to build according to the prevailing standards. Their lack of legal tenure makes them vulnerable to eviction and violence; it also severely limits their access to housing finance; both factors combine to make the poor less inclined and less able to improve the poor housing conditions that currently affect their health and productivity. The poor are also often prevented from developing their house as an asset from which income can be generated. Complicated procedures and lack of transparency add to their problems; it generally takes the urban poor far too much time and money to legalize the arrangements they have made for shelter.

It can be argued that the prevailing high level of standards and regulations is morally wrong, in that it stimulates the emergence of dualistic cities which formally recognize a minority of the population as legal residents, while an ever-increasing majority of people live unrecognized in informal and illegal settlements, where they are at considerable risk. In the authors' experience, it is also bad economic policy: the simplification of standards and procedures will increase the provision of shelter and generate much-needed employment and income in the more labour-intensive informal construction sector.

There is hardly a country or a society in the world which does not regulate the manner in which its citizens can build and occupy houses. Methods vary widely between, and even within, countries, and while written laws may exist, there is often a set of conventions which guides artisans and master builders, irrespective of the building code. In the developing world, population growth and a colonial legacy of inappropriate laws and procedures has left nearly a billion people in urban areas without adequate shelter. Today urban development in the South is dominated by informal activities and conventional construction activity is declining. Any discussion of standards has to be qualified by a number of questions: Standards for whom? Standards for now or the future? How can adequate provision of shelter, water, drainage, roads and other services be made at an affordable cost? What is adequate? Who should control whom? What are the appropriate methods of reform? These are some of the fundamental questions that this book tries to answer.

This book is based on an extensive survey of existing policies, laws and practices, supplemented by case studies and examples from a number of countries. Chapter 1 explains the effect that standards have on people's access to affordable legal shelter, looking at the evolution of standards and the different ways in which they are applied and enforced. The catalysts for change are outlined in Chapter 2, and both existing revision procedures and innovative approaches are described. Two case studies, from Kenya and Zimbabwe, are presented in Chapters 3 and 4 respectively. Chapters 5 and 6 contain recommendations resulting from the survey and fieldwork.

Shelter needs

As the environment in which people build shelters in which to live and work changes, so must the way in which they build, to ensure that the occupants will be safe, comfortable and protected from diverse weather and natural disasters, pests, vermin and disease, and to guarantee that the shelter suits the needs of the occupants. The rules of urban building are so diverse and culture-specific that no one group of people can claim to have the best system, only the best system for their local needs.

High levels of dependency on the state in the last quarter of the twentieth century resulted in decreased public spending, discouraged public and private investment in many countries and reduced household incomes and the capacity to borrow. Investment in housing and related infrastructure suffered, especially in the South where structural adjustment programmes severely curtailed public expenditure on social services. A series of complex structural changes in the world economy have affected the pattern of urban living (UNCHS 1996), greatly increasing the flow of migrants into urban areas. These changes include the relative depreciation of the exchange value of natural resources; the rapid growth in international trade coupled with a phenomenal expansion in the financial services business (the total capitalization of the world's stock markets increased more than sixteen-fold in the period 1974–94); the globalization of the media business and organizational systems in manufacturing and production; advances in information and documentation technology that have vastly expanded the operational scope of companies; and the increased mobility of capital across borders. As governments have reduced regulation, liberalized their economic activities and transferred into private hands a wide range of public assets, their role as providers of shelter and other essentials of social well-being has diminished.

The challenges facing those building cities today are much greater than those of only twenty years ago. Today large cities have become para-states in their own right, with the average population of the world's hundred largest cities exceeding five million inhabitants in 1990 – greater than the population of many thriving and vibrant nations. Changes in both economic and social conditions have profoundly affected the pace and quality of urbanization. The transition from agriculture to services as the dominant economic activity in most countries, changes in household size and age structure in the North, the eclipse of colonialism, and the demise of communism are only some of the factors shaping the world today.

It is estimated that about half the world's population now live in urban centres. This statistic represents a dramatic change, not only in terms of the density of people, but also in the way they live. Most urban residents live in Asia and Europe (see Table 1.1). In Africa and Latin America there has been a significant reduction in the average age of the population, with children accounting for about 50 per cent, whereas in Europe and North America the population is gradually ageing and household size is shrinking. In marked contrast to the situation in the South, over a quarter of all households in Europe consist of only one person, and the average household size is less than three people. A quarter of all European families are headed by one parent, and one marriage in three ends in divorce. These changing demographics are important, as household size is an important determinant of residential space requirements. Room sizes and space standards as well as water supply and sanitation criteria need to be based on both the number and the living habits of the residents.

Urban residents in the North on middle or high incomes can usually buy, build or rent adequate accommodation, but those on low incomes often find themselves trapped in substandard housing or, in the worst case, homeless. In the South the situation is much worse. The majority of households are on low incomes, and much of the housing available is of such poor quality that it seriously threatens their health – and in some cases their lives – and keeps them in a state of poverty.

The World Health Organization (WHO) has identified ten features of poor housing that contribute directly or indirectly to poor health (Table 1.2). All these features are common in housing environments inhabited by the poor.

Outside the home, environmental risks can arise from uncollected rubbish, poor drainage and the many bacteria that thrive in solid and liquid waste. Additional hazards result from:

- accidents on the roads, footpaths and in open spaces
- buildings erected on dangerous sites, such as flood plains, steep slopes and polluted ground
- exposure to dangerous chemicals, whether agro-chemicals or industrial (some unplanned settlements are situated close to industrial sites)
- air pollution, which in the industrialized countries is linked to a rise in the number of asthma attacks, especially among children, an increase in chronic breathing problems among elderly people, and in respiratory tract infections for children. Sulphur dioxide, suspended particulates, lead, ozone and carbon monoxide are some of the pollutants that cause concern.
- toxic and hazardous wastes. The high cost of storing and disposing of such substances tempts industrialized countries to dump such waste in the South, where the poor are the most likely people to be exposed to such waste. Regulations to deal with toxic wastes are non-existent in many countries.
- excessive noise levels in locations close to airports, major highways and industrial operations and construction activities. Noise levels were reported to reach 90 decibels during rush hours in some parts of Shanghai (UNCHS 1996).
- natural hazards such as earthquakes, floods and landslides.

Table 1.1 World population and urbanization trends

	Total population (millions)			Average annual population growth rate (%)		Urban population (millions)		Urban population (% of total population)		Population in cities of more than one million (% of total population)			Population in the largest city (% of urban population)	
	1980	1997	2015	1980–97	1997–2015	1980	1997	1980	1997	1980	1995	2015	1980	1995
World	4 429.9	5 819.6	7 101.4	1.6	1.1	1 748.2	2 676.0	39	46	14	16	18	18	17
Low income	1 385.6	2 035.6	2 758.8	2.3	1.7	307.7	577.7	22	28	6	9	13	16	19
Middle income	2 217.3	2 856.9	3 370.4	1.5	0.9	824.3	1 389.9	37	49	12	16	18	19	16
Lower middle income	1 792.5	2 282.9	2 663.0	1.4	0.9	559.0	966.2	31	42	10	13	16	16	14
Upper middle income	424.9	573.9	707.4	1.8	1.2	265.4	423.7	62	74	22	27	27	24	20
Low and middle income	3 602.9	4 892.5	6 129.2	1.8	1.3	1 132.1	1 967.7	31	40	10	13	16	18	17
East Asia and Pacific	1 359.4	1 751.2	2 050.6	1.5	0.9	288.4	578.0	21	33	8	11	14	13	9
Europe and Central Asia	425.8	474.0	487.3	0.6	0.2	240.1	317.7	56	67	14	16	18	15	15

continued on next page

Table 1.1 World population and urbanization trends (cont.)

	Total population (millions)			Average annual population growth rate (%)		Urban population (millions)		% of total population		Population in cities of more than one million % of total population			Population in the largest city % of urban population	
	1980	1997	2015	1980–97	1997–2015	1980	1997	1980	1997	1980	1995	2015	1980	1995
Latin America and Caribbean	360.3	493.9	624.3	1.9	1.3	233.8	366.5	65	74	24	28	28	27	25
Middle East and North Africa	174.1	279.6	393.9	2.7	1.9	83.7	161.9	48	58	17	21	23	31	27
South Asia	902.6	1 282.3	1 651.9	2.1	1.4	198.5	345.5	22	27	6	10	13	9	11
Sub-Saharan Africa	380.7	612.3	921.3	2.8	2.3	87.6	198.0	23	32	5	8	12	28	30
High income	826.9	927.0	972.1	0.7	0.3	616.1	708.4	75	76	31	33	35	17	16
Europe EMU	275.9	290.6	286.8	0.3	-0.1	203.7	222.4	74	77	25	25	25	16	15

Source: World Bank 1999

Table 1.2   Features of the housing environment that have important direct or indirect effects on the health of the occupants

- the structure of the shelter (which includes a consideration of the extent to which the shelter protects the occupants from extremes of heat or cold, insulation against noise, and invasion by dust, rain, insects and rodents)
- the adequacy of the water supply – both the quality and quantity
- the effectiveness of the disposal (and subsequent management) of excreta and liquid and solid wastes
- the quality of the housing site, including the extent to which it is structurally safe for housing and the extent to which provision is made to protect it from contamination (of which provision for drainage is among the most important aspects)
- the consequence of over-crowding – including household accidents and airborne infections whose transmission is increased: acute respiratory infectious diseases, pneumonia, and tuberculosis.
- the presence of indoor air pollution associated with fuels used for cooking and/or heating
- food safety standards – including the extent to which the shelter has adequate storage space to protect food from contamination
- vectors and hosts of diseases associated with the domestic and peri-domestic environment
- the home as a workplace – where occupational health questions such as the use and storage of toxic or hazardous chemicals and health and safety aspects of equipment used need consideration
- violence, especially against women and children; also exposure to criminal behaviour

Source: Adapted from World Health Organization 1989

These features of poor housing and environmental risks and hazards also highlight the type and scope of regulatory instruments that can be used to control housing quality and, ultimately, improve the lives and prospects of residents.

In recent years greater emphasis has been placed on the quality of housing stock and minimum affordable standards, rather than on the quantity. Experts used to be obsessed with the number of houses needed per 1000 people, but in reality these targets were never reached and were meaningless. The problem of accurate assessment is made worse by the absence of a universally acknowledged definition of what constitutes a house or dwelling. Depending on how 'home' is defined, there could be anything between 100 million and one billion homeless people worldwide. This estimate could include people who sleep outside or in public buildings, night shelters for homeless people, poor quality accommodation, refugee camps and temporary shelters. The term 'homeless' could also be extended to include people living in shared and overcrowded accommodation, as well as women exposed to domestic violence and children subjected to sexual abuse. About 2.5 million people were homeless in the European Union countries in the early 1990s. A large proportion of these (70 per cent) were people under 40. Applying the same standards to Africa or South America would produce atrociously high figures.

At least one billion people live in absolute poverty, without adequate food, clothing and shelter – of these, more than 90 per cent live in the South. Over 600 million people in urban areas live in houses and neighbourhoods that are 'life- and health-threatening' because of poor living conditions, including inadequate water, sanitation, rubbish removal and access. Improving housing conditions can significantly reduce the impact of poverty. An international comparative study of housing quality undertaken by the Housing Indicators Programme (World Bank 1999) provides data on the shelter situation in 1990 in 52 cities covering about a tenth of the world's urban population. The study highlights some important facts:

- Richer countries have larger and better quality housing stock than their poorer counterparts, with a larger proportion of dwellings built of permanent materials and having piped water on the plot.
- There are large differences in housing quality between countries with comparable per capita income, probably a result of differences in government housing policies, especially those relating to the supply of land, materials, infrastructure and finance.
- In high-income countries the average floor area per person is nearly six times that in low-income countries (see Table 1.3), while the number of people per room is under a quarter as much.
- The faster a city is growing, the more likely it is to have a high proportion of houses built of temporary materials.
- Some municipal authorities in poor countries spend less than US$10 per person per annum on shelter-related services and infrastructure, while those in high-income countries spend as much as $1000, or even $2020 in the case of Helsinki. These figures cover capital and operating costs for roads, sanitation, and refuse collection.
- While the house price to income ratio is remarkably similar between countries, there are considerable variations in house sizes and prices. An average house in Tokyo (41m^2) costs more than two-and-a-half times as much as one in Washington, DC (161m^2).
- Cities that are growing rapidly generally have high rent-to-income ratios. (Comparisons of rental levels are made complex by rent controls and subsidized public housing.)

Interesting facts, but this and other international studies raise more questions. What are permanent materials? What type of national policies contribute to raising housing standards? To what extent is room occupancy influenced by cultural, rather than economic, factors? Are yardsticks of acceptability and legality comparable between nations? Important questions in a world where nearly two-thirds of the housing stock in low-income countries consists of unauthorized structures. Not surprisingly, this proportion declines as per capita income rises. It is not clear whether higher incomes lead to better houses, or better houses result in higher incomes.

Is regulation necessary?

Why should law-abiding citizens be regulated when building the house of their choice on their own land with their own money? Academics, investors and developers hold conflicting views about whether or not regulation – in the form of standards and codes – is necessary. On the one hand, the arguments against regulation are that the bulk of urban residential development is (and always will be) unregulated; that regulation slows down the development process and favours the rich; that it increases the cost of housing; and that it is burdened with heavy baggage from colonial days that is no longer relevant to present needs and cultures in the South. In addition, some believe market forces ensure

Table 1.3   An international comparison of housing quality

Income categories	Floor area per person (m²)	People per room	Percentage of permanent structures	Percentage of dwelling units with water connection to their plot
Low-income countries	6.1	2.47	67	56
Low–mid-income countries	8.8	2.24	86	74
Middle-income countries	15.1	1.69	94	94
Mid–high-income countries	22.0	1.03	99	99
High-income countries	35.0	0.66	100	100

Source: World Bank 1993

product quality: good products sell, poor ones do not. Moreover, unwritten rules and social norms already influence the type of housing built and materials used, the amount of space between houses, and the location of houses in relation to other buildings and facilities such as places of worship, graveyards, rubbish tips, streets, open spaces and places of work.

The proponents of regulation, on the other hand, point to the complexity of modern urban living and the vast array of threats that arise from overcrowding, accidents, fire, disease, pollution, natural hazards, and so on. There is no way, they argue, to ensure and safeguard residents' health, let alone their survival, security, and well-being, without enforcing a comprehensive set of regulations. In addition, owners of housing built according to regulations and with secure tenure are generally more inclined to invest in their property.

Two Chinese engineers write that:

> The use of technical housing standards and codes is a fundamental method used to organize modern construction projects. With the guidance of regulations, standardization of administration in housing projects can be achieved; quality can be improved and guaranteed; speed of construction can be accelerated; material can be saved; funding can be reasonably used; new technology can be adopted; human beings' health can be assured; safety can be achieved; and efficiency can be improved.

Housing standards (technical regulations) must be met under Chinese law but in practice there are some difficulties during implementation. It is well known that effective implementation of housing standards depends on all parties involved in any construction project. The government has set up approval processes pertaining to every stage of construction. Different government organizations and agencies are involved in this work; clients, designers and contractors are required to implement related standards by themselves.

Shirong and Ming 1999

In China, as elsewhere, a wide range of housing standards are enshrined in the statute books as part of construction, housing, urban development and public health legislation. The need to define rights, obligations and duties in plain language has resulted in a legalistic approach to the formulation and documentation of standards. The unintended result is that standards are usually difficult to understand, and often do not take account of social and cultural requirements. Even lawyers admit that:

Research on law would make greater contribution to development if it ... examined the social origins and functions of law, explored the relationship between legal rules and institutions and specific developmental efforts, and examined the actual and potential impact of law on developmental goals.

International Legal Center 1972

The allegations made against the legal profession may also be levelled at policymakers and building professionals, who tend to isolate housing standards both from the housing that results and from many people or groups who use the standards. Standards and regulations do not apply only to the way in which a house is built. There are in fact six key areas in which standards apply and which affect poor people's ability to secure adequate housing:

- land ownership and security of tenure
- indigenous building materials production
- affordability
- cost of procedures
- enforcement
- financing.

Land ownership and security of tenure

Land is a prerequisite to house construction and a key component in determining housing accessibility. In many developing countries urban expansion is occurring through the illegal occupation of public and private land at the periphery of towns and cities. Squatting is often the only affordable housing option for poor people. Faced with a housing shortage, yet also responsible for safeguarding private property rights, governments have attempted to solve the squatting 'problem' in various ways, including the mass demolition of informal settlements and evictions of squatters. As these attempts failed, they have opted for 'in-situ regularization' instead of 'relocation and redevelopment' (Mohammed 1997:235). Land occupation is not a secure form of ownership, but already 'millions of established squatters have accumulated land rights through adverse possession' (World Bank 1993:155).

Not all squatters are poor. Land grabbing by the affluent is equally problematic in developing countries and politically very sensitive. Buying and selling activities where numerous interests – traditional, colonial, commercial, individual and public – converge, is further complicated by ineffective, and sometimes corrupt, land registration and transfer systems. Numerous bureaucratic bottlenecks and costs make land transactions time-consuming and expensive. Many government simply do not have the systems and procedures in place to establish a comprehensive picture of existing land ownership, nor the means to register or transfer ownership in an efficient and open manner. When land use is highly controlled, the impact, in terms of access and affordability, can also be detrimental.

> Land use and zoning regulations ... restrict the availability and hence raise the price of residential land ... [In] Seoul, Korea, rural-to-urban land conversion is severely restricted because of rigidly enforced greenbelt regulations ... [which] has resulted in explosive increases in the price of land and housing, severely decreased housing affordability, and persistent housing shortages.
>
> World Bank 1993:83

During the 1980s, the process of acquiring and developing urban land in Peru took 83 months if the developer complied with all the established requirements. Such a waste of time and resources 'must be viewed as the main restriction which makes access to formality so expensive that ... the only course is informal urbanization' (De Soto 1989:142).

Simplifying procedures and building capacity in land management agencies can improve accessibility. In Colombia, for example, the reform of service provision and land subdivision regulations from 1979 to 1980 resulted in increased accessibility to housing. In Mexico, a study found that 'an average of 25 per cent of the cost of new residential construction is attributable to clearly excessive local regulation' (World Bank 1993:41). FOVI, a housing trust fund within the Central Bank of Mexico, 'offers financial and technical assistance to participating states to computerize their land registration systems' (World Bank 1993).

Given the value and scarcity of land in most urban locations, any revision of standards must consider minimum plot sizes. Urban and peri-urban settlements of the colonial era were spacious and accordingly expensive to service. Harare's older streets offer ample evidence of an environment built when 'land pressure' was not a consideration. Plot sizes are a matter of not only land availability or affordability, but also political motivation. At the time of independence, popular and political opinion was generally critical of the Government of Zimbabwe's attempts to reduce plot sizes, and it subsequently *increased* the statutory minimum from 200 to 300m^2 (see Chapter 4). However, in India, pressure on land led to a considerable reduction in minimum plot sizes, which are now 26m^2 in some urban centres.

It is perhaps not surprising, given the magnitude of investment required to secure adequate housing, that the reduction in risk associated with increased land regularization results in greater investment by household 'owners'. 'Where governments acknowledged the existence of the settlement by providing infrastructure services and issuing long-term leases, as in Pakistan, or occupancy permits, as in Zambia, domestic investments increased substantially' (World Bank 1993:116). Research in Peru also suggests that 'the level of investment in housing is ... determined by the measure of legal security which the state confers on the settlement' (De Soto 1989:24). The national average differential in housing investment between legally recognized and illegal settlements was estimated to be in the order of 9:1, and was shown to be as high as 41:1 in two neighbouring settlements, one deemed 'permanent' and the other 'removable' (De Soto 1989).

Increased security generally offers the poor a safety net, an asset and collateral which generates increased investment. The granting of government-owned land to squatters is a form of 'progressive subsidy' which does tend to reach the poor, and it can be an effective policy measure where public land is accessible or where adequate resources are available for land acquisition.

Indigenous building materials production

'No matter what is promulgated in an endeavour to set desirable building standards, the quality of the end result of any building exercise rests with the materials used and the work-manship employed' (Barritt 1995:4). A desire to lessen their dependency on imported, industrialized building materials and the associated need for foreign exchange are key factors motivating governments to develop standards that allow – and encourage – local production of building materials. The constraints imposed by existing standards, however, 'hampered the adoption of simplified designs and the more widespread use of local materials in the formal housing sector' (Athman 1992:15; see also Lowe 1998a:16).

Legislation created during colonial times is notorious for its dogged insistence on indus-trialized materials and design practices. Reducing the costs of building materials is an important way to increase accessibility to housing by decreasing not only the need for foreign currency, but also the high costs of transporting those materials. Cement is one notable example of a high-cost, high-status material used in house building that is costly in both monetary and environmental terms: 'à un coût de revient tres onéreux au regard du pouvoir d'achat de chaque citoyen' (a heavy price in relation to the purchasing power of each citizen; Wodobode 1996:2; see also Ganesan 1979).

Several international agencies have supported initiatives to introduce national and regional standards for locally produced building materials. UNCHS, the Commonwealth Science Council (CSC) and the African Regional Standards Organization (ARSO) see production and usage standards as an effective mechanism to support local materials and construction sectors by reducing costs and increasing consistency of quality, and thereby increasing demand and market access. The lengthy procedures and international efforts instigated by the Earth Building Centre, Grenoble School of Architecture (CRATerre-EAG) to introduce pan-African standards for earth-based building components, for example, have shown that collaboration on a regional basis can establish the technical credibility of 'alterna-tive' building materials and enable governments to introduce the standards at a national level (Wodobode 1996). Despite numerous setbacks, CRATerre-EAG drew on years of research, experience and consultation with experts, civil servants and politicians to put in place agreed standards.

In the commercial sector, TERKOCAM in Cameroon advocated the incorporation of stabilized soil blocks (SSBs) into national materials standards. Profit is an important motive for producers, but official standards do help 'alternative building technologies to gain recognition and thereby improve the supply of indigenously produced building components and meet the demand for affordable housing' (Kuete Sonkoue 1996). It is therefore important that small-scale materials producers are encouraged to observe national standards in the manufacture of their products – it increases demand for their products.

Materials testing and standardization will also support the production and usage of local building materials by reducing costs, enhancing market acceptability, improving professional confidence and increasing knowledge. Primarily by eradicating the duplication of efforts, building and materials research institutions play a key role in establishing and monitoring standards: liaison with them is essential (Tanzania Ministry of Works 1977). Standards also offer 'critères pratiques pour leur mise en oeuvre' (practical guidance for implementation) for stakeholders involved in design and construction (Barama 1996).

'Lack of standards and performance criteria discourages innovation and places the regulatory official in a difficult position of accepting or rejecting innovation. If there is doubt he must primarily be concerned for the regulatory requirements and health and safety of the occupants' (Moudzingoula 1996). (The public appears not to recognize this concern or responsibility in developing countries, where the building control function is seen instead as a means for local authority officials to demand payment from those needing approval.) Interviews with municipal engineers working with communities in Nakuru, Kenya, highlighted how their confidence in SSBs was built up through the processes of field-testing soils and blocks, and finding that they complied with the Kenyan National Bureau of Standards' rules (Lowe 1999a). Without such authoritative back-up it is not surprising that any professional would err on the side of caution and choose conventional, proven options. In addition to informing officials, NGOs (non-governmental organizations) have been instrumental in devising standards for technologies that meet the demand for enhanced durability and generate income for small- to medium-scale producers in developing countries. The *FCR/MCR Toolkit* produced and published by the Swiss NGO SKAT is a notable example.

An international workshop organized by ITDG, CSC and ARSO highlighted the significance of standards in meeting demand and supply requirements and identified earth, clay fired bricks, lime pozzolanas and fibre-reinforced cement tiles as key materials requiring national standards. Suggested courses of action to gain standards for these products include greater involvement by African countries, greater information exchange, training, appropriate technology transfer, innovations in production, co-ordination between international agencies on research and development, practical demonstration and international donor support to build institutional capacity (ARSO/CSC/UNCHS Workshop 1987). The UNCHS also subscribes to the view that building regulations and standards based on performance criteria are needed in order to encourage research into both local building materials and the development of techniques ignored and not yet included in national building codes.

Affordability

What is required is technical assistance to plan, design, build, budget, and operate that which is affordable, not 'right'.

Dowall 1992

The continued application of colonial standards, or Western-influenced standards, place legal housing beyond the reach of the majority of people. A study of urbanization by the United States Agency for International Development (USAID) says 'all Caribbean countries have agencies that build housing for low-income groups ... such programmes have entailed high cost and the middle-income groups have been the major beneficiaries' (Mohammed

1997). In the Caribbean, cost estimates for housing developed in accordance with prevailing regulations showed that only the wealthiest 15 per cent of the population can afford to build legally (Mohammed 1997; see also Matthews Glenn and Wolfe 1996). Similar observations made in Zimbabwe suggest that existing legislation constrains construction: the 'existing regulations and the incentives that structure the market had priced the low-income product out of the market, leaving low-income housing to welfare policy or the informal sector' (Rakodi undated). The under-supply of housing is also causing price rises in the rental sector. Zimbabwe's own experience of housing provision by way of site and services schemes demonstrates the impact of this so-called 'low-cost housing solution': it has 'severely constrained the rate at which housing units ... can be completed. European-style modern building standards were maintained and strictly enforced ... The expense of such building materials and construction ... has meant that many people simply cannot afford any of the government's low-income housing options' (Potts 1994:211).

Both public sector provision and the approach taken in housing programmes should be analysed when considering the reach of planning legislation, which 'is even more limited ... as the state often changes or adapts the usual standards in its own developments' (Matthews Glenn and Wolfe 1996:63). In Botswana urban development is governed by the Urban Development Standards of 1981, but there has been a drift away from what were pragmatic guidelines in which economy in design and the principle of 'affordability' were key concerns, towards a general trend of building to more luxurious standards, which has recently resulted in very expensive large public housing schemes in Gaborone.

Cost of procedures

The lengthy and costly nature of application procedures also has a large impact on the affordability of legal housing. 'Informal housing developments in Egypt were rendered more attractive by [the] strict planning and building regulations which greatly increased the cost of formal sector housing' (El-Batran and Chandel 1998). Thus procedural costs act as very effective barriers to individuals, and to small- and medium-scale developers.

> [An] examination of dramatic differences in supply responsiveness between the Republic of Korea, Malaysia, and Thailand indicates that these three countries differ sharply in the degree of legal and regulatory complexity and in the stringency of enforcement ... In the mid-to-late 1980s developers in Malaysia were required to satisfy 55 different steps ... which might take five to seven years before they could deliver ... [while] in Bangkok the entire process for subdivision, building, and land titling takes approximately 100 days. A major result of Malaysia's regulatory requirements is to increase dramatically the risk associated with participating in the residential construction industry, [which] effectively limits participation ... in formal supply in Malaysia to relatively large and well-capitalized firms. In Bangkok, by contrast, the residential construction industry is extremely fluid, with many small firms eager to find a market niche that they can quickly fill.
>
> World Bank 1993:85

Policies that improve the responsiveness of the supply side of the market to changes in demand can be the best way to lower the cost of development.

In housing supply, materials and housing production, flexibility in the delivery sector has been found to be critical to national productive capacity. In comparisons made by the UN's Housing Indicators Programme, studies of the Thai housing sector in Bangkok and the

Korean sector in Seoul found that the greater degree of central control in the Korean housing sector has an impact on its ability to respond to demand. In Seoul increases in demand result in higher prices rather than increased output, whereas in Bangkok smaller-scale operators were able to respond and raise their level of activity to meet the market opportunities unconstrained by demanding legislative procedures.

What is the cost of bureaucracy? Approval for Kenya's Komarock Housing Project took almost fourteen months, a period during which the building cost increased by more than 30 per cent, resulting in an increase in cost of KSh50 million (Agevi 1990). Developers in many other African countries experience the same problem. Abdelhalim (1999) reports that while the cost of a building permit in Egypt seems reasonable according to the law, in reality it costs about ten times as much because official engineers from local authorities can create hundreds of reasons to block the procedure or refuse to release a permit unless a bribe is offered. The law states that permits should be issued within one month of the application, but residents find that their permits may take up to two years. The requirement in Kenya and Zimbabwe for approval to be granted only when professional drawings are produced is another onerous burden for those on a low income.

Yet there is hope. In response to these barriers, practical initiatives, such as standardized housing design options for self-help builders made by the Association for Settlement and Commercial Enterprise for National Development (ASCEND 1996), have been developed in Jamaica. A similar initiative in Kenya resulted from NGO/public sector/professional sector liaison and collaboration, including assistance from members of the Architectural Association of Kenya (AAK). Individual structures were designed for low-income communities in participatory design workshops that were subsequently approved *en bloc* by the Municipal Council of Nakuru (see Chapter 3).

The World Bank states that governments should abandon their role as providers (a view concurrent with the paradigm of governments as enablers espoused in the Habitat Agenda and other development agendas), but ensure that their legislation helps others to be providers. Putting these ideas into practice is difficult, however, as vested interests aim to maintain the status quo and strongly resist any change.

Enforcement

Systems of building regulation based on prescriptive, top-down approaches need to have the institutional capacity to 'police' standards. Many developing countries do not have the capacity to enforce building standards. Legal systems in different countries reflect their historical origins. For example, there are clear differences between the British and French systems (see Appendix 1). The alternative approaches already discussed come from systems that tend towards self-regulation. People are encouraged to set their own standards at a neighbourhood level, and are therefore motivated to comply with that system.

Public sector 'control agencies' are often criticized for being under-resourced, bureaucratic, slow, and expensive – and sometimes for being corrupt and incompetent. Even in the industrialized countries, which have the resources to enforce building controls, many buildings are defective. In Denmark, efforts to improve the quality of the housing stock have led to the development of a new system.

Set up under the Danish Ministry of Housing in 1985, the Building Defects Fund was given three tasks:

- to cover the cost of repairing any defects in buildings covered by the fund, primarily non-profit housing built by the state
- to prevent future building defects by ensuring that all new buildings are quality assured
- to build up a database on defects and defect-prevention strategies based on information gathered from five-year inspections.

The fund takes direct responsibility only for the five-year inspection, leaving the normal supervision to the building owner under contractual practice; the inspector's job is to assess the building and record any defects. The aim of the scheme is to assure quality during design and construction and thereby 'prevent defects rather than allocate responsibilities for the cost of making good damaged work' (Atkinson 1995:135). While it applies only to state housing at the moment, the five-year inspection is being incorporated into '"AB92: General conditions for works and supplies in the construction sector", [and] as awarding contracts under AB92 becomes normal practice, the five-year inspection is expected to become normal' (Atkinson 1995:134).

Financing

Access to, and the cost of, credit is another critical factor in enabling low-income groups to acquire housing. Commercial providers are reluctant to advance credit to the poorest, who often lack collateral or any other guarantee. In Bangkok, the Government Housing Bank granted a loan to the National Housing Authority on the condition that the authority was responsible for collecting the repayments, as the 'GHB was reluctant to lend directly to the residents' (UNCHS 1986:40).

Financiers require a return on their money, and expect building standards to ensure a quality housing product, so that if a borrower defaults on a loan the bank will be able to sell the house and recoup its investment. Credit institutions rarely loan money for construction using local materials, but adhere strictly to a policy that obliges house builders to use modern industrialized products that are thought to guarantee inherent value and durability in any structure built using them. A building society official attending an ITDG workshop in Zimbabwe said that for him the 'farm bricks' (made by artisans), which were allowed under the revised standards, were not good enough.

Work in Delhi took affordability as the point of departure and highlighted the need for formal standards in accessing credit; the high cost of credit leads to a reduction in standards as the higher cost of financing the housing process, from informal money lenders for example, leads to the use of low-cost and low-quality materials (Mehta et al. 1989:55). Credit suppliers in the informal and NGO sectors generally take a more flexible approach towards compliance with official standards. All the same, financial procedures, informal or otherwise, require all parties to have a clear understanding of the terms involved and precise definitions of their obligations and responsibilities.

Definitions

The terms 'building regulations', 'codes' and 'rules' are often used interchangeably. They all share a legal standing. Quite often they constitute subsidiary legislation to a statute, for instance a public health act or a local government act, whereas 'standards' are technical yardsticks or measures that a building material, service or method must satisfy.

The definition of a specific regulatory instrument largely depends on the system of government and policies in place. In a dictatorship or authoritarian regime a leader's pronouncement, even on technical matters, is a decree that must be followed. Even in democratic systems we find that government departments often have their own internal building manuals and standard specifications, for example for schools, health centres or public housing. In fact, public projects rarely have to go through the same approval process as private ones. In Kenya, for example, the Chief Architect in the Ministry of Works is not obliged to obtain planning approval from local authorities for projects that he designs for the central government. (A list of definitions is given in Appendix 1.)

The evolution of standards

The earliest references to standards in Europe come from the Romans, who were concerned with the quality of brick walls. They 'made use of a punitive system whereby if a building collapsed with fatal consequences they executed the builder' (Barritt 1995:1). The Roman tradition partially affected building methods in the Mediterranean cities of the Maghrib (North Africa), where another dominant influence was the 'law through building guidelines as a prime factor which shaped the traditional Arabic–Islamic city' (Hakim 1986). In Tunis, for example, such guidelines were in use for many centuries. Principles included the concept of doing no harm to others, rights of original usage, privacy, inheritance and rights and obligations concerning pollution. Standards were also an important concern in the East. It is reported (Philippe 1986) that the oldest regulations regarding the construction of cities and their architecture are found in the *Zhouli*, a book dating from the Chinese Zhou Dynasty (11th–3rd century BC). 'In this book, the city is conceived as an image of the universe.' The traditional Chinese concept of *feng shui* refers to the art of building cities, houses, tombs and other structures to be in harmony with nature and to respect the mountains and bodies of water that are manifestations of a higher power than human beings.

In Germany, the earliest standards were established during the nineteenth century, in 1872, to govern the size of bricks; they remained in force until 1952 (Hahn 1997). In the UK the processes of urbanization and industrialization brought about the need for regulations to safeguard public health, especially in the growing metropolitan areas, where there was the threat of disease spreading from the working-class neighbourhoods to the residential areas of the ruling élite (Briggs 1990).

As colonialism spread, so it brought with it foreign ways of controlling house construction. 'The model imposed on colonial possessions in Africa and Asia in the nineteenth and early twentieth centuries, and the model that was followed in Latin America, [was one of] formal laws which provided the legal foundations for urban settlements, and doctrinal legal scholarship which provided an interpretation of those laws within a restricted intellectual framework' (Fernandes and Varley 1998:19). Practitioners in the disciplines concerned with the regulation of human settlements, especially in the rising field of urbanization, 'acquiesced in the approach to law put forward by legal scholars: that the law was an unproblematic phenomenon which had no connection with the social sciences' (Fernandes and Varley 1998:19). Colonials imposed their existing laws on their overseas territories, ignoring or discounting indigenous laws, which were often relegated to the status of 'customs', of interest only to anthropologists, not lawmakers. In many parts of Africa and Asia, however, these customary building rules are still relevant (see, for example, Box 1). An international study carried out in 1975 in Asia and Latin America found that 'one of the reasons for the relatively inefficient functioning of human settlement … is the conflict

> **Box 1 Traditional building rules in Hausaland**
>
> The rules governing the location, size, spacing, and construction of houses in traditional African societies are preserved in indigenous knowledge which is passed on from generation to generation of builders. A well-documented example is the expertise and power of the master mason in Hausaland. In his extensive study of the aesthetics of traditional architecture in Hausaland, Hamman Tukur Saad of Ahmadu Bello University in Nigeria writes (1981) about the physical organization of the residential compound, dwelling orientation, the role of the master mason in society, the art of mensuration, and the weight of public opinion as an enforcement agent. Houses are in the form of compounds and grow by accretion, rarely being built in one go. The compound is surrounded by a boundary wall (or stick fence in rural areas) to afford privacy, provide security from intruders, and define the owner's territory. The entrance has to face a direction which is not only protected from the elements (monsoon rains and harmattan winds) but also pleasing to supernatural beings. West is therefore preferred wherever possible, while north and east are normally avoided.
>
> The compound is inhabited by family members, relatives, dependants, and animals. It has room for guests and grain stores. Room measurements, ceiling heights, and other cardinal dimensions are determined by the master mason using his body as the measure. The foot, the cubit, the stride, the outstretched arms, the palm, and the knee are only some of the dimensions used to set out the various elements of the building. A donkey with a back pack should be able to pass between compound walls without impediment, and this dimension determines street widths. A compound owner who attempts to obstruct free passage faces sanctions in the form of gossip and cursing by donkey owners. Public opinion ultimately forces him to demolish any unacceptable accretions.
>
> *Source*: Hamman Tukur Saad 1981

between official and cultural standards' (Mabogunje et al. 1976), that is those standards accepted by a number of people based on social beliefs and traditional practices, and those set down in legislation and based on professional and 'scientific' recommendations.

In a similar manner, legal instruments governing the built environment are seen as primarily technical in nature and have remained the preserve of professionals concerned with safeguarding public interest. In developing countries, laws imposed by colonial powers have changed little. In Tanzania, 'the existing building regulations as embodied in the building code were formulated in the 1930s and partially revised in 1954' (Athman 1992:15). In much of the developing world, standards were imported by foreign professionals from a very different context and often a very different time. While ex-colonial powers have revised their national legislation governing the built environment, many developing countries have not.

The code custodians

Around the world there are many different regulatory regimes and institutional frameworks used to administer housing standards.

Institutions

There are numerous types of institutions established to safeguard public and private interests in the built environment, just as there are many people with associated interests, including planners, designers, implementers and users of housing, land, infrastructure and services. The built environment links people and organizations in a myriad of ways, so it is not

1963

New building legislation comprising of Grade I and II by-laws

1979

Low-Cost Housing By-Laws Review Study commissioned by the government

1985

An interministerial and multidisciplinary committee constituted to devise ways and means to implement the 1979 recommendations. Unfortunately, no progress was made on this.

The reality that could not be accommodated by earlier by-laws

1990

ITDG organized a national Seminar Formation of a task force to oversee implementation of revised building by-laws. Its work slowed down due to financial constraints.

1993

Wasted period

1992

Code 92, a set of amendments to the building code as applicable to low-cost housing and a manual of *deemed to satisfy solutions* were published and distributed particularly to local authorities. The Task force also presented refined plans for the formation of a permanent Review Board

July 1995

Code '92 gazetted as Code '95 by the Ministry of Local Government

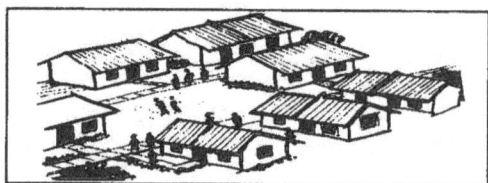

Sept 1996

A major Survey on building standards and procedures in eight major towns completed

Revised by-laws allow construction of decent and affordable houses using local and appropriate materials.

Dec 1996

A Presidential Commission on Building Laws, By-laws and regulations constituted

1997 and 1998

National Workshops on enabling housing standards convened

Figure 1   Standards revision process in Kenya

Source: Yahya et al. 1999

surprising that confusion exists over which statutory body and instrument governs what and how. Political considerations, vested interests and the human nature of those responsible for legislation and its application mean that the subject of housing standards is full of tension, compromise, conflicting agendas and inertia. In Kenya, for example, the authorities have grappled for years with the revision process (see Figure 1), but the weight of bureaucracy and conflicting interests have served to prevent the introduction of well-researched and well-intentioned changes (see Table 1.4).

Table 1.4   Agencies responsible for formulating and enforcing residential standards in Kenya

	Policy formation	Standard setting	Plan approval and inspection	Enforcement
Housing Department	♠	♠		
National Housing Corporation	♦	♦		
Department of Physical Planning		♠		
Ministry of Health	♠	♠	♠	♠
Commissioner of Lands	♠	♠	♠	
Nairobi City Council	♠	♠	♠	♠
Local Authority	♠	♠	♠	♠
East Africa Power & Lighting		♦		
Water Authority	♠	♠		♠
Attorney General's Office		♠		
Provisional Admin./Chief				♠
Lending Institutions		♦	♦	♦
Employers		♠		
Labour Department		♠		
Confederation of Trade Unions		♦		
Architects, Engineers and Designers		♦		
Bureau of Standards		♠		

continued on next page

Table 1.4 Agencies responsible for formulating and enforcing residential standards in Kenya (cont.)

	Policy formation	Standard setting	Plan approval and inspection	Enforcement
Housing Research Department Unit	♦	♦		
Donor Agencies	♦	♦	♦	
NGO/CBOs	♦	♦		♦

♠ public measure   ♦ quasi-government and private measure

Source: Yahya 1980

Peruvians benefited from a reduction in the time required to register land when new decentralized institutional capacity and procedures were introduced; the old system, during its hundred-year existence, had managed to register just 40 per cent of formal land ownership and 5 per cent of informal land. Recent changes in ministerial responsibility for regulation mean that one ministry develops regulation, while another one is responsible for the local authorities who will have to enforce it. Such division is likely to lead to conflict in all but the most co-operative, unpartisan, public sector hierarchy. In Peru 'no action was taken at central government level, possibly because conflicts between various authorities persisted. It did result in some relaxation of standards at the local level, but the actions were arbitrary and uncoordinated, and therefore not effective nationally' (Schilderman 1992). Contradictions between separate legislative items governing the same matter are also not uncommon.

'Residents are often cynical and disillusioned with public institutions. And in both countries [Kenya and Zimbabwe] corruption, and to some extent political issues, cause widespread dissatisfaction and undermine the credibility of the building control system' (Schilderman 1998:1). In the Orangi project in Pakistan it was 'observed that costs are reduced by 30 per cent if government agencies and contractors are not involved in development work because the elements of corruption and profiteering are eliminated' (Siddiqui and Khan 1994:283).

One school of thought suggests that there is a need for two types of standards institutions, one temporary and the other permanent. Temporary institutions would be concerned with the processes and provide back-up services, such as technical committees, while permanent bodies created by government at a high level would review regulations, as in Jordan, where the 'government established a High Commission for the National Building Code of Jordan with direct accountability to the Prime Minister' (UNCHS 1985:36). The approach adopted for the new National Code in India was 'comprehensive', that is a secretariat was appointed to gather information on all state by-laws for analysis and reformulation and to organize a series of seminars in each of the states. Temporary structures may have a role to play in the revision process, but more permanent capacity is needed to ensure the continuous monitoring and updating of regulations.

International donors can have considerable influence on institutional practices in the South. In Pakistan, for example, the World Bank set conditions that included the 'creation of a separate department for squatter settlement upgrading' (Kioe-Sheng 1982:30). The provision and facilitation of cost-effective housing requires flexible approaches while deriving benefits from inclusion in the mainstream institutional framework. Experience from other countries, however, suggests that such a project-specific approach diverts attention and resources from wider issues of sustainable urban development.

The following list summarizes the diversity of institutions that may be involved in the development and application of regulations (see also Figure 2). The diversity of interests within such a range of organizations means no one is homogeneous. An important distinction can be made between professionals and the politicians within such bodies: the former may be aware of practical realities, what is needed, and what is possible, while the latter may be more concerned with winning votes.

- *Ministries* Numerous, and will include, for example, the departments of Health and Sanitation, Town Planning, Building Control, Industry, Industrial Development, Scientific Research, etc.
- *Bureaux* There may be a few of these specialized operations, such as the national bureaux of standards or research.
- *Committees, sub-committees and working groups* Predominantly comprised of experts in related disciplines and civil servants.
- *Local authorities* The range of contexts in which they operate, as well as the diversity of functions they undertake, means these institutions are critical links in the housing supply chain.
- *Parastatals* The UK Building Research Establishment was originally supported by public sector funds, for example, but was subsequently privatized, highlighting the trend towards market-driven approaches. Other parastatals include international trading standards associations such as ISO and ARSO.
- *Research and academic establishments* These closely linked or integrated commercial and academic research establishments are often vital in providing the knowledge required to assure technical and scientific integrity in standards, for example CRATerre-EAG in France and commercial research and certification organizations in the United States. Academics also play a significant role as educators of the technicians, professionals and politicians of the future. The tendency to perpetuate the use of industrialized materials and techniques is all too often reinforced by educational systems that are themselves modelled on Western standards.
- *Private sector* Operators in this sector influence standards both indirectly, as, for example, experts on committees, and directly, as government resource people or pressure groups that aim to influence regulations in view of their shared interests, for example the Brick Development Association in the UK, or its counterpart in Burkina Faso, the Société des Briques de Faso.
- *Lobbyists* Apart from private sector interest groups, those people with strong ideological beliefs who actively lobby legislators on behalf of a particular cause, for example the environmental lobby
- *Professionals* This group will include individuals operating as designers, planners, constructors, consultants, etc.
- *Financiers, banks, building societies, co-operatives* A wide group of businesses, such as Banco de Materiales in Peru.

- *Communities and individuals* A wide range of people and groups, including self-help builders, artisans and private sector contractors, all of whom influence the way in which standards are applied in practice.
- *Development agencies and NGOs* Both local and international organizations, such as UNCHS, ITDG, SKAT, CRATerre-EAG, DA, etc.
- *Alliances* An unusual but growing group, for example CODINORM, in the Ivory Coast, an association established by government remit but implemented by the private sector, is given the responsibility for developing standards following rules similar to those of international standards organizations (Aka 1996). The process is undertaken by committees and sub-committees involving technical professionals and 'opérateurs économiques' (commercial operators).
- *Donors* Usually large agencies such as the UN, World Bank, and Inter-American Development Bank who work both directly and indirectly to influence national and international legislation.

A major problem is how to co-ordinate the efforts of all the relevant national institutions and ensure that they are adequately funded. In Burundi the Standards Bureau (BSB) had difficulties developing national standards because of their lack of resources and need for improved documentation and dissemination; there was also said to be a lack of standardization between the various bodies responsible for different regulations relating to housing (Nzinahora 1996).

After the Second World War British influence was still evident in institutional frameworks in the Caribbean, even though British funding was not significant. Assisted by the UNCHS and sectoral reform programmes, and funded by the Inter-American Development Bank, several governments, including those of Jamaica and Trinidad and Tobago instituted reform, but the 'institutional framework remains fundamentally the same' (Mohammed 1997:235).

In Algeria, standards for earthen construction were established in 1987, but by the early 1990s local standardized testing methods still did not exist and therefore the technology was not being used. Earth construction still lacks status and the reported deficiency in facilities may be a smokescreen for a lack of political determination to address the issue and facilitate the use of low-status building materials. It is evident, however, that scarcity of human, physical and institutional resources at national and local levels severely restrict the effectiveness and efficiency of regulation in the built environment, particularly in the public sector, where new professional skills, such as community mobilization and support for participatory technology development and use (see Box 2) are required. (Other lessons from Kenya are presented in detail in Chapter 3.)

The technical professionals, like many others, may think that they have a monopoly on technical expertise. Although it is important to acknowledge the existing skills base within the construction sector, it is also necessary to appreciate the needs and skills of the informal builder who works for himself. Collaboration with professionals in the social sciences is also essential.

Given the institutional maze that surrounds the process of planning and building approval, it is not surprising that it is inaccessible to lay people. There are few examples of the 'one-stop shop', an approach that has been recommended as a way forward. Indeed, when approval is granted, enforcement practices by their nature can appear, from the builder's point of view, as 'interference by the state'. First-hand experience in the UK demonstrates the

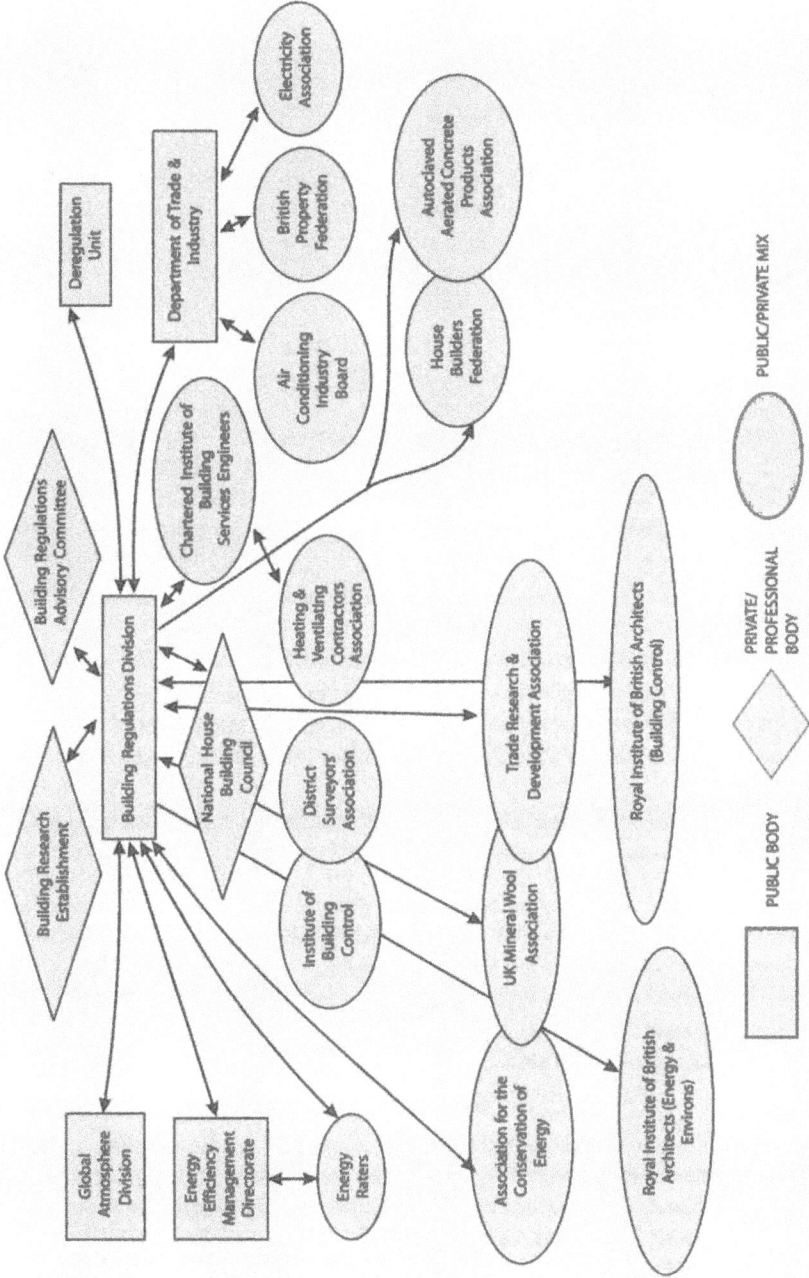

Figure 2 Participants in the revision of the UK Building Regulations Part L. A summary with examples of the institution types involved in the development and application of regulations

Source: Shove 1998

Box 2   Local capacity in Nakuru, Kenya

Before the revision, the Municipal Works Inspector of Nakuru felt unable to walk about the neighbourhood where he now regularly comes into contact with local people and supports them in adopting technologies permitted under the revised by-laws. Working primarily with landlords and neighbourhood associations, the inspector has helped to generate employment for artisans and local workers, and created new rental accommodation and small business units (mixed land use is permitted). Despite individuals' enthusiasm and local success, the engineers and head engineer admit that they have failed to scale up the experience.

Councillors are a source of delay in approving building permits because they often have little in-depth knowledge of the issues concerned, and there is no money to train them. The capacity of local authorities to interact effectively with communities is limited, but several initiatives supported by the international donor community are working with councils in Kenya and elsewhere to use existing resources more effectively and to develop new strategic thinking (for example, the Localising Agenda 21 Programme, Municipal Development Programme of East African Region and the Urban Management Programme sponsored by UNCHS, UNDP, and World Bank).

Source: ITDG Kenya

adversarial nature of the building control officer–builder relationship. Building control officers in the UK see their role as a supportive one, 'it's on site that a lot of information exchange occurs', yet they are often faced with people who do not want to listen (Lowe 1999b). The reverse is also true, that is that the attitude of public sector officials can be unhelpful, if not obstructive or abusive.

A land-sharing initiative in Bangkok highlights the issues that arise when the housing process depends upon negotiation between the parties involved (UNCHS 1986:38). Key factors were found to be:

- organizational strength and cohesion of the slum community when facing eviction; a unified front was required in dealing with the landlord
- landowner type, whether private individual or public institution
- existing density (lower densities facilitate sharing)
- effective mediators; if common aims can be found between the community organizers, housing authority, influential civic figures and political parties, then there is a good chance of solving the problem.

Self-regulation has proven to be a viable way to counter the lack of institutional capacity and to impose sanctions that do not penalize those in greatest need. Community-based standards like those developed in Sri Lanka under the One Million Houses Programme are the result of a participatory process that creates a sense of ownership and communal commitment to the collective standards. This idea is developed further in the next chapter.

National or local codes; double or flexible standards?

The need for flexibility and context-specific standards is problematic because housing standards and the programmes incorporating them 'tend to be administered by central agencies ... The problems and procedures associated with centralized administration tend to impose a uniformity of standards' (Martin 1980:19).

In a country as large as China, however, it is easy to see that 'the geo-climatic conditions, such as weather, ambient temperatures, soils, rainfall, [and other] natural resources are extremely different in various parts of the country. It is important to develop standards that are suitable for local use. Therefore, local technical standards are developed based on local natural conditions' (Shirong and Ming 1999). However, it is not just the physical conditions that play a part in housing standards. In the Kenyan town of Nakuru, two housing estates have very different housing needs because they have evolved historically to suit different cultures: one estate is occupied predominantly by Muslim residents, the other is not. If standards are to accommodate such environmental and human diversity, they must be adaptable.

A UN seminar considered the adoption of flexible standards in Tanzania, where the greatest difficulty was felt to be the distance central authorities were from the place of implementation. During the debate feelings ran high, as some people perceived it as an issue of 'double standards' (Martin 1980). Similar emotions were expressed by local authority officials in Zimbabwe during a seminar in March 1998, organized as part of the international research by ITDG.

The Chinese regulatory regime is based on two types of laws and regulations, administrative codes dealing with transactions and institutional relationships, and technical codes regulating the exploitation of nature and technology. The latter, which are mandatory, are designed to harmonize all the technical issues encountered in construction operations. They comprise five aspects:

- quality requirements and relevant methodology in engineering survey, design, construction and acceptance
- technical requirements concerning safety, hygiene and environmental protection in construction
- technical codes, symbols, units, architectural modules and regulation of engineering drawings dealing with construction activities
- methodologies for testing, checking and reviewing work related to construction engineering
- information technology required in construction.

Although it makes common sense to do so, standards are not always set with regard to the context in which they are applied. The standards in Tashkent were applied according to the directives issued by Moscow (about 3000km away), which were based on the conditions and needs there (Djabbar 1990). Similar incongruity has been documented in the standards used throughout Chile.

Local by-laws enable local authorities to interpret national legislation and to take account of local variations. The shift from prescriptive to performance standards can also accommodate various methods, designs and technologies to achieve the desired quality. However, such a shift requires a change of attitude and an increase in local capacity. Local authority staff may find it much easier in the short term to adopt a national code, which has less risk associated with it than the potentially better but unknown alternatives.

The American system is different from that of most industrialized countries. In the United States the building control process has become, for the most part, a private sector enterprise involving a wide spectrum of federal, state and local regulatory bodies, professional societies, trade associations, manufacturers, builders, developers and the academic community. In total there are approximately 5000 building codes in use throughout the United States, developed by 500 organizations. Many of the larger cities and some of the states use their own codes. Yet 85 per cent of all state and local governments have either adopted one of the three model codes or based their regulations on them. Examples of the many different codes applicable to wind loading in coastal states highlight the variation in building requirements. While many of the building control functions in industrialized nations are decentralized, many Americans are now arguing in favour of universal standards. 'The constitution of the United States leaves the authority to regulate building designs and construction to the states' (Gross 1991:75). This authority has in the past been exercised by local-level bodies such as cities and counties. The recent trend has been for states to reclaim the authority to develop and implement state-wide codes.

National and state-level standards can act as barriers to international trade. Europe's standardization efforts aim to harmonize the Common Market in order to reduce non-tariff barriers. Currently any construction products crossing national boundaries are subject to numerous European directives. (For an in-depth description of the institutional arrangements in Europe see Atkinson (1995), which also has a detailed explanation of the complex arrangements involved in agrément certification for building materials and production processes, and the 'product–usage couple'.) It is too early to assess the potential effects of the World Trade Organization's impending global dominance; national standards could be regarded as non-tariff barriers restricting the importation of processed materials from the North.

In preparation for a review of its building regulations the Indian government took stock of existing regulatory approaches abroad, and selected the following main features as the basis for their new code:

• Buildings were classified according to whether they represented a fire hazard.
• Administrative instructions and regulatory issues formed the core of the code.
• Standards and technical issues were given only a mention in the code and remained separate documents.

The India Code has two distinct parts: one deals with administrative instructions and regulatory aspects, the other with technical issues. 'The idea was that each of the states was allowed the opportunity to reformulate its own set of building by-laws based on the first portion of the National Code but that the second portion of the code, i.e. the purely technical issues, remained a standard reference document for all states' (UNCHS 1985:40).

The diversity of approaches is ably summarized by R. Nagarajan: 'Model regulations and codes are formulated by national standards bodies in New Zealand, South Africa, and India; by professional bodies and special committees in the US and Canada, and by government agencies in the UK, Australia, and certain other European countries' (Nagarajan 1976:124). There are four basic models of regulatory systems (see Appendix 1), the Anglo-Saxon, German-Nordic, Napoleonic, and planned-economy models. The type of system in place reflects the history and colonial affiliation of the country concerned. The Napoleonic model is used in France, Belgium and many other French-speaking countries, including Francophone Africa, while regulatory systems in Anglophone Africa reflect British origins.

International and national policies on housing standards

Despite some activity at national level, there are few initiatives to make sure the law is working in practice. Many countries have employed a top-down, expert-driven approach in reviewing policies, with little further action to disseminate, create understanding of, and put into practice revised standards. One notable exception was Sri Lanka's housing programme, driven by the persistent political will and sensitivity to the needs of the poor of the Minister, and later President, Ranasinghe Premadasa. Initiatives in Sri Lanka allowed the designation of special project areas and the adaptation of standards locally, demonstrating a willingness to recognize need. A desire to avoid the proliferation of slums in all areas also formed part of the rationale. The 'Sri Lankan government opted for allowing different regulations in different localities rather than for lowering the standards for everyone ... [and] by allowing more flexibility to special project areas only, they remain firmly in control' (Sirivardana 1999).

The growing demand for affordable, adequate housing is not a new phenomenon. The need to provide shelter has been a concern for politicians and professionals for many years. National governments, local authorities and international donors have formed alliances and adopted various approaches in order to provide housing and associated services for those in need. As the limitations of public sector funding and resources have become more evident, the methodologies employed have changed. Low-cost housing became a notorious misnomer. As governments moved from acting as providers to becoming enablers, preference was given to site and service approaches, and then to community self-help and non-governmental provision facilitated by public and private sector alliances. Over the years projects undertaken in the name of the poor have been ineffective at reaching them, proving to be expensive, often usurped by middle-income people, while the poorest continue to be marginalized from the little state assistance that exists.

Throughout the decades that saw the decline of colonial rule and changes in government and development practice, millions of people have met their immediate need for shelter by creating their own housing solutions. It was in Latin America that informal sector activity was first perceived as being part of the housing solution, not the problem (Turner 1982). The legal system adapted to popular and new political thinking. Writing of the Barriadas (informal settlements) Law of Peru, Manaster concluded that it is 'a strong example of the important process by which law is adapted and developed. The kind of pragmatic adaptation of old legal concepts to new problems which we see in this law is the kind of first step which Peru and many other countries must take if they wish to confront the squatter crisis effectively' (Manaster 1968, quoted in Fernandes and Varley 1998:25).

Significantly, international development agencies appear to have accepted the premise espoused by Manaster, a fact reflected in numerous policy documents. During Habitat I, the United Nation's first international conference on human settlements, held in Vancouver in 1976, it was suggested that 'a national policy for human settlements and the environment should be an integral part of any national economic and social development' (UNCHS 1980). Furthermore, UNCHS states that 'standards for shelter and infrastructure and services should be compatible with local resources, be evolutionary, realistic, and sufficiently adaptable to local culture and conditions and be established by appropriate government bodies' (UNCHS 1980).

A review of the African National Plans of Action, drawn up for the second international conference on Human Settlements, Habitat II (UNCHS 1996), shows that eighteen countries considered standards as an important issue in terms of national policy. The need for review was acknowledged, though mainly proposed in a top-down, expert-driven approach. Although eighteen is a relatively small number in a continent with over fifty countries, it does indicate some interest in integrating housing standards issues into the policymaking process.

The Habitat Agenda shows that policymakers and politicians see a role for standards in meeting the need for 'adequate shelter for all'. The numerous references, over thirty in all, recognize the importance of involving people in the review of legislative frameworks and instruments in order to address the lack of housing, land, infrastructure and services. The UN Global Plan of Action (UNCHS 1980) advocates legal frameworks that inform and empower people to participate. It recognizes the significance of environmental standards and makes various recommendations to:

- 'expand the supply of affordable housing through appropriate regulatory measures'
- 'review and adjust the legal, fiscal, and regulatory framework to respond to the special needs of those belonging to vulnerable and disadvantaged groups, in particular, people living in poverty and low-income people'
- 'review restrictive, exclusionary, and costly legal and regulatory planning systems, standards, and development regulations'
- 'adopt performance standards as appropriate'.

The UNCHS also gave consideration to the issue of standards for housing and building materials in a 1985 seminar involving professionals from several countries. Attention was paid to African standards and their significance, highlighting criteria for good standards and requirements for reformulation and decision-making issues.

As a contrast, the World Bank, driven by banking principles and economics, highlights the significance of housing in global development and the need to remove 'supply side barriers'. Based on its involvement in housing provision in numerous countries the bank identifies the need for governments to turn attention away from programme interventions towards regulatory and institutional reform and support. 'The regulatory environment may function effectively through a variety of forms, depending on cultural traditions and historical circumstances, but each system must create a comprehensive matrix of relationships among recurrent actors – those who consume, build, service, finance, and regulate housing' (Peru, Ministerio de Vivienda y Construccion 1977). Given the higher proportional expenditure on housing when regulations are in place and enforced, 'regulatory systems [have] led to shortages in the supply of housing' with greater impact on the poor and, in particular, the urban poor. The World Bank states that what is required are:

- *Affordable standards* Land use and building regulations that allow flexibility in lot sizes; effect on price should allow economic development with low-cost housing in compliance with codes
- *Compliance* A well-functioning legal system means increased compliance with affordable standards, low bureaucratic costs and little delay
- *Squatter tolerance* Responding to squatters, while protecting property rights and public open spaces; supplying regularization and infrastructure for squatters

Despite such international awareness, the lack of regulatory reform in the last two decades has been blamed on government initiatives that are able to circumvent regulations on a 'special basis' (Sherer 1987), thereby taking away any impetus for broader change. There is a need for policymakers to assess fully the trade-offs between environment and affordable housing and the effects of regulations in order to make informed choices. Offering guidance on the reform process, the World Bank suggests a regulatory audit that identifies all the players, quantifies the cost implications, and helps to target reform towards specific institutions and regularization, while being particularly mindful of the political issues and implications. One political concern is the extent to which regulations reinforce social inequality. Mabogunje sums up: 'Standards ... serve more as a means of social stratification than as a means of reconciling the shelter needs of the population with a maintenance of a reasonable level of environmental quality' (quoted in Agevi 1995). Fernandes observes that the 'failure of housing policy in Brazil has resulted in a chronic deficit' (Fernandes 1995:111). While *favelas* are 'the virtual expression of social inequality and of the contradictions underlying the structure of society' in which the homeless invent their own housing, it is also an 'indispensable solution given the lack of alternatives' (Fernandes 1995). Some national governments have, nonetheless, tackled this politically complex and sensitive issue; the example of Kenya is outlined in Chapter 3.

2

CURRENT THINKING ON STANDARDS DEVELOPMENT AND REVIEW

Catalysts for change

This chapter presents an overview of the main features and trends in current thinking on housing standards and related codes and regulations. A large number of documents, reports, books and published papers were analysed, and although the literature on standards *per se* is fairly limited in volume and intellectual scope, there are nonetheless large amounts of material relating to housing policy issues in general, to the technical aspects of shelter provision and to specific projects. In fact, many innovations originate as project components, and eventually trickle into the larger realm of workshops, conferences and published articles. The questions this chapter tries to answer are: What and who stimulates change in regulatory regimes? How do changes occur? What is the general pattern regarding the thrust and scope of reform? Have any significant innovations been evident in recent years? Have there been any noticeable impacts, beneficial, or otherwise? The answers and analysis will set the stage for the two detailed case studies that follow this chapter.

There are many diverse factors that influence politicians and policymakers to revise legislation governing the built environment, but the main reasons for making revisions are political stability, poverty reduction, participation and market expansion. Kenya's reformulation exercise was prompted by conflict between the existing legislation and the government's efforts to promote low-cost housing. In Uganda changes contained in the Building Control Bill 1996 (still awaiting parliamentary approval) are necessary because of the five-fold increase in the country's population since the 1964 Building Code was passed, and because of the need to remove rules that deter housing development for the poor.

User-led changes: dissatisfaction or opportunity for change?

Regardless of the reason, many changes are likely to conflict with building regulations and planning controls. People adapt their housing as a matter of natural life cycle changes, rising aspirations, and increases in family size. Residents make changes to their houses for different reasons, including their need to make their own mark, to make a home with which they can identify, their need to generate income from their housing by renting some or all of it to tenants or by running a business from home. Research suggests that the factors that encourage or discourage change can be divided into three groups: factors that affect the resident; the dwelling; and the context (Rezende 1993):

The resident

- security of tenure
- resources available, for example, costs, alternative options, mobility
- characteristics of the resident, especially confidence, age, gender, skills and ability

The dwelling

- type of dwelling, for example, single- or multi-storey; plot layout
- technology type; key factors being familiarity and accessibility of the materials and construction techniques used
- immediate surroundings

The context

- geographic context, climate and seismology
- economic situation, the price of materials, the ability and need to generate income
- housing situation, for example overcrowding
- laws and regulations
- attitudes and general climate of acceptability.

The most obvious, and most often-cited, reason for insisting people build according to regulations is the potential danger created by the addition of structurally unsafe extensions or alterations to a building's fabric. In addition, ventilation and lighting levels (for both the homeowner and, sometimes, the neighbours) tend to be reduced by user changes. Whether or not the majority of changes represent real danger or whether they demonstrate that people usually build well is arguable. Recent research in Bangladesh has shown that user changes 'brought more rooms as well as more room per person, increased house size, and improved service levels and physical conditions' (Tipple and Shahidul Ameen 1999). Experience in Egypt suggests that end-user modifications can even inform the process of change: 'more important than proposed guidelines is the change in the attitude of professionals resulting from the experience of [witnessing good] user transformation. Existing housing policies and codes of practice should be reviewed in the light of actual transformations in different projects through empirical in-depth studies' (Salama 1998:39).

Over-densification will, however, lead to increased loads on infrastructure that will require higher levels of maintenance. This, and some potentially dangerous structural additions, will have to be weighed against the positive benefits for individuals, communities and national economies. The financial and human resources that are invested when users improve their housing adds significant value and new housing stock, while enhancing and diversifying the built environment.

Social and political pressure

'The image of informal areas does not fit into the civilized face of Egyptian cities' (a high-ranking Egyptian official, as quoted by Abdelhalim 1999). The socio-political complexity of the housing agenda cannot be denied. At the time of independence in countries such as Kenya and Zimbabwe there was significant pressure on governments not to lower standards despite the rising demand and limited resource base. The Zimbabwean government's 'commitment to modern, high-standard dwellings was partly ideological, but now seems more influenced by concerns over image, rather than people's needs' (Potts 1994:211). This implacable stance, especially at the time of independence, and unwilling-ness to lower standards epitomize the sensitive, complex issues that govern standards.

Rising expectations among individuals and society played a key role in raising the standard of housing in Britain in the 1920s, and there was considerable pressure on the government to provide good social housing. The case for high standards was put in 1923 by John Wheatley, at that time a Labour front bench spokesman on housing, who accused the government of building hutches rather than homes, of, 'stereotyping poverty in housing ... and giving parliamentary acceptance to the permanency of class distinction' (Durand-Lasserve 1996:97). For cost-conscious officials and politicians in local and central government, the goal is always to build as many houses as possible as cheaply as possible.

Throughout the twentieth century UK governments of different political persuasions have argued for, and against, minimum housing standards. A Labour government intro-duced the Parker Morris standards in 1961 to govern the minimum floor area as a means of improving the quality of working-class housing. The same government did not want to impose the same minimum space standards on private developers, however, for fear of curtailing the construction of smaller 'starter units'. Conservative governments, pursuing their policies of market liberalization, argued in favour of deregulation throughout the 1980s and 1990s, but did not deregulate building or planning control in England and Wales (Goodchild 1997:98).

In industrialized countries the clout of the environmental lobby has grown significantly in recent years, and governments have pledged, in the Kyoto Protocol, to take action to limit their nations' negative impact on the planet, particularly by reducing greenhouse gas emis-sions. Lowering energy consumption and emissions from building materials production for the housing sector form a part of this agenda, but the 'introduction of additional controls is dependent on the scale of ambition' (Goodchild 1997:117). The need for change will have been a factor in the recent alterations to the UK Building Regulations Part L: Conservation of Fuel and Power, which seek to limit carbon dioxide emissions.

Research undertaken by the International Council of Scientific Unions, responding to growing concern about the human environment, identified the environmental aspects of human settlements as a major field for study. 'One such topic, regarded as of the highest priority, is the evaluation of the rationale for standards ... especially in the developing regions of Africa, Asia and Latin America' (Mabogunje et al. 1976:1). The aim of the evalu-ation was to provide increased understanding of the essential human needs in a wide range of settlements leading to the 'development of new standards and criteria which may ameliorate the current environmental crisis in human settlement' (Mabogunje et al. 1976). Academic research has also influenced several governments to review standards. Developing country universities and research institutions are paying increasing attention to the subject, largely as a contribution to efforts to promote sustainable urban development policies.

International institutions such as the World Bank and the United Nations wield considerable political influence through their large investments in countries, programmes and projects. There are several examples of pressure from international donors resulting in changes to national legis-lation, such as in Kenya and Uganda. In Cameroon the United Nations' Development Programme (UNDP), Industry Development Organization (UNIDO), and CRATerre-EAG collaborated with national government bodies to introduce standards for stabilized earth, while in

Ghana the initiative was taken with support from the UNCHS and the Commonwealth Science Council. In Kenya, despite local awareness, 'pressure to review ... was to a large extent from external actors, particularly the World Bank and USAID', who are key players in the country's large urban shelter projects (Yahya and Agevi 1997). Changes in international policy paradigms have influenced approaches adopted in human settlement interventions in many countries. The new thinking, as expostulated by Turner in the 1960s and 1970s, coupled with international research recommending new approaches, found support from both the World Bank and the governing Pakistan People's Party, who were upgrading and regularizing settlements in Karachi (Kioe-Sheng 1982:29). The marriage of a good idea, adequate resources and political commitment is essential for success.

Public health and safety

Public health was the first banner under which the built environment was regulated; the outbreak of cholera in 1831 in the UK alarmed British politicians, if only temporarily. A further outbreak in 1848 resulted in pressure for health controls to be extended. The need for standards in the provision of water and sanitation is evident to anyone concerned with safeguarding public health. However, the gradual harm that poor housing causes to inhabitants is sometimes less apparent, for instance in the case of poor ventilation in Kenya (Wanjohi 1997), where medical researchers found that inadequate ventilation in traditional Maasai houses had a significant impact on the health of the occupants, especially as solid fuel (cow-dung and firewood) is used for cooking and heating. Government enquiries, as well as the work of medical and statistical professionals, have helped to identify the interrelationships between social conditions, housing types and location. The WHO has also emphasized the connection between health and housing.

The government of Zimbabwe, among many others, took an adamant anti-squatter position: the informal sector has had to fit within the existing stock of formal housing, which has led to the drastic densification of legal housing as 'backyard shacks' have multiplied. This drop in the supply of housing raises the rental value of existing stock, making the renting of rooms more profitable and attractive. Absentee landlords often form a significant proportion of owners of units in government schemes and are said to contribute to the deterioration of environmental standards, for example by opting not to pay the often higher service charges for amenities such as water, leaving their tenants without access to the existing infrastructure. The psychological impact of overcrowding, though difficult to quantify, cannot be ignored; numerous instances of extended families living in extremely cramped conditions have been reported in Zimbabwe's national press, highlighting 'the sheer physical discomfort involved, the physical health risks, and the moral and cultural taboos' being broken (Potts 1994:213). Studies in Indonesia have also shown that 'high population densities, high building densities, lack of indoor and outdoor living space, and poor quality of housing facilities are perceived as problematic ... [and that] in addition to a physical dimension, crowding is perceived as having an important psycho-social dimension ... [This study also showed how] the lack of windows and ventilation causes a damp indoor ambience that constitutes a health hazard' (Clauson-Kaas et al. 1997:120).

Work with pastoral people in Kajiado, Kenya, has clearly shown that improving housing and the surrounding environmental conditions reduces vector-borne disease and infections of the upper-respiratory tract. Improvements to rented houses in the Kwa Rhoda community in the Kenyan town of Nakuru, such as adding fireplaces and chimneys where there were none before (see Chapter 3 and Appendix 4), have reduced the incidence of bronchial disease.

Eliminating risks to public health from the use of hazardous materials is also important. Many countries have revised regulations to ensure occupants' safety, for example the outlawing of asbestos in Western countries. Yet, despite this total ban in some parts of the world, 'hazardous' materials are the mainstay of some low-income housing markets. Asbestos roofing sheets and discarded metal and plastic materials previously used to package chemicals and pesticides are reused extensively in shanty towns, and, indeed, demand for such materials has created business opportunities for middlemen and small-time dealers who are not unaware of the dangers involved.

Ensuring the structural integrity of any building is essential if it is to meet its purpose and prevent injury to people and damage to property in the event of collapse. The recently introduced Construction (Design and Management) Regulations in the UK aim to improve the performance of design and building practices and have introduced new duties for all of the parties involved in construction in the UK. Similar concern is evident in other countries. Cairo is notorious, not only for its large population living in cemeteries (Abdelhalim 1999:7) but also for the dangerous and unauthorized extensions to multi-storey apartment blocks that have collapsed at times, killing many people. As a result, the government insists on building housing for the urban poor, instead of contracting it out or letting the market provide, in case corners are cut, and it also regulates strictly all private sector housing (Abdelhalim 1999:8).

Technical change

In industrialized nations there are two significant trends in the continual pressure to revise standards:

- technical changes, resulting in increased levels of computerization and automation in construction processes and products, which force standards agencies to incorporate advances in knowledge from research
- harmonization, between states in the USA (Gross 1991) for example, and across numerous national boundaries in Europe, in an attempt to facilitate international trade by reducing non-tariff barriers.

At the same time rising standards of living and the concomitant rise in people's expectations have resulted in an on-going round of revision that seeks to raise the level of material provision in European housing, such as thermal comfort levels. Building regulations have become more stringent, and new provisions have been added, while few have been taken away. In industrialized nations generally, the building regulations are seen as key 'vehicles for [the] transfer of advancements in building technology' (Gross 1991). Standards are also perceived as both instruments of change *and* examples of society norms, not only as responses to innovations: 'regulatory documents are the outcome of certain ideas or social prescriptions for the right way to live, and in turn, these documents become media or vehicles by which social values are perpetuated' (Anderson 1996:47).

The inability of standards institutions and politicians to incorporate changes in materials and techniques into standards has been a matter of concern in developing countries. This inability stems from inadequate expertise, the high cost of new technology and the rigidity of existing building regulations. The need for enhanced flexibility in the face of rapidly changing environments and advances in technology has led to an increasing preference for performance-related, rather than prescriptive standards.

National economic interests

The insistence on national financial autonomy is an important factor in causing change, because economics governs most political decision-making. Some of the earliest alterations to housing standards resulted from colonial economic interests. In 1959 both Malawi and South Africa lowered standards in settlement areas to attract low-income earners to urban centres to meet the demand for labour. Standards had to be low enough to enable the less-well-paid workers to erect houses for themselves within these areas (Pennant 1990:191; see also Crooke 1981:13). In Uganda Grade II standards were introduced because of the need to attract migrant workers and to avoid evicting people from peri-urban migrant settlements. A subsequent national review consulted with all town clerks to ascertain usage of standards and barriers to usage, and the results were fed into the Building Control Bill 1996.

The current economic reality in developing countries makes support for the indigenous construction sector of paramount importance. In Cameroon, for example, the 'devaluation of the CFA, the Structural Adjustment Programme, and the worsening economic situation' are all suggested as reasons for supporting national efforts towards standardization of compressed earth blocks (Lowe 1998a). Even in the richer countries, economic considerations are paramount. While people on good incomes are willing to pay for luxury and space, those on low incomes do not have the choice.

In the UK the decline of public sector funding and dominance of a market-driven ethos in the public housing sector, with the associated push for cost effectiveness, has been instrumental in reducing standards. House construction in this sector has in recent years become the preserve of housing associations, which are clearly governed by rules associated with government funding. Financial rewards for using cost-cutting measures have led to a reduction in the quality of materials, components and finishes used.

Market economy societies and rapidly industrialising nations expect much higher standards of living than past generations. Economic growth in China has led to a demand for bigger and better housing and, consequently, increased work in the construction industry. It is a matter of national policy that standards, which are becoming more luxurious, are constantly reviewed.

Private sector interests

People and companies that supply products and services to meet the private demand for housing take great interest in the revision of building standards. In the UK approximately 1400 local authorities governed local house building through by-laws, each with minor, but significant, variations. 'This presented great difficulties for designers and builders operating nation-wide ... To improve this situation the Public Health Act of 1961 enabled the Minister to make national building regulations', the first edition of which was produced in February 1966 (Barritt 1995:2). The need for uniformity was also a strong factor in reforms made in India in 1965, when all states had their own by-laws; over 2000 local bodies and 35 municipalities were responsible for building control and 30 government departments published their own codes of practice (UNCHS 1985:38).

Private sector operators have continued to influence the process and direction of change in standards through several mechanisms: as experts on review committees; as specialist advisers to, or in partnership with, government departments; and through representation by professional interest groups and associations. In the Ivory Coast, for example, CODINORM is an institute managed by the private sector under government control to develop standards (Aka 1996:3). In Jordan, the comprehensive review of codes was driven by parties 'within the construction industry, consulting firms, the Engineers' Association, and contractors [who] felt that the regulations and codes were inadequate. This led to the use of excessively high factors of safety' (UNCHS 1985:35). The need for economy in practice was evidently at work, but was supplanted by the need for professionals to safeguard their own interests by ensuring that public health and safety requirements were met. As a result, there was a sudden increase in high-rise construction and misuse of sophisticated construction equipment, which led to frequent disasters in construction. Moreover, the local engineers felt insecure without any technical and legal basis for their practice. This private sector involvement, if not properly monitored and restrained, can have the contrary effect of raising costs and increasing exposure to structural failure.

Legal controls should also aim to safeguard against bad practice by the private sector; for example, the infamous construction sector 'cowboys' in the UK. The informal nature of employment and practices are seen to require regulation to safeguard the public against the operator who would cut standards to enhance profit. It is with potential litigation in mind that many professionals claim regulations need to be comprehensive documents that are clearly and precisely drafted.

Legislation is sometimes seen as necessary to control the tendency of market-based competition to reduce standards. In the case of housing association provision in the UK, research undertaken by the insurance sector highlighted the tendency of associations to reduce housing quality in new construction because of the pressure to achieve 'value for money' – a situation that occurred because clients (usually local authorities) failed to stipulate in their tender documents any 'quality floor around which the competition was taking place' (Atkinson 1995:12). Indeed, insurance companies and financiers clearly have a vested interest in the quality of housing, and their requirements often determine whether people with low incomes are able to access housing. Building societies in Zimbabwe, for example, concerned about the lifespan of mortgaged property, have opposed materials such as farm (artisanal) bricks.

Materials producers have a stake in the revision of standards, especially in having their materials incorporated, so that they can supply large and public sector contracts. Members of the Brick Society of Burkina Faso lobbied successfully for the inclusion of extruded earth blocks in national codes. The extent to which industrialists and materials suppliers can and/or should influence the work of national standards institutions needs further thought, especially as governments in developing countries are finding it increasingly difficult to fund such institutions, which then have to rely on private sponsorship and international aid, which may cause bias.

This kind of political pressure co-exists with the personal aspirations of people who want to build a house using materials that they feel are appropriate. Manufactured (often cement-based) products usually fall into this category, and 'such prejudices are only reinforced by lack of standard performance criteria' (Walker 1995) for local housing technologies. In Latin America, as in Asia and Africa, popular preference is given to 'matériales nobles'(durable materials) in house construction (Burga 1987:22), though investment in durable building materials will occur only if ownership is assured and if the money is available.

Alternative materials and techniques are at last starting to be recognized as they are included in statutory documents. However, the rarity of standards based on performance has been a major constraint to innovation. The prescription of predetermined solutions clearly does not encourage people to find alternative solutions; however, innovation requires technical and institutional capacity and can be expensive.

Disastrous events

The spectacular impact of 'natural' disasters means that they often cause the systems that exist to safeguard life and property to be reconsidered. The first standard in the UK, prohibiting the use of reed for roofing in London, resulted from the devastating fire of 1212. The Great Fire of London in 1666 was responsible for the introduction of further legislation (Knowles and Pitt 1972:28). In the Philippines, building regulations aim to reduce the impact of typhoons. The force of phenomena such as earthquakes and typhoons is felt most by people living in 'non-engineered' housing; the single most significant factor in the loss of human life is collapsing structures. Governments and funding agencies become aware of building standards in the aftermath of disasters, and question the prevailing standards. The Fars earthquake in Iran highlighted the fact that local building regulations did not require buildings to be resistant to earthquakes.

It is after disasters that 'external' experts are most likely to influence governments, and not always for the better. Indonesia's post-earthquake standards revisions in 1979 were based on the very high Japanese standards, despite the clear socio-economic differences between the two countries. In recognition of the need to provide adequate protection against natural disasters, a co-operative programme was set up between financial and technical institutions in Peru and the USA (Fattal 1998), despite the very different situations in the two countries.

Given the impact of natural disasters on the built environment, it is easy to understand that the lack of regulation can be very costly, but imposing higher standards to mitigate vulnerability to disasters is also expensive. Risk reduction is achievable only if the proposed measures are within reach and put into practice. In Canada, a policy of liberalizing standards in search of flexibility has been implemented by authorities on the west coast, 'where all codes concerning live/work quarters waive seismic requirements provided the building is otherwise structurally sound' (Anderson 1996:44). In this way expensive retro-fitting or outright demolition of existing stock is avoided. A delicate balance has to be maintained between emergency needs, which could occur only once in a lifetime, and the goal of providing housing and infrastructure at affordable costs.

Revision procedures

The most successful developments are those that benefit from the views and involvement of the people who live there.

Cotton 1998:16

The involvement of end users might seem a logical approach in this day of market-driven, customer-centred economies, but the principle that users are the best people to judge what they want has not penetrated the thinking of housing sector officials, bureaucrats, politicians, civil servants, professionals or technocrats, who tend to claim superior knowledge of what is 'right' for people. This section considers the people who are usually involved in the revision of building standards – and those who should be.

The process of standards review in China, represented in Figure 3, exemplifies the kind of process followed by many countries, at least in theory, in reviewing building standards. In some countries diagrammatic representations of the processes involved have been likened to a 'snakes and ladders board', that is a game of rapid rises, declines, pitfalls, chance, and uncertain moves and outcomes.

Although Figure 3 shows discrete stages in a time-bound process, the revision of standards is often a continuous, if sporadic, process that spans years. Compare this with Figure 1, which outlines the procedure that was followed, and is still being followed, in Kenya.

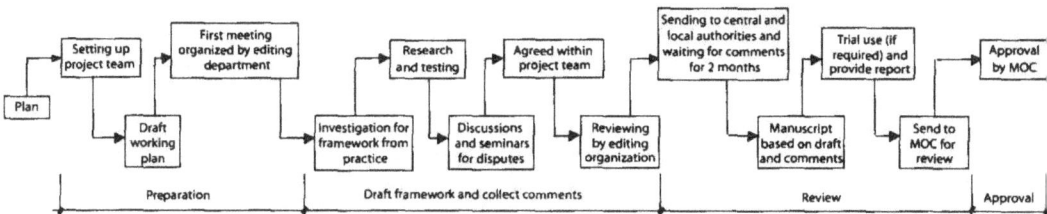

Figure 3   Standards revision process in China

Source: Shirong and Ming 1999

Review processes in Europe

In Europe it is difficult to find a consistent pattern of housing standards review in terms of methodology, timing or organizational arrangements. National history and culture have a strong influence on how problems are approached. High-density, technologically advanced societies located in harsh climates do have common concerns, however. Thus energy savings, damp protection and fireproofing are important issues, along with the adoption of new inventions and techniques, and apportionment of liability in case of structural failure.

The UK review system is governed by the British Standards Institute (BSI), which follows well-established procedures by serving notice of any pending reviews in their institutional news-letter *Update*. Once notice has been given, a consultant or a small panel of experts produces an initial draft document. In the construction sector, responsibility lies with the Department of the Environment, Transport and the Regions. A hierarchy of consultative committees and sub-committees will also be involved. The initial draft document is issued for 'public comment', a process that aims to build consensus. In 1989 a review of consumer participation in the process took place and resulted, in 1992, in the establishment of the Consumer Policy Committee, with representatives from many different consumer interests (BRE 1994:36). In 1993, this committee was supplemented by the Construction User Group. The majority of representation work from private sector and user groups is undertaken on a voluntary basis, however, and 'the voluntary nature of BSI work can cause problems for users' (Home 1993:36) as they may lack sufficient awareness of notices or fail to obtain draft documents for comment. Individual representatives may be badly briefed or fail to communicate the extent and nature of proposed changes and their potential impact on their constituencies, and the 'cost of attendance in the UK is borne by individuals, their firm, or professional or industry associations' (Home 1993:36). Clearly any private and/or community-based organizations would have to be very interested in the legislation to secure and allocate resources to such activities.

The Danish National Building and Housing Agency has overall responsibility for building regulations in Denmark, while enforcement lies with the local authorities. Technical coverage in the regulations differs little from the European Union, and their eventual replacement by European standards will be relatively straightforward. A peculiarity of the Danish system is the role played by the Society of Engineers, which has been responsible for most codes of practice since 1893, 'many of which, following public acceptance, are issued as Danish Standards' (Atkinson 1995:132). The Society also plays a role in testing, through the Danish Association for Material Testing.

Sophisticated and highly structured conformity testing, certification procedures and industry standards denote the German preference for achieving quality and security rather than promoting technical innovation. 'The aim is to protect building owners, as well as the general public, but at a cost' (Atkinson 1995:135), and this approach would seem to carry substantial weight in Europe. Indeed, 'The German approach was one of the key influences on the Commission's proposals for the Construction Products Directive' (Atkinson 1995:136). This approach involves stringent third party testing and awarding of stamps of approval, and control of production quality, which is governed by membership of, or contract with, an approved quality assurance association. Such associations are funded partly by government and partly from fee-based services to industry.

The French legal system evolved from Napoleonic origins. Principles are implemented through decrees issued by the prime minister after consultation with relevant ministers and with the constitutional court, which has considered a detailed application in the form of orders issued by the responsible minister. This system is said to have three particular merits:

- Documents are logically ordered and explained.
- Legislation is codified and made available periodically through bookshops.
- Relevant legal documents are published in full, loose-leaf versions in the weekly construction journal *Le Moniteur*.

This system is said to be more easily understood by those who implement it and less dependent on interpretation by the legal profession than, say, the English system. A brief comparison of the German and French systems is presented in Box 3 (more detailed information is contained in Appendix 1).

In the UK, the formal process of developing building legislation began in 1848 and continued under the remit of Public Health Acts until 1961, when the minister responsible for construction established the first national Building Regulations (1966). Several important acts were passed in 1974, including the Health and Safety at Work Act; subsequent studies and experience led to the 1984 Building Act and a further act specifically for London in 1986. In 1985 Building Regulations were supplemented by 13 Approved Documents which aimed to increase accessibility by providing illustrations and explanations as to how regulatory requirements could be met.

The piecemeal evolution of building control regulations in the UK, where bits and pieces of existing regulations were bolted together, was a factor that prevented the kind of radical change that was in fact necessary (Jimenez 1982:225). A redraft of the whole of the legislation was undertaken and promulgated as the Building Regulations 1991. Further changes to the Approved Documents were made in 1992 and 1995.

**Box 3   A comparison of systems regulating construction
in Germany and France**

The German system

More control by authorities, less responsibility for constructors. Strict control during the construction process:

* Stringent regulations based on full national standards (DINs)
* Designs checked before building permits are issued, where necessary by an independent licensed structural engineer
* Products either tested against DINs and subject to factory production control, or approved by DIBt, the German Institute for Building Technology, Berlin
* Technical site inspection, with much attention given to final inspection to uncover deficiencies.

The French system

Less control by authorities, more responsibility for constructors. No technical control by authorities during design or construction:

* Building permits issued against signature of an architect that design meets planning, health, fire and safety regulations with the possibility that compliance is checked by a government engineer in the first three years after completion
* Clearly stated guarantees for soundness of, and fitness for, intended use within specified time limits
* Requirement for building owner's damage insurance and constructor's responsibility insurance during and after construction
* Mandatory requirement for independent technical control for high-risk situations
* Importance placed on *reception* or practical completion as start of damage.

Source: Atkinson 1995:141

International review processes

There are examples of international collaboration in developing or reviewing national standards. International agencies' focus on, and funding of, policy and institutional reform has led to some initiatives, such as the one in Peru that reviewed standards governing low-income housing and seismic performance (Fattal 1998:VI–17). This initiative was undertaken in two stages:

* Research and testing activities were carried out on soil stabilization and acceptable standards for improved seismic-resistant structures.
* Two pilot projects were designed and built in communities previously affected by earthquakes.

Guidelines for human settlements were produced by an international forum, drawing on the experience of several Asian and Pacific countries, and they suggest that no standards should be set without:

- the conscientious documentation of existing conditions
- the perusal of existing policy guidelines
- the listing of feasible or relevant options
- checks on the specific project conditions (ESCAP 1979).

This approach was typical of the 1970s, when there was a general awareness of the need to place standards within a policy context, although concern about participation and dissemination had yet to develop.

One very successful international collaboration was the initiative to develop pan-African standards for compressed earth blocks. It followed on from several successful initiatives to produce national standards, and aimed to establish transnational standards to improve the commercial viability of local building materials by widening their potential market. The process was a lengthy one, drawing on NGO, government, academic and private sector expertise. Extensive research and experience in working with this material enabled CRATerre-EAG and the University of Grenoble to develop draft documentation covering all aspects of the production and use of the blocks. A series of international consultative meetings culminated in a week-long gathering in Cameroon to 'finalize' the standards (Lowe 1998a). Participants in this process represented numerous countries, disciplines and organizations. Such a complex and costly exercise would not have been possible without a strong sense of belief in its worth and the determination, by the lead agencies, to see it through. Financial support was also essential, and in this instance it was given by the Centre for Development of Industry. The participatory approach adopted deliberately aimed to create interest in, and ownership of, the resultant standards, and the biggest impact in terms of construction outputs is evident in countries where political and material support exist and practical demonstration occurred.

These examples of international collaboration highlight the extent of participation that is possible given sufficient motivation and resources. The approach adopted in many countries is top-down; private and public sector interest will usually be represented, but only rarely will end users' opinions be heard. In Kenya 'reviews had been *ad hoc* events which were non-participatory' (Yahya and Agevi 1997:11). Likewise in Zimbabwe there is 'no documentation to suggest wide consultation took place ... [which in turn means that] considerations of affordability and sustainability did not take centre stage' (Mugova and Musandu-Nyamayaro 1997:7).

Review processes in Africa

The case of Uganda demonstrates the diversity of public sector bodies involved in reviews as well as the consultation that takes place. A broad-based national committee was set up 'because of the wider implications on most building development works ... It consisted of representatives of key Ministries of Lands, Housing and Physical Planning, Labour and Social Affairs, Works, Transport and Communication, Local Government, Health', and other institutions involved included the National Water and Sewerage Corporation and the National Housing and Construction Corporation and the National Bureau of Standards (Uganda 1992:73). Advice was also provided by a legal adviser, a UNCHS (Habitat) consultant and local consultants from the Uganda Association of Technical Professions. Furthermore, 'relevant information from town clerks of all municipal and town councils on the building rules, the extent they are used, and constraints they face' was obtained (Uganda 1992.; see also Byaruhanga 1998).

Standards' review literature suggests that professional bodies and associations are repre-sented, although this is not always the case. In research undertaken in Zimbabwe and Kenya individual professionals who expressed an interest and perceived the issue of standards as significant had in fact been unaware of the processes when they occurred, and a large propor-tion said that they would like to participate in such activities in future.

What changes?

The evolution in standards may appear natural; as societies 'develop', policies and thinking shift, technological capacities change, resources differ and aspirations tend generally to grow. Regulatory legislation has also been updated over the years to incorporate an increasing number of concerns relating to the built environment. This section considers some of the changes in approach and material provision that have been made. Reviews of standards in Africa, for example, have been governed by concerns over political stability, poverty reduc-tion, participation, and market expansion (Yahya 1998a:20). Factors considered in reviews include:

- tenure and access to land
- environmental health
- technology
- poverty
- urban/rural interfaces
- self-regulation and governance
- information technology
- women, children and the disabled
- the old
- quality management and sustainability
- consolidation and partnerships.

The literature suggests that reviews are rarely as extensive as the list above in their coverage of issues; the focus is on fewer areas, but is no longer as narrow as it once was. The earliest emphasis was on safeguarding public health and safety. After the 1848 cholera outbreak in the UK, for example, growth in central control was significant. The Public Health Act was a landmark in social reform, establishing a national standard and describing the responsibil-ities of local authorities. However, as the act empowered but did not compel local health boards to pursue sanitary reform, its effectiveness was limited. Subsequently, with changing circumstances, such as an improved standard of living, a general awareness of public health aspects, the development of technology and gradual understanding of the role of housing in promoting social integration, the narrow emphasis on health was reviewed.

Shifting development paradigms have influenced the approaches adopted by the public sector to housing provision. In Egypt, for example, the site and services policies pursued in the 1970s and 1980s were the result of a dramatic move from supplying 'high quality' finished housing units. This change met with resistance; 'officials resented the reduction in the government's role as well as the length of the self-help process and the "unattractive" (i.e. unfinished) aspect of site and services' (El-Batran 1998). The resumption of the earlier policy, to supply completed units, has been criticized (see Abdelhalim 1999) because it is inappropriate for most people on low incomes. For example, in Zimbabwe insistence upon core rooms, WC and washroom completion before people could officially take up residency was a major hurdle as it made the homes too expensive.

The inability of site and services projects to meet the rising demand for affordable housing was perhaps as much a function of the sites chosen as the high standard of finishes imposed on them, however, as these schemes are frequently located far from sources of employment and adequate means of transport (El-Batran 1998).

Prescription or performance?

A significant trend in the changes that have been made to regulatory mechanisms has been the drift from prescriptive- to performance-based standards, which combine materials choice, quality, methods and workmanship. South Africa has adopted a system that evaluates the 'fitness for purpose of standardized materials and systems' (see Box 4, page 54). The same trend is evident in industrialized countries. In the UK the 'manner of control was to make simple statements of how the work was to be done' and assume the desirable performance would be achieved (Barritt 1995:2). Many changes occurred after the Second World War because of the rapid development of analytical approaches and new technology. In 1953 by-laws specified purely functional requirements; local authorities could state what a system of construction must achieve. The benefits of more general legislation 'concerned with the proper definition of tasks and formulation of performance standards ... gives engineers maximum freedom in choosing' (Laquian 1983). Designers and builders are thus permitted to use their own methods if they can be proven to satisfy performance criteria or 'deemed to satisfy provisions' giving 'common building methods' that are considered capable of meeting the requirements. These changes are reflected in the revised UK Housing Corporation Guidelines in which Scheme Development Standards are less prescriptive than they were before and comprise, for the most part, a series of questions such as 'Does the dwelling layout minimize noise transmission?', 'Is circulation space sensible?', and so on.

This flexible approach will work only if there are adequate levels of information, support and education to facilitate the process of choosing and to publicize the range of options. In the UK, for example, ample resources exist and builders and developers can look to a variety of institutions for support in making their choice and proving compliance, and for examples of conventions, procedures, and mechanisms to help them make the right decision, including:

- British Standards
- national standards of member states of the EC (or elsewhere if it can be shown to be equivalent)
- Agrément Certificates issued by the British Board of Agrément
- national technical approval by member states of EC if equivalent to an Agrément Certificate
- EC marking denoting compliance with harmonized standards of EC
- tests, calculations, or other means carried out in accordance with recognized criteria
- past experience, such as buildings already in use demonstrating that materials are sound
- samples taken that prove compliance with the requirements (Barritt 1995:4).

Efforts to support builders and developers by demonstrating or outlining options will depend on effective information and dissemination tools. Chapters 3 and 4 present examples of the methods used in Kenya and Zimbabwe respectively to disseminate the regulations or standards, although these are isolated efforts by NGOs and activists and can in no way match the institutionalized and systematic information channels available in the UK.

Many countries have no mechanisms to support the dissemination of this type of information, or it may not be accessible to people wanting to build. Yet everywhere government's preference for performance-related standards means that they are superseding prescriptive legislation. In India, the government decided to develop a National Building Code that is recommendatory in nature, and provides technical support to the building regulations and acts. The drafting team was to adopt performance as the basis of the new codes, where 'previous codes were rigid and specific as to detail' (UNCHS 1985:40). Their thinking was influenced by a review of foreign codes, in particular Canadian legislation, which is also recommendatory. 'Where no Indian Standards are available for such alternative types of construction or materials, their suitability and safe working stresses have been approved by a national institution such as the Central Building Research Institute, Roorkee; the National Test House, Calcutta, etc.' (Nagarajan 1976:128).

Physical properties

One of the earliest factors considered by experts aiming to provide improved quality was floor space. Imposing a limit on the allowable density of inhabitants regulates overcrowding, and ensuring adequate space in social housing was important for breaking the links between poverty and poor housing. The Parker Morris standards, established in 1961, were a long-standing benchmark in social housing design in the UK (see Table 2.1). They were endorsed by the Royal Institute of British Architects as recently as 1983 in their report 'Homes for the Future' (RIBA 1983).

Under the revised Indian National Building Code the special consideration given to low-income housing is exemplified in a permissible reduction in floor area. The code states that for standard housing 'the area of kitchen where separate dining is provided shall not be less than $5m^2$ with a minimum width of 1.8m'(Yitna 1994:127). This compares with the special requirement for low-income housing: 'The size of a cooking space shall not be less than $2.4m^2$ with minimum width of 1.2m' (Yitna 1994).

Various countries have seen changes to permissible floor area, as well as plot sizes, often expressed as minimum standards. In Zimbabwe, minimum plot sizes jumped to 300 from $200m^2$ at independence, but revised standards introduced in 1992 reduced them from 300 to $150m^2$ (see Chapter 4). In 1982 Sri Lanka introduced an amendment to the Urban Development Authority Law No. 41 of 1978 which provided for the introduction of areas for special treatment and their detailed planning, development and redevelopment. The amendment enabled low-income settlement areas to be declared Special Project Areas where the $150m^2$ minimum plot size was inapplicable and an alternative site-specific set of standards could be used. Thus a new set of housing and settlement rules for the urban poor came into being: 'It was a major breakthrough in the practice of inclusive thinking' (Sirivardana 1999).

Social housing standards in the UK, which applied only to government-built housing, were for some time more generous in their provision of space than the smallest privately supplied units. This difference was justified because families on low incomes and in social housing were less mobile and less able to 'upgrade' when life cycle changes such as increased family size might dictate otherwise. Moving can in itself be too expensive, and the stock of social housing has never kept up with demand. Thinking shifted in the 1980s, as demonstrated in 'Homes for the Future' (RIBA 1983), to incorporate much broader issues within

Table 2.1   Parker Morris floorspace standards

Dwelling	Expected occupancy (number of people)					
	6	5	4	3	2	1
Floorspace (excluding storage) (m²)						
Three-storey house	98.0	94.0				
Two-storey centre terrace	92.5	85.0	74.5			
Two-storey semi- or end-terrace maisonette	92.5	82.0	72.0			
Flat	86.5	79.0	70.0	57.0	44.5	30.0
Single-storey house	84.0	75.5	66.0	57.0	44.5	30.0
Storage						
Houses [1]	4.5	4.5	4.5	4.0	4.0	3.0
Flats and maisonettes (inside)	2.0	2.0	2.0	1.5	1.5	1.0
Flats and maisonettes (outside)	1.5	1.5	1.5	1.5	1.5	1.5

[1] Some of this may be on the upper floor, but at least 2.5m² should be at ground level.

Note: Two WCs are required in two- and three-storey houses, in maisonettes of five or more persons, and in flats and one-storey houses with six or more persons.

Source: Goodchild 1997

the housing debate, that is energy conservation, costs in use and quality of the external environment. 'In contrast, from the late 1980s onwards the Housing Corporation emphasized cost-effectiveness in a way that has, in the view of most observers, largely eclipsed any commitment to design standards' (RIBA 1983). A drop in the average floor space provided was subsequently recorded.

Despite the influence of market forces on social housing in the UK, a change in thinking is still evident, with housing being viewed more holistically. The growing concern with the social and functional aspects of housing has given rise to studies of user requirements and cultural differences in living patterns. Increased emphasis has been placed on the social and psychological aspects of housing, and user studies have become standard practice. Table 2.2 shows how increased affluence has raised minimum standards relating to domestic fittings and appliances such as fixed baths, central heating and artificial lighting.

Table 2.2   Minimum fitness standards for dwellings in the UK

The fitness standard 1954–89	Scottish tolerable standard 1969 to date	New fitness standard 1990 to date	Definition
●	●	●	Adequate repair
●	●	●	Structurally stable
●	●	●	Substantially free from rising or penetrating damp
●	—	●	Substantially free from condensation
○	●	X	Satisfactory access to external doors
●	●	●	Adequate natural lighting and ventilation
●	●	●	Adequate piped supply of wholesome water
●	●	●	Satisfactory facilities for drainage and sanitation
●	●	●	Satisfactory facilities for cooking and waste disposal
—	●	●	A sink with hot and cold water
—	—	●	Wash basin, fixed bath or shower
—	●	*	Internal WC
—	●	●	Satisfactory artificial lighting
—	●	●	Satisfactory heating
—	—	—	Adequate insulation
●	—	—	Satisfactory in terms of overall condition

● part of original standard;   ○ introduced in 1969; X in the case of multi-occupied properties, adequate means of fire escape are required under a revised section 352 of the Housing Act 1985; * the precise definition is of a 'suitably located water closet'.

Notes: The list of criteria is a general indication of the contents. The detailed wording varies. The detailed wording and application also varies for houses, flats, and houses in multiple occupation (HMOs). In an HMO, different households may share a WC without the property failing the fitness standard.

Source: Goodchild 1997

In Kenya, a much poorer country, revisions to standards for low-income settlements have permitted:

- a reduction in minimum room sizes
- a reduction in circulation space
- two-room units with provision for subletting and extension
- the reduction or complete omission of finishing requirements such as plaster, paint, and suspended ceilings
- the substitution of expensive building materials such as corrugated iron sheets for concrete tiles
- the reduction or omission of fittings to allow for future provision
- a reduction in plot sizes
- more economical layouts
- changes in the allowable use of open space
- the use of cheaper options in standards of services provided, such as reduced road thickness and widths, and fewer culverts
- the provision of security lighting instead of street lighting
- the provision of water and sewerage along common boundaries to facilitate access from both sides.

Housing designs complying with these standards were considerably cheaper: a unit cost of KSh65 000 in 1983 was reduced from 1985 to 1987 to KSh45 000 for a similar flooring area. (Appendix 3 highlights the differences between the 1968 and 1995 Kenyan building codes.) These cost-cutting measures, coupled with suitable technologies (such as stabilized soil blocks), can reduce housebuilding costs by as much as two-thirds. Unfortunately, there is still a tendency for architects to overdesign to impress their clients and make themselves known.

In Tanzania, a similar cost-reduction approach led to the exclusion of glazed windows, suspended ceilings, waterborne sanitation and electric wiring from the minimum standards; it was 'assumed occupants may be able to install these at a later stage' (Tanzania Housing Bank 1978) thereby enabling incremental investment and construction to take place. This approach enabled low-income households to start building with their own resources, helped, if necessary, by small loans from the bank.

Building materials and elements

Governments are now aware of the need for alternatives to expensive, highly industrialized, imported materials, and many revision processes have begun to allow the use of more cost-effective alternatives. Performance standards have facilitated this transition.

In Zimbabwe, the revised standards are still prescriptive, but they do allow a wider range of materials, and the requirement for walling thickness has been reduced from 230mm to 150mm. In Malawi, people on low incomes are permitted to use low-cost traditional solutions such as sun-dried bricks and beaten earth floors within designated Traditional Housing Areas. Unfortunately, a lack of political commitment to meeting the needs of poor people meant that such schemes were often located on the periphery of towns, making them undesirable places to live because of the major transportation problems (Potts 1994:125). Transport and other relevant planning issues need to be taken into account when developing standards for low-income settlements.

Social housing in the UK is thought to have suffered a reduction in overall quality because developers, driven by the need to save money, used low-quality materials such as 'chipboard floors [which are] ... more vulnerable to water damage from leaks ... [and] cheap partition walls with less acoustic insulation' (Goodchild 1997:104). Although the resultant housing is no longer as costly in capital terms, there is no real improvement in cost-effectiveness, because the expenditure is effectively transferred to the running and maintenance costs.

Standards types

There is a remarkable diversity of standards types. Figure 4 summarizes the categories governing housing in China, for example, and other countries are no less complex.

In Tanzania policymakers devised several standard types of houses to cater for a variety of circumstances, and called them minimum, desirable, temporary and emergency (Vagale quoted in Lowe 1995:34). Minimum standards were first developed in 1977 for the Tanzanian Housing Bank with the aim of instigating progressive 'change in lending conditions which would result in an acceptance of traditional house structures as a sound basis for the lending of improvement loans' (Siebolds and Steinberg 1982:118). There is little else recorded as to how these types have an impact on people or housing.

Table 2.3 lists the various categorizations of housing standards based on the models discussed so far. From this it is possible to appreciate the wide array of possible permutations. Conservation by-laws can be used to promote heritage conservation in one part of a city, for example, while the general building code applies to the remaining area. This is the approach used in ancient Swahili settlements on the East African coast, such as Lamu, Mombasa Old Town and Zanzibar Stone Town, where conservation measures have been designed to be compatible with low-cost housing needs. Another example is the city of Dakar in Senegal on the West African coast, where there are special rules (Decree 91–748) to guide the upgrading of unplanned settlements. It is not necessarily desirable to have a 'comprehensive' code to suit all situations at all times. It is more useful to rely on a certain basic level of standards, supplemented by selective measures, such as those indicated in Figure 4 and Table 2.3, to suit particular situations as appropriate. Table 2.3 could in fact be further refined to form a matrix with physical/sectoral categories on one axis and historic/elective on the other.

Consumer-led standards

Despite the growing recognition that it is important to take account of end users' views during the review of building standards, experts still dominate the process in many countries. In Ghana, the first 'serious review' of national standards resulted in very little change. 'The only novel idea to come out of the review is that developers can now start building if the local government has not processed an application within three months' (Goodchild 1997:5); flexible standards by default maybe! Even then, three months is a long time in a sector where every day counts.

End users' requirements and preferences are prioritized, primarily when existing informal settlements are to be upgraded and relocation is not an option. Since government is no longer the provider, community and private sector resources have to be invested to improve neighbourhoods, and it is the communities' participation in planning and delivery that should set the pace and standards if collaboration instead of conflict is to result (Kioe-Sheng 1982:31).

In Bangkok, development council rules were relaxed to enable reconstruction initiatives to increase densities and building height without requiring the inclusion of a lift. 'It must be

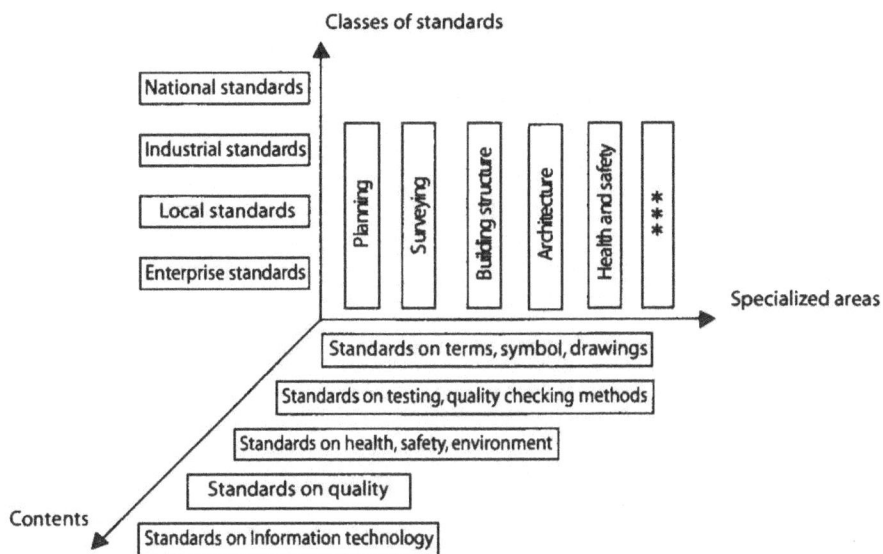

Figure 4   Classes of housing standards in China

Source: Shirong and Ming 1999

Table 2.3   Categories of housing standards

Physical	Sectoral	Historic	Elective
Use	Geographic	Evolution	Quality levels
Residential	Local	Customary	Absolute minimum
Mixed (e.g.	District	Statutory	Minimum
commercial/	National		Desirable
rural/industrial)	Urban		Emergency
	Peri-urban		
Elemental	Class-based	Heritage	Method
Land	Rich	Colonial	Prescriptive
Building	Mid-income	Conservation	Performance
Services	Low-income	Upgrading	
Planning	Poor		
	Poorest		
Materials	Density		Volition-based
Natural	Single storey/family		Guidelines
Processed	Multi storey/family		Adoptive
			Mandatory

Source: Authors

noted, however, that the highest density of all projects was found in Manangkasila, where community leaders themselves sketched the site plan and determined that most families would receive 20m^2 sites' (UNCHS 1986:72). The same project feels that small room sizes, low-cost materials and infrastructure standards safeguard the interests of the poorest by improving access to decent shelter.

The most significant variations to standards in land use and ownership patterns exist where authorities are trying to increase housing accessibility for the poor. The land-sharing approach taken in Bangkok proved beneficial to both squatters and landowners, as it resulted in access to housing and income-generating opportunities respectively. The Community Land Trust initiative in Kenya secured land tenure for the community and minimized the negative effect of the land market on the poor residents by retaining a right to purchase housing and other improvements located upon its land from willing sellers. A 'resale formula' has been adopted to determine a fair price to compensate the seller, but there is no great inflation of prices, as there can be in the private sector, so housing improvements and access to land remain affordable. The rules governing the trust and its management aim to ensure that it represents all interest groups in the community (Mshila 1997). A reduction in bureaucracy helped people in Mexico to access regularized land, while a relaxation in land and infrastructure requirements applicable to small-scale developers in Colombia resulted in 'an increased degree of legal development facilitating the processes of land servicing and mortgage financing' (World Bank 1993). Thus improved land delivery practices can augment the stock of legal housing and help the expansion of mortgage markets.

Innovative approaches

Human migration and the establishment of new settlements are undoubtedly age-old phenomena, but large-scale urbanization and spontaneous 'squatter' settlements are more recent trends. The initial state reaction to the 'problem' of squatters and the 'illegal' neighbourhoods they create was to evict or simply demolish them. The move to site and services schemes evolved as a more inclusive approach to solving this problem, but even this 'low-cost' solution remained beyond the reach of most poor people. The high standards of housing and infrastructure adopted for these schemes often made them relatively expensive and therefore unattractive to the poorest, who were often 'down raided' by middle-income earners who also lacked housing but had the resources to buy. This section considers some of the alternative approaches to standards.

Successive governments have been forced to recognize both the political power wielded by, and the social need met by, *pueblos jovenes* (informal settlements) in cities in Peru. Between 1950 and 1990 urban settlements grew by 1200 per cent – and most of this growth took place in the informal sector, operating outside of, or in defiance of, state laws. Research found 'a set of extralegal norms which did, to some extent, regulate social relations, offsetting the absence of legal protection and gradually winning stability and security for acquired rights' (De Soto 1989:19). Recognizing this type of 'law' may point to ways in which housing and neighbourhood standards can be established successfully within communities: 'It is the "law" that has been created by informals to regulate and order their lives and transactions, and as such is socially relevant' (De Soto 1989). A similar philosophy lay behind Sri Lanka's One Million Houses Programme (see Box 5, page 61).

Faced with the impracticability of the legal system, the Peruvian state chose to work directly with housing co-operatives and informal brokers to help acquire and transform land. People

Photo 1   Houses at various stages of improvement in a Columbo slum upgraded under the One Million Houses Programme

violated a system that did not accept them or meet their needs to 'build a different system which represents a minimum of essential rights ... in the case of informal housing these are property rights' (De Soto 1989:55). This policy had important repercussions: between 1961 and 1981 privately owned housing in Lima increased by 375 per cent, while rented housing decreased by 34 per cent. This flexible approach had a greater impact on low-income residents as a group because they had been most held back by earlier rules, and home ownership in this sector has increased greatly, probably preventing Lima from becoming one large slum.

Traditional and local materials

The quality of any structure will always depend in part on the materials and components employed in construction, which are also the main costs. The need to reduce dependence on imports and increase the use of local materials has been discussed (see Chapter 1); experience demonstrates that the inclusion of appropriate building materials into formal standards is both desirable and possible. Stakeholders of many types have been involved in developing building materials standards on an international and national basis.

Peru's authorities were perhaps the first to recognize formally traditional materials in their national standards. The potentially disastrous impact of earthquakes made this decision all the more significant. The materials most commonly used by the builders on low incomes are *quincha* and adobe, both earth construction techniques whose resistance to seismic activity had to be improved. Research and development on these labour-intensive, locally available materials was successful and improved their performance. Their widespread availability, application and low cost are key elements in the self-help housing sector.

Government review processes in Kenya benefited immensely from an (admittedly limited) bottom-up approach when the national task force of experts visited informal

Photo 2   A house in Soritor, Peru, built using a traditional technique called *quincha* that was improved through research and development

settlements, measured dwellings and saw for themselves the types of materials and designs people used. The conclusion they drew was that it was essential to find 'the lowest common denominator for health and safety upon which improvement may be made' (Yahya and Agevi 1997:11).

Much of the work to formalize appropriate building technologies has been undertaken with the support of – and has sometimes been driven by – international agencies. UNCHS was a prime mover in developing Kenya's national standards for MCR/FCR (micro/fibre concrete roofing) tiles, for example. NGOs have been involved too, as they know standards are a way to guarantee quality for users and to offer guidance to designers and builders to help them directly or to help them persuade others of the validity of the technology in question. International NGOs have also created international partnerships in order to develop national material standards. The Swiss NGO SKAT, for example, which has been instrumental in publishing a 'Toolkit' series that guides the whole production and implementation process, has collaborated with Sofonias in Latin America to extend the reach of this roofing technology.

The UN also actively supports initiatives to make standards applicable to their locality and purpose: numerous seminars drawing together diverse stakeholders have aimed to support international and national initiatives. The UN definition of standards focuses on the users: 'a new concept of standards must be for people, especially in the low-income group ... standards must be flexible, utilise the performance concept, and present a wide range of options, which cover equally wide range of levels of satisfaction' (ESCAP 1979:26).

The regional approach taken by CRATerre-EAG to support compressed earth block production was driven by the desire first to ensure that earthen construction technologies were not discredited through poor performance resulting from low standards of production and application, and second to support national initiatives by eliminating research and development costs for countries in the South, avoiding duplication at national levels, while supporting increased market access and acceptability (Lowe 1998a:18). The participatory approach that they used evolved in order to overcome strong opposition at a national level, and to create consensus and, ultimately, to ensure ownership of the resulting standards. The technical working groups and plenary discussions held at international seminars meant that the final wording of the standards was the product of much debate. This work also enabled CRATerre-EAG to realize where the gaps in knowledge lay. It was able to initiate new research to fill those gaps, thereby advancing knowledge about an environmentally friendly, cost-effective technology.

NGOs also have an intermediary role to play in the development of technological capacity to implement new standards: the capacity of local building materials production has to be built or reinforced in order to create and meet demand. Some examples include training women to manufacture FCR tiles in Kenya, training artisans to build improved *quincha* houses in Peru and, more recently in Nakuru, Kenya, training artisans to make the newly approved stabilized soil blocks.

In industrialized countries manufacturers seek approval for their products from Agrément certification schemes or national standards bodies, such as the British Standards Institute's 'Kitemark' scheme. Products are certified on the principle of fitness for use (see Box 4). Many building materials and technologies have demonstrated their

Box 4   Agrément South Africa and the use of the performance concept

Obtaining market acceptance of innovations in building and construction in South Africa

In the 1940s and 1950s applications for building approval were governed largely by local by-laws. By the 1960s standard building regulations had been introduced and were intended to be applied nationally, but they were not appropriate for all situations. At about the same time, system building began to be used in both post-war Europe and South Africa.

System-built state-funded housing ran into problems, however, and the director of the National Building Institute of the Council for Scientific and Industrial Research persuaded the Minister of Public Works (whose department was responsible for housing construction) that South Africa should adopt the French system for assessing and approving non-standardized building and construction products and systems. This system established performance-based criteria against which the fitness-for-purpose of the product could be assessed. Agrément South Africa was established through a Ministerial Delegation of Authority in 1969. Among other objectives, the Delegation charged Agrément South Africa to facilitate the adoption of appropriate innovation in the industry.

By the 1980s, the National Building Regulations and Building Standards Act had been passed. These regulations are largely functional and compliance with the Act can be demonstrated by:

- complying with South African Bureau of Standards' Code of Practice 0400: the application of the National Building Regulations (generally used for conventional construction)
- using a rational design by a competent person (most often used in 'one-off' situations – for example shopping/office complexes)
- obtaining an Agrément certificate (when there are non-standardized components or aspects of construction).

There are numerous examples of products that were initially non-standardized – for example there was no applicable South African Bureau of Standards (SABS) standard specification or code of practice – but which later came to be regarded as conventional and for which a standard has been drawn up. Some examples are:

- drywalling
- hard-drawn copper tubing
- pulverized fly-ash cement
- solar water heaters
- certain plastics for baths, pipes, etc.

Not every system or product follows this path, however, and in such cases Agrément certification may remain the preferred option of the manufacturer or contractor.

Agrément South Africa uses a methodology that can be applied to a variety of subjects. The most recent developments have been approaches by the South African Bitumen Tar Association for assessment of their products for use in roads, and by the National Roads Agency regarding the evaluation of bridge deck seals.

Source: Kraayenbrink 1999

fitness for use over the years but new, or unquantified, technologies can be certified in order to establish the limits of their usefulness. By coupling the material's behaviour with a defined context, the Agrément certification creates a conceptual coupling called 'product-usage', that is, it classifies the performance of products and delimits the range of their potential. The Agrément system enables designers and users to assess how suitable a certified product is to their context and purpose, thus reducing the risk, and therefore cost, to themselves. Reliability derives from the legal standing and from the institutional capacity to uphold the quality of testing, monitoring and production at all levels. In France, it comes from the Scrivener law of 10/1/78 and its revision of 1994, and a sophisticated institutional set-up that links public with private sector interests. A stamp of approved quality is a valuable sales tool, so many companies take part not only in statutory, but also voluntary, testing and certification, enabling them to distinguish themselves from others in the market place. Private sector operators have also played a part in developing standards in African countries. AGRI-CONGO's action research, for example, has helped to develop compressed earth blocks in that country.

The South African certification system, called Mantag, is based on performance standards for low-income housing. The following principles were adopted:

- The evaluation of fitness for purpose is based on essential health and safety consider-ations only, and the criteria relate to simple, single-storey detached buildings.
- Mantag certification provides technical information and advice to help potential building occupiers, owners, local authorities, financial institutions and designers to assess the suitability of a given method for a given set of circumstances.
- Assessment includes the feasibility of incremental upgrading of the performance of the structure.
- Evaluations include systems developed with self-help building in mind.

Kraayenbrink 1999: 14

Incrementality

Incremental construction is often the only viable option for the poor, and standards should recognize this fact. The majority of standards aim to ensure that the final product meets established criteria, but the cost of implementing these criteria is often prohibi-tively high. The requirements on sites and services programmes in Kenya – that houses must be completed within eighteen months – made them very expensive to many target beneficiaries. 'Housing is process not a product' (Turner 1976), and by definition must be built in stages; it is often only the speed of that process that the authorities set beyond the possibilities of people with severely restricted resources. However, it is possible to accommodate an incremental approach in housing, infrastructure design and construc-tion (Díaz 1984:28).

It is easier to see the rationale for incremental standards in the case of improvements to existing housing stock. When *de facto* standards are low and demolition and reconstruction is not an option, then step-by-step upgrading offers a way for poor people to meet their needs in line with their resources. The 'upgradable plots approach is relevant for Indian cities because it is cost effective, quick, simple and does not compromise standards in the long run ... No other approach is capable of incorporating these qualities ... making land and services affordable through spreading the costs rather than by lowering the standards, [so] low-income families will still be able to get access' (Banerjee and Verma 1994:213). Incre-mental improvements are the norm in practice, yet few formal planning processes enable this method, despite the evident advantages. It has also been observed that the sustainability of these processes improves when incremental standards are supported with financing.

A comparison of two human settlements, one planned informally, the other formally, is summarized in Table 2.4 and highlights the fact that investments in housing improvements are not always as expected, and do not always result from security of tenure, but sometimes act as a means to obtain it (Reimers and Portela 1995). Development objectives have to be carefully considered against issues of land tenure when attempting progressive housing strategies.

Research undertaken in the informal settlements of Bangladesh emphasizes the need for authorities to recognize the changes made by users that improve the quantity and quality of housing available to the poor (Tipple and Shahidul Ameen 1999). Often such end user initia-tives are viewed as the unfettered creation of slums, yet the study clearly shows that the biggest change required is in official attitudes, in order that incremental improvements are encouraged: 'It is important to forsake detailed development control from above and encourage local solutions' (Tipple and Shahidul Ameen 1999: 183). The same study points to the lack of access to finance as the biggest constraint operating against end user housing improvements.

Table 2.4 Comparison of investment in formal and informal settlements

	The informal settlement *San José de Chirica*	The formal settlement *El Gallo*
Summary of development	In 1978, 60 rural families invaded the city. The supported community leader was responsible for decisions on street clearing, layout, plot delineation and allocation. New arrivals approached the *junta* and/or leader who allocated land; the size, location, etc., depended upon family size, need, demand, friendship and favours. As demand rose, so plot sizes decreased. No deed or tenure was given, but households had to demonstrate occupancy (i.e. live in the house). Temporary dwellings were built rapidly, then progressively improved in terms of quality of construction materials and size. The settlement progressively reached urban-like standards and finally official recognition; 90 per cent of dwellings are built by individuals.	Also located on peripheral urban land, cleared in 1964 and 'urbanized'. Both settlements were built as self-managed processes. Households provided labour for infrastructure and agencies supplied project plans, materials and technical assistance in El Gallo. Residents participated in the planning of the initial layout, and successive stages of development were totally self-managed; 70 per cent was privately financed, constructed and managed.
Observation of the evolution of streets, blocks, and plots over the lifetime of the development, based on roofed dwelling area and consolidation as indicated by improvement in construction materials.	Some non-permanent shelters averaged 43m² Some non-permanent shelters grew from an average of 9m² to 38m² before permanent buildings were erected Non-permanent structures were used as primary shelters, while more basic family needs were met, for example services and infrastructure provided, income sources discovered or generated, more favourable social environment developed.	Temporary shelters averaged 45m² Temporary shelters remained unaltered until permanent structures of 78 to 88m² were built. It took longer to reach each stage of development. Because tenure was secure, it was not necessary for the owners to show consolidation to try to gain tenure. The piecemeal construction observed by many housing researchers was only evident in the informal settlement.

continued on next page

Table 2.4 Comparison of investment in formal and informal settlements (cont.)

San José de Chirica	El Gallo
Many temporary shelters were upgraded with durable materials. Showing consolidation was a means to obtain legal status and create pressure for infrastructure provision. Area increases were similar to El Gallo, though in San José the successive increases were reached in half the time.	Savings accumulated during a similar period enabling permanent structures to be built.
	Some in El Gallo spent sixteen years in temporary shelter without upgrading.
The non-permanent stage differed with regard to investment patterns. Informal households continually invested in housing improvements over time (a characteristic for which an allowance was made in El Gallo).	Land formed part of the housing proposal and therefore desirable urban standards were met in the planned use of open and closed areas, which remained constant. Standards included allowance for small crops and poultry raising. Subdivision was very difficult and only occurred in corner plots. Started by matching official standards for plot areas and densities.
In either settlement it is difficult to assess which of the development processes was more convenient for residents, though inhabitants in San José spent at least twelve years in non-permanent shelters.	Progressive provision of infrastructure and services released pressure on living conditions enabling longer stay in non-permanent shelters. Despite formal planning premises, consolidation of infrastructure was slow and far from acceptable by conventional standards.
At the beginning of the process people's living conditions were difficult (i.e. no services or infrastructure), but they were compensated by having access to large plots of land. Land use evolved rationally, a natural self-defined process of intensification that moved towards an urban-like environment in terms of layout, services, dwelling area and construction quality, which meet low-income housing standards.	

Source: Summarized from text of Reimers and Portela 1995

Land regularization and tenure security

Several state initiatives have aimed to regularize the situation for urban informal settlements. In Trinidad and Tobago the Regularization of Tenure (State Lands) Act enabled any squatter with a history of residence on the land to make a claim for a 30-year lease (Matthews Glenn et al. 1993). Despite good intentions the scheme failed to increase access to regularized land because the criteria and procedures employed were too restrictive.

An NGO initiative called Sou Sou Land, which began almost inadvertently in Trinidad, was able to draw on the lessons of the informal sector, while using the professional skills of an economist, a lawyer, a journalist and others to house a group of squatters who had been issued with an eviction order. They acquired a large tract of abandoned agricultural land on which to house the former squatters, and aimed to avoid the pitfalls that had been the downfall of earlier projects. Based on simple but planned designs with adequate allowances for the incremental development of infrastructure, the major differences from previous efforts were planning, community and financial mobilization, self-help and ownership of the land by the participants, and the stipulation that the subdivisions could be upgraded and legally regularized at a later date. 'The nature of the company's operations developed in response to participants' needs and demands. The most viable projects were those that paid close attention to these factors. The projects based upon the directors' utopian ideas ran into problems of participant acceptability and later of financial insolvency' (Mohammed 1997:237).

During the International Year of the Homeless in 1987, Sou Sou Land was highlighted by the UN as one of ten innovative success stories. 'Endorsement [by the government and legal institutions] became possible only because what had previously been a programme of illegal land development had had its approach endorsed as state policy.' The approach fitted well with new thinking in international development and policy. Ten years on, however, it was found that the 'model has only been partially adopted by the Trinidad and Tobago government, and to an even lesser extent other governments' (Mohammed 1997:234). Institutional differences appear to constrain governments from adopting processes like those implemented by NGOs or community-based organizations (CBOs). Innovation was further restricted by the conditions imposed by multi-lateral agencies, especially the Inter-American Development Bank. Such agencies were until very recently preoccupied with efficiency and cost recovery, and had no capacity for dealing with, or supporting, NGOs and CBOs.

The government's Project 100 was an attempt to replicate the Sou Sou Land experience, but it lacked many of its positive aspects. A government-run programme creates different expectations among participants. Lower standards were not accepted, and the state agencies responsible for setting standards did not factor in incremental improvements, self-help, or community savings. Project implementation was slowed down by bureaucratic planning, tendering, and financing procedures. After eighteen months only 800 out of a potential 10 000 residential lots were developed, and they were restricted to subdivisions because of 'problems of legal vesting' (Mohammed 1997). The lowest income groups were excluded, and dependency on the IADB's loan and conditions meant the programme ground to a halt.

A broad programme known as 'housing with services' in Chile, including land subdivision and allocation, was based on each family's social and economic needs, and the state provided a subsidy of up to 75 per cent of the costs incurred in purchasing land, redrawing plots, providing services and building latrines (Mercado and Uzín 1996:16). State subsidies of land are generally thought by planners to be an effective means of helping the poorest people, yet examples exist to demonstrate that the *modus operandi* during planning and implementation has just as significant an impact on the final outcome. Land subsidies in Bolivia were made possible because of innovative delivery strategies, for example (Mercado and Uzín 1996:18). The national university played an important role in the survey of land and existing buildings. Given the high level of professional fees, voluntary input by architectural students was a welcome contribution that enabled plots to be formally defined, the settlements concerned to be mapped, and thereby officially recognized, so facilitating land registration and acquisition. Free technical assistance was also provided to enable self-help improvements through technical training and support. Credits for housing improvements were only granted on the need 'to solve health and safety deficiencies'. Despite these positive aspects, however, fifteen years on the project was said to have failed because of the inadequacy of one or more of the technical, legal and financial delivery mechanisms.

Unrealistic expectations could be said to be accountable for the failure of some sites and services projects in Zimbabwe. It was clearly demonstrated that the provision of ultra low-cost core houses was economically expedient: 26 386 units were built between 1978 and 1981 compared with 9882 units between 1974 and 1977. The political climate was such, however, that neither the government nor the target population was prepared to accept such low standards, which were 'anathema in independent Zimbabwe' (Potts and Mutambirwa 1991). The Zimbabwe story is told in greater detail in Chapter 4.

Success in persuading governments to grant property rights to the poorest sections of society has been slow, and often occurs only after considerable political momentum has gathered and effective pressure has been applied. In Brazil, the popular uprising among *favela* dwellers was so huge that politicians were forced to recognize it. Immediate solutions were necessary, especially to the explosive issue of land tenure. The enactment of the PRO-FAVELA legislation, which officially and unequivocally recognized the *favela* dwellers' legal rights to the property on which they lived, was a landmark.

In Peru, the Institute for Freedom and Democracy (ILD) proposed a system for the regularization of ownership that attempted to link the informal practices and the legal system. Approved by legislative decree in 1988, the *Registro Predial* was created to register regularized plots using simplified procedures. In three-and-a-half years, the programme registered 142 000 plots in the Lima area; 220 000 plots were registered nationwide by June 1995. The key features of the programme include:

- new laws recognizing proof of property as defined by the informal sector (for example, duration of occupancy and allowance for transfer and mortgaging of registered plots)
- the creation of a single, decentralized body with the sole purpose of registering land and giving titles
- new procedures that integrate community, rather than individual, plans for setting boundaries; lawyers and engineers employed rather than public servants for verification and community information gathering; and a simple and efficient geographical accounting system.

Lima city has spread mainly through *urbanizaciones populares*, the result of a housing process dominated by self-help: 'la autoayuda, el autoempuje, y la autoconstrucción' (roughly translated, self-help, self-motivation and self-build) (Burga 1987). The ILD was instrumental not only in the land reforms outlined above, but also in increasing access to finance from the formal financial services sector. The participatory approach adopted in designing and implementing the registration system shows a clear commitment to the principle of working with informal communities, and to mobilizing public and political support. As a result, ILD's Property Rights Law was enacted, with full support from all parties across the entire Peruvian political spectrum. By taking the services into the settlements and engaging with the people, the system developed in response to feedback from all stakeholders, and it remained simple, efficient and accessible.

User-led standards

Although many national standards in the South have been transferred inappropriately from other countries, it is logical to learn from existing practices. Traditional housing is often the most efficient response to the need for human habitat; it is suited to the site's environment and inhabitants' lifestyle, and it uses local construction materials and resources. Empirical studies of existing habitat can be systematized into standard designs and form the basis of Housing Design Standards, Urban Design Standards, and recommendations for efficient dwelling design. 'Extremely poor' settlements in Brasilia improved rapidly from sites with demarcated plots along unpaved roads to an active neighbourhood linked by bus to the city, demonstrating 'their ability to mobilize resources in order to build their houses within a short period of time. Many shacks were replaced by houses within a short period of time' (Acioly 1994:255).

Communities in Botswana were equally resourceful in meeting their housing needs when helped by an enabling environment. 'The simple observation was made that many people had already erected a wide variety of house types and that presumably all of these were affordable. Based on this observation, the Ministry approved a policy permitting individual plot-holders not only to build their own houses but also to plan them, provided they could gain assistance from technical staff in the Self Help Housing Authority (SHHA)' (Van Nostrand 1982:45) 'The open-mindedness of the proposed housing programme was reinforced by the adoption of a simple and easily comprehended building code. This defined a "habitable room" as a building of not less than nine square metres, having a door, two windows, cross ventilation, and a minimum head height. Plot-holders were permitted to use whatever materials they desired, provided these were of a permanent quality' (Van Nostrand 1982:46).

Initiatives in Zambia to establish standards based 'on culturally derived patterns of usage' ran into the problem faced by many who carry out 'market surveys', that is, that people say they want one thing when in practice they demonstrate a preference for another. 'In the issue of plot size we noted research had already shown that although people wanted big plots (and who does not?) the reasons for wanting the space could not be justified by the amount of gardening activity ... those families which were active in cultivation grew maize and groundnuts outside the town ... Where people had the chance to set out their own layout, and decide the shape and size of their plot, the actual plot size was much smaller than the standard plot, even where land was not a constraint ... Plots laid out under these circumstances were wider, and gave a much more spacious appearance' (Martin 1980:14).

There is a notable absence of discussion on the issue of gender in relation to housing standards. Within the body of literature reviewed for this study, the needs of women are mentioned only four times. One is a reference to innovative housing projects in which women produced MCR tiles in Kenya (Agevi 1990:29); the second considers the needs of women in their domestic role, that is, space allocated to cooking (Yitna 1994:128). The third reference also pertains to spatial requirements: in Tanzania, the government increased the size of high density plots to a minimum of 15m × 30m for four reasons, the last of which includes 'the construction of courtyards where females live and do their daily activities' (Athman 1992:15). The final reference is found in relation to the community-based processes developed in Sri Lanka, where a minimum representation of women was assured in setting the new standards (see Box 5), and work in women-only groups was facilitated.

There is a increasing need to consider technology choices in terms of women's needs. In some countries self-help construction is traditionally undertaken by women, and they are likely to be displaced unless new technologies are introduced carefully. The rapid increase in female-headed households, especially among the urban poor, is another compelling reason for designers, implementers, and regulators to give women's needs careful consideration.

A reluctance to 'reduce standards' can be circumvented using *ad hoc* dispensations and applying project-specific standards. Efforts to regulate low-income settlements at a national level usually require prior definition of 'special areas'. Even the most supportive governments avoid a general lowering of standards by confining provision to allocated areas. Some local authorities in Kenya, faced with the high costs of existing standards and under pressure from major donors, adopted lower planning and building standards for incidental projects, on an *ad hoc* basis.

There have, however, been some inspirational attempts to accommodate those on a low income in a manner that does respond to their needs, while avoiding the stigma of 'informality' or 'illegality'. This section draws on a few experiences that demonstrate that alternative means of increasing access to adequate, affordable housing do exist and can succeed. In Malawi, three decades of emphasis on minimal site and services led to the establishment of traditional housing areas. THAs, especially designated settlement areas, enabled people to use traditional construction materials and technologies. This approach may have had

Box 5   Minimum intervention, maximum support by the state

Maximum involvement of the builder families

Sri Lanka's One Million Houses Programme is perhaps the most extensive example of a people-led housing process, in terms of both the area it covered and the time it lasted. The scale of this initiative was in itself significant as 'this was quite different to doing projects or pilot projects. There was a depth, a scale, a clarity, and a commitment which was rare' (Sirivardana 1999:14). Standards were established using a people-centred approach, facilitated by professional and technical support staff.

Building codes were formed by 20–25 participants during a two-day workshop; 3–5 resource people and 15–20 community members (with at least seven women) addressed a range of questions about building regulations and their enforcement. 'Community members interact as partners with the staff of the National Housing Development Authority, the local authority and non-governmental organizations. They discuss the problems of the community, identify solutions and formulate plans of action.' After the initial community action planning workshop, half-day issue-based workshops are organized to consider any subject the communities want to raise, but which often includes

- planning principles and technical guidelines
- community building guidelines and rules
- orientation to housing information services.

The Urban Development Authority has made provision in its laws concerning planning and building standards for reduced standards in those settlements designated
as special project areas. A reduction in minimum plot size, from 150m² to 50m², fits
the limited land availability. Other basic rules include: 'No one should build beyond
his or her plot boundaries, and all plots must have a minimum open space of two
feet at the front and back' (Sirivardana 1999: 25).

The following kinds of questions are answered in the participatory workshops:
• What are the issues?
• What should the guidelines be?
• What should the rules be?
• Who must observe the rules?
• Who checks that the rules are observed?
• What can the community development council do to enforce the rules?
• How can the municipal or urban council enforce the rules?
• What should the sanctions be?

The new relationship between housing standards and support-based participatory
housing development is systematic and cross-cutting. A new ideological setting
'basically relates to a new set of values, where the poor are sovereign and subjects of
their own process of self-development' (Sirivardana 1999:13). The corollary is that
the state now becomes a sensitive supporter and partner, the other partner in the
dialogic relationship.

significant effect nationally, acting as a model of 'appropriate and affordable housing' development that gives the poor a chance to access housing (Amis and Lloyd 1990). Subsequent
political pressure to retain Lilongwe's image as a garden city led to initiatives to upgrade
THAs, however, and resulted in a rise in standards, commercialization – with plots being
bought rather than allocated – and overcrowding (Potts 1994 and Schilderman 1998).
Lower standards were accepted in several other African countries after many years of
passive resistance by the authorities, yet little effort has gone into dissemination, so that
these innovative national standards have had little impact to date (Romangnolo 1996).

The impact of revised standards

There has been little systematic research aimed at assessing the impact of building standards
or their revisions. In Zimbabwe 'no assessment of the effectiveness and affordability of the
revised standards has been made since they were released in 1992' (Mugova and
Musandu-Nyamayaro 1997:16), and ITDG Zimbabwe's own survey of users suggests that
most people have not noticed any change since the revisions took place.

Some of the stated objectives for making alterations have been ambitious, for example 'to
remove the segregation of people' (Athman 1992:15); 'to create technological continuity'
(Lowe 1998a:18), and so on. This section outlines some of the evidence that shows the impact
of change in local and national regulations.

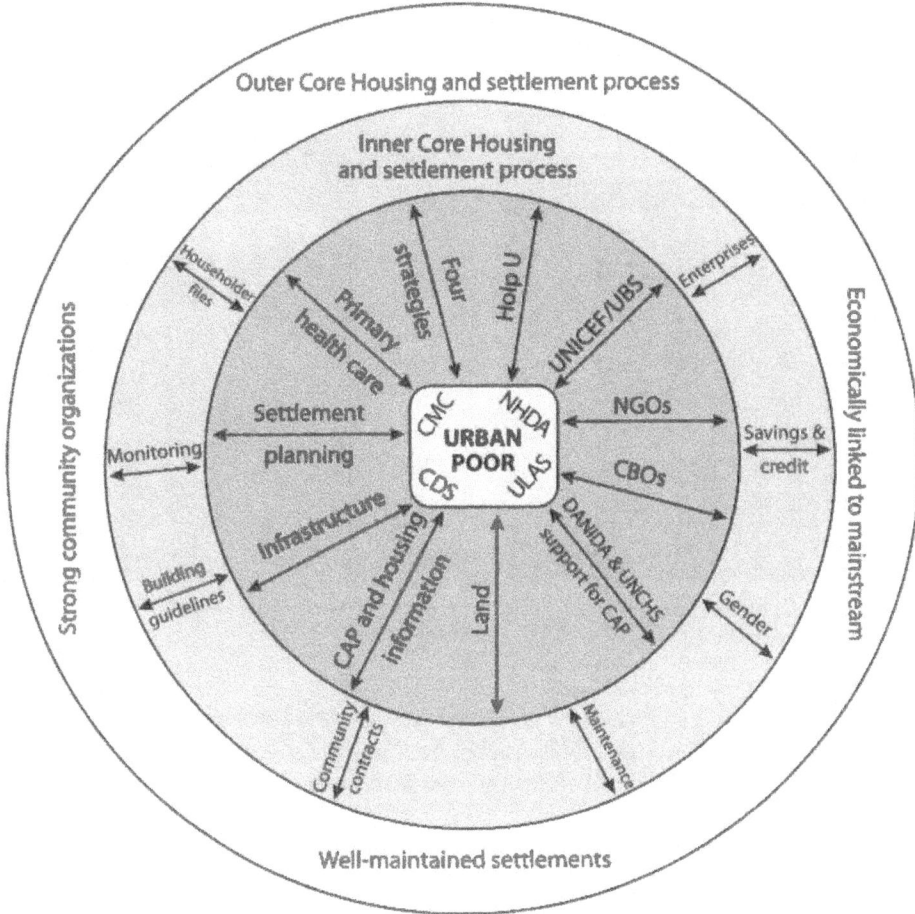

Figure 5 The One Million Houses Programme: the conceptual umbrella

Source: Sirivardana 1999

Less expensive shelter

ITDG's experience working with people in low-income settlements in Kenya and Zimbabwe has demonstrated clearly that people are able to use alternative building materials which enhance the physical environment and to build in a cost-effective manner. In Nakuru, stabilized soil structures have been built with the support of the Municipal Council, creating visibly improved dwelling units; demonstration structures in Chitungwiza, a peri-urban settlement in Harare, cost 30 per cent less using newly permitted materials when compared with 'conventional' materials.

Lower standards and infrastructure provision in Botswana (in the self-help housing areas) 'help to keep the scheme affordable to the poor' (Yahya 1998b). The application in Kenya of the 1985 Low Cost By-laws demonstrated the potential; the design standards used for the Umoja II project have enabled the construction of housing units for individual

Photo 3   One of the new model houses built according to the revised standards in Chitungwiza

ownership with waterborne sanitation and other services for the lowest price achieved since independence. The project was partly funded by USAID, which went to great lengths to ensure that Nairobi City Council relaxed the rules to accommodate the poor.

Material cost reductions

In Peru ministerial support was given for a reduction in standards in designated areas. In this way it was possible to use local materials and adopt a self-help approach; the resulting reduction in cost per unit floor area was estimated to be one-third the cost of conventional materials (Fattal 1998:IV–20). Such experience can also have a long-term influence; in this case the Building Code is currently being amended. Similar examples are available from other countries. Cost comparisons between improved traditional materials such as *quincha ameliorada* and conventional materials show savings of 20 to 40 per cent (Díaz 1984:19). Considerable savings were made when building schools in India over conventional reinforced concrete construction, thanks to the adoption of materials and technologies usually considered substandard.

Procedural cost reduction

Procedural requirements and associated costs have been shown to act as an effective barrier to many people's participation in the formal housing process. The Municipal Council in Nakuru, Kenya, has reduced costs by cutting bureaucratic procedures and approving plans 'en bloc' (Yahya and Agevi 1997).

In Trinidad and Tobago, legal revisions enabled squatters to claim a 30-year lease on land that they had occupied for some years. Impact was severely limited by the eligibility criteria applied, however, which included cut-off dates and continual occupancy requirements. The adversarial nature of the process was also an effective barrier to individuals, who would have needed to engage legal professionals, and it also overloaded state organizations. It was estimated that it would take 30 years for the existing institutional capacity to deal with all the potential claims (Matthews Glenn et al. 1993). In response to the apparent difficulties encountered, the approach changed to a settlement-wide process, rather than a lot-by-lot method, resulting in the Squatter Regularization Programme of 1989.

A reduction in land registration procedures under such accelerated delivery programmes is clear: a process that previously took at least four years to complete now requires one month. Apart from the capital cost, there are numerous other expenses relating to bureaucratic procedures, and simply being delayed incurs the subsequent cost of inflation and non-ownership. Where construction finance has been borrowed, every day counts in terms of interest due and rental income (or occupational benefits) forgone.

Cost-effectiveness in the review processes is also important if the capacity to make changes is to be enhanced. In Burkina Faso, the established structure for research and standardization aims for 'une réelle synergie entre les acteurs'(a real synergy between actors) (Tiemoko 1996:4); synergistic benefits should be incorporated in the processes required for regulation and control, that is, maximizing the benefit from existing resources rather than creating the need for more or for external resources that are unsustainable.

Livelihoods and commercial viability

Some evidence that artisans are able to generate new sources of income from newly accepted building technologies is beginning to emerge in Nakuru. Some of the aspirations held by instigators of change have been to facilitate growth in the local contracting sector and increase access to public sector work, but there is no accessible information on whether this has been achieved. Experience in West African countries suggests that steps taken towards the standardization of earthen building components have helped the few professionals using such appropriate technologies, although the poor do not yet have full confidence because they are not able to exploit the technical information provided in the standards. The knowledge gap is clearly impeding the adoption of desirable innovations.

Informal sector residents also work mainly in the informal sector, often creating their own jobs. The location of housing, and thereby access to potential markets, is crucial to the long-term viability of any settlement. Many peri-urban housing initiatives have failed because the authorities were unwilling to recognize this point. The use of housing by the informal sector as a place of work is also a common phenomenon, which is yet to be recognized by policymakers and regulators. Mixed-use planning and construction can help those with the greatest need for jobs, while supporting popular initiatives has been shown to be effective in adding value to the built environment and can do so in the realm of small- and medium-scale enterprises. Several initiatives in Kenya are now beginning to look at the need for regulatory reform and financial structures to support the small business sector.

Access to finance

Incremental development allows the houseowner to build up equity gradually, relying less on loans. Using cost-effective alternative technologies has been a significant obstacle to accessing formal sources of credit, however; the inclusion of alternative technologies in official standards could permit insurance companies to insure buildings of improved adobe, for example, and consequently enable the savings and loans industry to finance such

Photo 4 New technologies generate significant job opportunities. These women are making fibre concrete roofing tiles in a large housing scheme at Koma Rock, Nairobi

construction through mortgages (Fattal 1998:VI–20). Similar thinking lay behind approaches adopted in Latin America and was critical in the revision that took place in Tanzania in 1977. The housing finance industry has been rather slow in taking up available opportunities, however, and financial innovations have been few and far between (Siebolds and Steinberg 1982).

Experience working with all stakeholders in Kenya has also highlighted the reluctance of conventional financiers to lend money to people who want to use 'substandard' housing for collateral. 'Local authorities are not alone in maintaining the "status quo", as a number of housing finance institutions are also reluctant to support public housing developments that do not conform to the present stringent building by-laws' (Agevi 1990:29). In some Asian countries, government efforts to increase low-income housing stock are hampered by both the inability to attract the private sector developers and the absence of long-term credit facilities geared to the poor. International efforts to develop small-scale and micro-credit programmes have focused more on trading and industrial production than on housing.

Improved security and choice of location

When housing and land allocation standards are revised with the poor in mind, they can have a noticeable impact on access to secure and affordable shelter. The regularization of informal land in Egypt was allowed after external pressure (from the World Bank and USAID in particular) was brought to bear and a series of new laws and decrees was introduced: 'finally in 1984 a law provided a framework for allowing the settlers to regularize their situation by buying their plot' (El-Batran and Chandel 1998:228). There were, however, discrepancies in implementation between governorates; by 1987 only 5 per cent of potential land claims had been filed because of the high price put on government land.

Photo 5   Integrating homes and workplaces is vital to people living and working in the informal sector

Formalization of squatter settlements in Bangkok through land sharing is reported to have had a significant impact, with the housing stock gradually improving to a level much above the standards that people had under insecure land conditions. By enabling residents to upgrade with the support of the National Housing Authority, 'overcrowding within developing units has been reduced ... [there have been] improvements in housing quality ... [and] floor area grew by more than 75 per cent on average, from 25m^2 per household to 45m^2'. Unfortunately, it is also reported that these initiatives were undertaken in defiance of the existing rules pertaining to housing density and plot coverage, so 'adherence to municipal regulations in the future will necessarily limit land-sharing projects' (UNCHS 1986:72).

Security of tenure has been shown to result in increases in local economic activity, as 'residents of the low-income settlements are usually eager to start the construction or improvement of their houses' (Kioe-Sheng 1994). Experience in Bhopal, India, highlights that appreciable levels of shelter consolidation can be achieved over time through incremental investment. Neither the granting of leasehold tenure or *'patta'* to squatters nor environmental improvement schemes have had much effect on improving shelter, although a *patta* at least gives a household the explicit legal right to create a fixed private asset that can be mortgaged to mobilize finance for house building or employment generation (Mitra 1990). The World Bank's experience supports the premise that 'generally, the granting of tenure on government lands is a form of subsidy that is progressive, tending to focus benefits on the low-income groups' (World Bank 1993:116). The requirement that residents need to show occupancy and land 'ownership' also encourages people to build with permanent materials as a means of staking a claim on the property.

In Kenya, regularization through the community-based land trust has had an impact that is difficult to quantify or value, although 'the fear of eviction and demolition of structures by the authorities has disappeared' (Mshila 1997). The same paper reports that once people have security, they enhance their housing through the 'use of improved techniques and appropriate building materials'. The cost factor must not be overlooked, however, as access to land is enhanced by reduced costs. Cost implications associated with plot sizes are related to the subsequent cost of infrastructure provision. 'Apart from urban sprawl, provision of large plots leads to extravagant use of land' (Athman 1992:16). Similar issues were faced in Jamaica. Given their willingness to accept the low level of infrastructure, Sou Sou Land benefited from considerable reductions in unit costs, partly from the negotiating power held in buying large tracts of land from a depressed agricultural sector which 'resulted in raw land costs as little as one-seventh of the residentially zoned land in the formal market' (Mohammed 1997).

More and better houses

What are the possible effects of revised standards or housing stock indicators in terms of how many and how good? It was found in settlements adopting lower standards in Botswana that 'the level of overcrowding found in (cities such as) Harare and Lilongwe has not appeared and many plotholders are consolidating their residences to fairly high standards' (Potts 1994:217).

In Bangkok, where the rules apply to structures' height (up to two storeys) and plot coverage, but do not restrict permissible materials, it was found that average household expenditure on construction was US$760 in 1982–3 – more than double the value of the houses in the original settlement. Added to the physical improvements is the value of the regularized land, which creates problems when the higher income sector becomes interested (UNCHS Habitat 1986). The impact of incremental processes in Brasilia has already been discussed.

Changes in the social housing sector in the UK led to a reduction in the average area of newly built housing association units. A study by the National Federation of Housing Associations showed that in the year 1989–90, '53 per cent of housing association general needs housing was built with a floor area 5 per cent or more below Parker Morris' (Walentowicz 1992). By the time of a later survey, undertaken by Karn and Sheridan (1994) and covering the year 1991–2, the equivalent figure had risen to 68 per cent' (both quoted in Goodchild 1997:104).

In general, incremental, user-led changes have resulted in significant economic activity and enhancement of the national housing stock. In Peru, for example, 'the total squatter housing stock had a replacement value of US$8.3 billion in 1982' (World Bank 1993:16).

Building materials quality

Building materials' standards aim to ensure quality, consistency and suitability to the purpose for which they are intended. Under the European Directive 89/106, regulations subsume their right to be on the market to the fitness for use. The strict controls in industrialized countries virtually guarantee the quality of construction materials through a plethora of support resources and laws. In many countries, however, the resources and systems are not adequate to ensure that regulatory mechanisms work. It has been shown how some manufacturers are able to show compliance to voluntary standards in order to further enhance their market viability and create a competitive edge. In Burkina Faso 'LOCOMAT has partly encouraged the development of the SEB sector. Consequently the number of producers, therefore market availability, has increased considerably' (Lowe 1998a).

If standards are to have any impact, they have to be effective. Experience in the Ivory Coast shows that the effects on construction quality of earthen architecture has been as good as nothing – because professionals and public servants are ignorant of the new standards. Nonetheless, the use of alternative cost-effective building materials is no doubt assisted by official regulation to support production and implementation. The confidence of those people responsible for enforcing regulations is crucial to the uptake of any newly permitted material. In Nakuru, Kenya, during an evaluation of revised by-laws, the municipal engineer acknowledged the fact that he had been able to refer to national codes from the National Bureau of Standards to verify the validity of the materials in question, and this greatly helped the community members in producing and employing these materials.

Many projects are time- and resource-bound, with little scope for unforeseen delays. The international efforts led by CRATerre-EAG to establish pan-African standards for earthen architecture have been 'process oriented not means driven; to ensure the process continues until the desired result is achieved' (Lowe 1998a:17). The completion of the democratic process means the standards developed have already been translated into several languages, used as teaching materials and adopted by several national authorities. The regional approach was able to overcome the political inertia and opposition that so often ruins such collaborative initiatives. It must not be forgotten that the initiative came from France, a rich nation with the material and intellectual resources to invest in the future of a continent with which it has strong cultural and commercial relations.

Economic pressures on the social housing sector in the UK play a key role in reducing the quality of materials employed. Unlike in developing countries, it is felt in the UK that the long-term impact will not be from incremental improvements, but from an increased need for component replacement, effectively transferring capital costs to life-cycle costs.

Infrastructure adequacy

When developing new settlement sites, the provision of a minimum level of services is essential to create a safe and healthy environment. But what level of provision is required for the settlement to be of an adequate standard? Infrastructure tends to include water, sanitation, roads and electricity, but numerous initiatives labelled 'site and services' have adopted varying standards and demonstrated that initial provision of all these services can put unit costs beyond the reach of poor people. In Malawi, where a generally 'cheap and simple' approach was adopted, the cost of roads was found to make the average cost per plot too high, so 'it was decided to spread the development of the road works over successive stages' (Crooke 1981:29). The distribution of costs over time may not reduce final costs, but does enable greater access by the poor.

While 'scarce funds, low population, and light traffic use make low standards and costs of servicing both necessary and justifiable' (Crooke 1981), the acceptance of lower starter standards requires careful design to ensure the systems can cope with increased loads without requiring total replacement when population densities increase. Rapid urban growth in Zimbabwe and 'backyard shack' syndrome have resulted in severe pressures on the infrastructure, which ultimately leads to higher maintenance and servicing costs or breakdown. Experience in Malawi also demonstrated that the need for foresight is paramount; a water delivery system that was installed to cater for communal water points had to be replaced as the flow was insufficient to cater for on-plot connections (Crooke 1981:49). The high cost of infrastructure provision is influenced by two factors:

- The historically vague basis of the nature and performance standards of infrastructure makes it difficult to judge what are appropriate or acceptable reductions.
- Regulatory bodies hesitate to approve lower standards given the uncertainty around whether or not the unusual maintenance patterns and upgrading will be undertaken.

Where lower standards have been allowed, the result has been an increased degree of legal development, facilitating the processes of land servicing and mortgage financing. At the same time social infrastructure has to be provided if future human development is to be assured. Schools, primary health care, environmental standards and neighbourhood decision-making structures clearly have to be established to determine need and develop solutions. Work in India has shown that introducing cost-effective construction technologies into the formal systems of infrastructure provision is fraught with difficulties, but it can also result in increased provision for the same amount of resources; community planning and resource mobilization are critical, as is a cadre of supportive professional staff with a positive attitude.

In spite of these positive aspects of standards revision, it is important not to lose sight of the fact that public expenditure on infrastructure in low-income countries is already very low, and there is a limit to how much further cost reductions can be achieved. The UN reports that in the early 1990s annual government expenditure on water supply, sanitation, drainage, rubbish collection and electricity in South Asian cities averaged US$16.6 per person compared with US$656 in the cities of Europe and North America. The implication is that, while standards should be appropriate and affordable, the search for innovation should not be allowed to absolve governments and local authorities of their responsibility to ensure that adequate resources are directed towards physical and social infrastructure.

3
LESSONS FROM KENYA

Introduction

Although the link between poverty and housing standards has only recently become the subject of serious scientific study, it has been recognized in African development literature and policy documents for nearly half a century. The history of housing standards in Kenya began with differential housing rules in colonial times, progressed through post-independence egalitarian visions, and ended with the targeted strategies of the post-structural adjustment era. Kenya was one of the first African countries to codify systematically the standards believed to be appropriate for its newly urbanized citizens. In 1968, barely four years after independence, what are now known as Grade II By-laws provided a simplified code for use in the rural–urban fringe. This change set the stage for subsequent reforms, which are still continuing.

This chapter describes the Kenyan experience in formulating and updating standards for low-income housing. It traces the origins of the process, the main instigators and their motives, and the results that have been achieved. The information was collected mainly in 1997–8 from a variety of sources, including official documents, field surveys, workshops, focused group discussions and other participatory methods. This chapter is itself part of the review process, since it is meant to draw lessons for the future and to present an appraisal of successes and failures.

Urbanization

Kenya is urbanizing rapidly. After independence in 1963, rural–urban migration increased dramatically, and led to urban overcrowding. The urban share of its population has grown from 5 per cent at the time of the first census in 1948 to nearly 21 per cent in 1997. In other words, 5 877 000 of Kenya's national population of 28 145 000 are now living in towns and cities. Nairobi, the capital city, has an estimated population of 3.2 million.

The most pressing issues facing this urban population, as defined in the consultative process for Habitat II, include poverty, unemployment and poor access to land, energy, and basic infrastructure and services. The cost of conventional building materials is beyond the reach of low-income and vulnerable groups, many of whom do not have access to housing finance and credit. Over the last decade, inadequate settlement planning and management policies, coupled with the limited use of appropriate materials and technologies, have resulted in a marked deterioration of the urban environment.

Shelter policies

Kenya's first housing policy was developed in 1966–7 with technical assistance from the United Nations. Several institutions were created as a result of that policy, including a ministry dealing with housing, a Housing Corporation, a Housing Research and Development Unit, and a Housing Finance Company. By 1980 the policy had become outdated. A series of surveys were undertaken and led to the formulation of a new National Housing Strategy for Kenya 1987–2000. An important element of this strategy was the 'enablement approach', in which the government's role shifted from being a direct developer of low-income housing to one of working with, and facilitating, housing development by private entities.

The National Plan of Action, created in late 1995 in the run-up to Habitat II, includes more specific proposals, particularly for the enabling role of the government. These proposals fall under the general heading of shelter delivery systems for: markets; land for shelter; regularization of informal settlements; finance; basic infrastructure and services; building materials; construction; maintenance and rehabilitation; and vulnerable groups. The questions of shelter standards, building by-laws and planning regulations feature prominently in the plan, because it cuts across the pressing issues of affordability, land, materials, technology, durability and financing. The activities relating to housing standards and procedures in the plan are highlighted in Box 6.

Box 6 Summary of activities relating to housing standards and procedures in the Kenyan National Plan of Action (NPA) for Shelter and Human Settlements

Shelter markets

- Review periodically the legal and regulatory frameworks, including planning and building codes and standards
- Establish procedures that will make property transactions transparent
- Formulate and implement innovative programmes through relaxation and simplification of property laws, cadastre, improved value rating, building by-laws, and planning regulations, among others

Land

- Simplify land survey, registration, transfer and title documentation procedures
- Review and consolidate legislative and regulatory instruments influencing the planning of land for shelter development and related support facilities

Land markets

- Review, reformulate, and consolidate land rights legislation
- Review urban planning legislation in a responsive and harmonious manner

Access to land

- Review existing land tenure systems

Land administration

- Decentralize and simplify planning approval procedures
- Decentralize land administration and management at local level
- Harmonize and consolidate scattered land legislation that is relevant to citizen's shelter development needs
- Establish a partnership policy approach in legislative and regulatory reviews, recognizing the engagement of NGOs, CBOs, citizens, and the private sector in collective participatory approaches in shelter development

Building materials and maintenance

- Revise building codes and standards

Vulnerable groups

- Review and revise legal and regulatory frameworks that act as barriers within the shelter sector
- Formulate programmes and establish norms to eliminate social exclusions, prejudices, and discrimination in shelter transactions and services provision

Source: Kenya Ministry of Works and Housing 1996

Building standards and procedures

Building standards and procedures are one of Kenya's most important colonial legacies. The earliest building controls were developed in urban areas to ensure that settlers were not endangered by the potential spread of disease from areas settled by locals. The earliest attempts to introduce legislation related to building and planning can be traced to around 1900, when surveyors started plotting camps and townships along the Kenya–Uganda Railway, which was then under construction.

It was not until 1926 that the Nairobi Municipal Council introduced its first comprehensive set of building and planning regulations. Only Mombasa had earlier by-laws related to building. Other public health and building controls were introduced during the development of Kisumu, Nakuru and Eldoret, and these regulations formed the basis of norms adopted by local authorities administering smaller urban centres.

The main statutes governing building standards, design and materials today are the Building Code and the Public Health Act. Yet other building, planning and engineering standards, statutes and regulations are scattered in various legal documents, including town planning, land and housing laws; the Public Health Act; the Local Government Act; and subsidiary legislation. This muddle is made worse by the fact that there are a host of government agencies responsible for policy, legislation, enforcement and control of housing. The resulting confusion means that existing statutes (see Table 3.1) are, in some instances, contradictory.

Table 3.1   Kenyan legislation relevant to housing

The Building Code, 1968, consisting of Local Government (Adoptive By-laws) (Building) Order, 1968, and Local Government (Adoptive By-laws) (Grade II Building) Order, 1968

The Public Health Act, Cap. 242

The Housing Act, Cap. 177

The Rent Restriction Act, Cap. 296

The Government Lands Act, Cap. 280

The Local Government Act, Cap. 265

The Land Control Act, Cap. 302

The Trust Land Act, Cap. 288

The Streets Adoption Act, Cap. 406

The Water Act, Cap. 372

The Fire Inquiry Act, Cap. 103

The Land Acquisition Act, Cap. 300

The Guarantee (Loans) Act, Cap. 461

The Sectional Properties Act No.21 1987

The Land Planning Act, Cap. 303 (Repealed by the Physical Planning Act 1997)

Source: The Laws of Kenya

Of all these laws, the Public Health Act is the most far-reaching in respect of the power it wields over the built environment. For example, the Minister of Local Authorities can approve by-laws proposed by a local authority only with the agreement of the Minister of Health. The powers contained in the Public Health Act also constitute the main conflict between building legislation and the production of low-cost housing using appropriate building materials and techniques.

The act covers the:

- type of construction and materials to be used
- amount of space around buildings
- lighting and ventilation of buildings
- size of rooms to be used for human habitation
- prohibition of the erection and use of temporary or movable buildings for business or dwelling purposes
- prohibition of the use of buildings until an occupation certificate has been issued
- repair or demolition of unsafe, dilapidated, or dangerous buildings.

Local authorities are empowered by the Public Health and Local Government Acts to make their own building by-laws or planning regulations. However, local authorities have rarely exercised this right, partly because of a lack of resources and, with the exceptions of Nairobi and Mombasa, have instead just used those proposed by the central government.

The case for appropriate standards and regulations

Between 50 and 70 per cent of urban residents in Kenya live in informal settlements where a substantial proportion of construction makes use of earth and timber-based products. Local by-laws completely ignore this fact, specifying instead modern materials and techniques: cement and mortar, steel and electrical and sanitary installations that are appropriate for middle- and high-income housing, and commercial or industrial developments. Since the majority of low-income urban residents cannot afford these materials or techniques, most building in the rapidly growing informal settlements (whether on public or private land) contravenes both land-use controls and building standards.

The sheer volume of relevant legislation (see Table 3.1) is also confusing to developers, whose frustration is aggravated by individual interpretations of these statutes, as in several projects on the Dandora and Umoja estates in Nairobi. Housing development is consequently complicated and sometimes made more costly by the difficulties of obtaining building permits. The application of the legislation is slow, cumbersome and expensive. The situation is worsened by the many public, quasi-public and private sector groups that have vested and, occasionally, conflicting interests in the formulation and implementation of these standards.

For these reasons the official standards and norms are taken seriously by only a small proportion of private developers. For the majority, the standards and regulations are no more than minor irritants that they ignore. This renders the standards inadequate and irrelevant to community needs and aspirations, particularly to residents in unauthorized and low-cost shelter settlements.

The review process

Concerns over the suitability of the existing building regulations were raised in the 1960s, when Kenya was about to become independent. It became obvious that a critical appraisal was needed of all legislation affecting human settlements in light of the socio-political and economic trends of the time. After independence in 1963, new building legislation was prepared with the aim of providing regulations compatible with the needs, as seen then, of the country. The objective of the building code, which comprised the Grade I and Grade II Building Orders of 1968, was to produce legislation that would encourage experimentation and new ideas. In particular, the Grade II by-laws were designed to enable the inhabitants of the primarily agricultural peri-urban areas of municipalities to satisfy the building control requirements of the urban authorities, but in a semi-urban situation.

Setting the pace

In spite of these new building codes, which retained the former colonial requirements, there was a strong need to reform the planning, building and infrastructural legislation and regulations. Further review of the legislation was not a priority for the government, however, despite empirical evidence demonstrating the advantages of adopting appropriate standards, especially for low-cost housing. Not until the 1970s, when the government undertook the construction of massive housing schemes in major urban centres, did it become clear to the policymakers that the houses (such as the Dandora 'I' estate in Nairobi) would be unaffordable to the target groups unless the regulations were changed. The pressure on the government to review the by-laws and regulations largely came from two key players in urban development projects in Kenya – the World Bank and USAID.

In 1979 the government commissioned a major survey of low-cost housing by-laws, an act that made Kenya one of the first Third World countries to undertake such a study. Its purpose was to analyse the performance of the existing building control system and to develop measures to enhance its efficiency. The study was undertaken by a strong team of both local and international consultants, including architects, planners, lawyers, engineers, political scientists and environmental health specialists, but, crucially, without the involvement of end users. Given the tense atmosphere between the World Bank and the Kenyan authorities, between the 'progressive' (researchers, academics, planners) and 'conservative' (administrators, public health officials) camps, it was essential to include environmental health specialists. The study was characterized by the:

- desire to scale down a 'modern conventional house' to make it cheaper but without losing the modern attributes
- recognition of the need to reduce the standards much further but an unwillingness to do so
- willingness of authorities in each area to allow other standards to be reduced but not their own departments.

After numerous discussion papers and interim reports, the study made various recommendations to enhance rational urban development, with particular emphasis on low-cost housing, and to change the existing building code and the Public Health Act with a view to making them compatible with the needs of the urban majority. Then the report disappeared amongst the dusty files of the departments, authorities and committees that seem to characterize governments everywhere.

The report resurfaced in the mid-1980s, when an inter-ministerial and multi-disciplinary committee was constituted to devise ways and means to implement the now five-year-old recommendations. The team successfully sought government approval to adopt immediately those guidelines that did not require legislative changes. The government also supported a recommendation that the entire building code be revised and a central technical committee be established to co-ordinate and regularly monitor the performance of all building by-laws. Approval for legislative action on the building code was given, and the ministers for Works, Housing and Physical Planning and for Health and Local Government, together with the Attorney General, urged implementation of the by-laws immediately. Unfortunately, even with cabinet approval, none of the recommendations from the Kenya low-income housing by-laws review was implemented and the report soon disappeared into another bureaucratic bog.

Breaking the committee–study–seminar cycle

The review process had other significant outcomes, including a *Town Planning Handbook* produced by the Physical Planning Department and other research publications by the Housing Research and Development Unit (HRDU) of the University of Nairobi. The adoption of lower planning and building standards by Nairobi City Council in 1981 was a milestone. This important event was followed by other major municipalities such as Mombasa, Kisumu, Nakuru and Eldoret a few years later, but these standards were applied in an unco-ordinated way.

During this period many of the agencies that were trying to introduce innovative building materials and technologies became very frustrated. The old restrictive by-laws remained in force, even though many stakeholders continued to press for the revised by-laws to be implemented. By this time, a number of NGOs and academics had taken a keen interest in the debate. ITDG and Shelter Forum, for example, played a proactive role in studying the policy environment and organizing broad-based seminars and meetings.

In 1990 ITDG organized a national seminar to highlight the difficulties in implementing the 1985 recommendations and to formulate strategies to overcome those difficulties. The seminar's mandate was to form a plan of action that would identify and recommend policy, administrative, legal, institutional and technical courses of action. With this in mind, a task force that drew its members from a broad base in the public, private and voluntary sectors was set up chaired by the Ministry of Lands and Housing. It started its work with enthusiasm, but was eventually disbanded because of financial constraints.

While all members of the task force agreed about the need to update the regulations, not all concurred on the extent to which the sanitation rules should be revised. The members from institutes and NGOs, who had a better grasp of the actual situation, were still frustrated by the inability of the conservative planners to be really radical in their thinking. Coincidentally, at this point the financial constraints that were limiting the task force's contact with the major and secondary towns in the country led to a plan for the task force to visit Nairobi's main housing settlements, both formal and informal.

The task force measured the extent of people's plots, the sizes of their rooms and the thickness of the walls; it noted which materials were used for both walls and roofs, and what water and sanitation facilities were available. The members of the task force also counted the number of people living in each house. They were amazed at the way in which people were building and at the materials they were using. In retrospect, this first-hand, eye-opening encounter with reality finally persuaded the entire team that what was needed was not scaled-down standards with prescribed materials, but minimum standards from which everyone could start.

Task force members felt the standards must be related to the performance of the materials used and should not exclude the rough and ready materials with which most people were building. They had to allow people to start with a very basic structure and to add to it whenever they had the inclination and the money to do so. This alternative approach to the review, the 'bottom-up' model, identifies the lowest common denominator for health and safety, and sets a framework within which improvements may be made over time.

In 1992 funding was secured and consultants engaged to work on a smaller technical committee under the general guidance of the task force. The team presented a report containing standards that were flexible, enabling the use of inexpensive building materials and techniques and affordable infrastructure and services. The report also contained a comprehensive dissemination strategy, and highlighted the changes that would not require legislative revisions and could therefore be put into action immediately. Refined plans for the formation of a Permanent Review Board to update building and planning standards on a continuous basis were also included.

Code '92, a set of amendments to the building code that applied to low-cost housing and a manual of 'deemed to satisfy solutions' were published in 1993 and disseminated, particularly to local authorities. The revised by-laws were formally adopted by the minister for local government in 1995, after which they became known as Code '95.

Photo 6   The visit of the task force was a turning point for Kibera, the largest slum in Nairobi

The way forward

Four years after the revised by-laws were changed, 30 local authorities had adopted the regulations. (A comparative analysis of the old and revised by-laws is presented in Appendix 3.) The authorities in Nairobi, Mombasa, Nakuru, Voi, Nyahururu and Eldoret, among others, have relaxed their building standards. Agencies that support these authorities include the National Housing Co-operative Union (NACHU), the World Bank, USAID, GTZ, ITDG, and individual housing co-operative societies. NACHU-supported projects in Nairobi and Mombasa have promoted the use of lower building and planning standards, and lower standards have been applied on low-income estates such as Umoja I and II, Dandora, and Komarock in Nairobi; Huruma and Majengo in Eldoret; and Mwariki and Kwa Rhoda in Nakuru, where seven low-income neighbourhoods have been designated as eligible to benefit from the revised standards.

Even so, the implementation of reformed or relaxed standards has generally been on a project-by-project basis. The fact that the new standards have not been widely applied is attributed to four factors: poor information flow, lack of general institutional support at both local and national levels, inadequate resources, and bureaucracy. This trend shows that the challenge of reforming the building standards regime does not end with official recognition. An aggressive dissemination strategy is needed to teach local authorities and the general public about the benefits of applying the revised by-laws. Such a strategy would include workshops for civic leaders and technocrats, trainers and community-based leaders, and a hard-hitting publicity campaign through publications and the national media. The use of demonstration houses should also be adopted to test and demonstrate the viability of revised building by-laws and standards under different circumstances.

Photo 7   Mama Susan is delighted with her new single family home, built according to the revised by-laws in Kwa Rhoda, Nakuru

Dissemination of revised standards

The dissemination aspects of the standards review process in Kenya fall into three categories: pre-1995 efforts, post-1995 initiatives, and participatory house-type design. Dissemination is an unfortunate term, because it implies a flow of information and ideas from the centre to the periphery, which is rarely the best way to improve collective awareness. It also carries heavy connotations of media technology (broadcasting, press) and governmental administrative practices (circulars and district commissioners' rallies).

Pre-1995 efforts

Prior to the gazetting of the revised code in 1995 (the weekly *Kenya Gazette* is the prime official channel through which government departments announce important decisions), dissemination efforts were restricted to working sessions and workshops for experts drawn from the government, the larger local authorities, the University of Nairobi, selected NGOs and professional firms. From time to time there would be articles in Sunday papers on homelessness, unplanned settlements and the inadequacy of building by-laws.

The result was limited public awareness of the on-going efforts to change to building legislation. There is no doubt that this lack of awareness contributed to the slow way in which the Code '95 was adopted later on.

Box 7   The aims of the 1997 study of stakeholders' awareness of changes

The aim of the field investigations was to generate the necessary information and knowledge on:
- the impact of the Kenyan building code, including recent revisions, on low-cost housing delivery
- the level of awareness of the revised code among potential users
- opportunities for making standards more affordable and suited to local conditions and for disseminating simplified standards and procedures more effectively
- obstacles to further revisions of standards and simplification of procedures
- the capacity of local authorities to take full advantage of the revised code
- the extent and effectiveness of self-regulation

Post-1995 initiatives

A handful of activists who prompted the government to finalize the 1995 revisions were eager to see widespread adoption and use of the new provisions. The first priority, therefore, was to design a dissemination strategy and convince the Director of Housing not only to endorse it but also to find the necessary funding to implement it. However, hopes of securing support from a sympathetic donor did not materialize. Fortunately, Shelter Forum, a Kenyan NGO, was able to broker a partnership including ITDG, the Ford Foundation, the Department of Housing and local researchers. At the same time ITDG, inspired by the Kenyan experience, formulated an international project on code revision and enabling housing standards sponsored by the Department For International Development (DFID) in the UK. This project enabled intensive research and dissemination work to be undertaken. It was important to start documenting the review process as it occurred, and to assess the extent to which various stakeholders were aware of the changes being made. A survey was undertaken in 1997 (see Box 7) in eight towns using a questionnaire, in-depth interviews, and participatory urban appraisal. A total of 505 housing agents provided valuable feedback, 344 in the questionnaire survey and 161 during the focused group discussions.

Key findings of the 1997 study

The results of this study were expected to help prepare a methodology for the development, implementation and review of housing standards and procedures. In this way a majority of urban dwellers could gain access to legal and affordable shelter.

Awareness

Awareness among potential users of housing standards ranged from a vague acknowledgement to a detailed knowledge of standards and how they should be used. Awareness relates not only to the standards themselves but also to the associated issues of application and usage. In the case of non-professionals, 77 per cent were aware of housing standards, and 56 per cent had some knowledge of the standards in operation. All urban residents were able to identify, or see the relevance of, at least one standard within their immediate environment. Location, occupation and sex had no significant influence on the type of standards known to the respondent. Asked whether they were aware of standards in other countries, 20 per cent said that they were. About 30 per cent of respondents could relate standards to housing issues, while 20 per cent saw the necessity of standards being adaptable. These low percentages suggest that there is an urgent need for information, communication and training on all fronts.

When asked whether they knew about the procedures for building applications, 63 per cent of non-professionals said they did, and 44 per cent had actually used them; 35 per cent of all respondents considered them difficult to use, and 17 per cent easy. These figures seem high, considering the large number of renters in the sample. Nonetheless, 'application procedures' are not uniform or always formalized. In informal settlements, planning and building approvals are issued by administrative officers and landowners rather than municipal authorities. There is a general feeling of frustration among potential builders, and the need for transparent fast-track processing is evident.

Participation

Responses to questions on awareness show that the better the understanding of standards, the better the appreciation of standards review issues – that is, that an effective revision process must be built on a solid foundation of popular knowledge of the existing situation. Participation needs to be encouraged in various stages of standards' formation and application, including building control, code revision, production on site, and actual use of standards.

While some people in the poor and low-income neighbourhoods have some knowledge of housing standards, the majority are ignorant. Those who do know, however, have a broad understanding of related issues. Even among relevant professionals, not all (only 93 per cent) knew what housing standards were, and only 73 per cent were aware of the current situation.

The majority of respondents in both non-professional (65 per cent) and professional (93 per cent) groups felt that they should have been consulted in the recent review process so that they could have indicated their preferences and prioritized areas needing urgent attention. Some of the changes that the groups would have proposed include:

Professional groups	Non-professional groups
Developers to be punished for unauthorized development	Supervision of building works to be undertaken by qualified architects and engineers
Loopholes in housing administration legislation to be closed	Standard materials certified by Kenya Bureau of Standards to be used
Strict adherence to environmental quality standards	Provision of access to houses to enable ambulances, fire brigade and utility vehicles to pass for emergencies and day-to-day maintenance
Avoidance of unauthorized extensions, such as that on the Umoja Estate	

The overwhelming view of those who were familiar with building houses and who had used the revised standards was that they were not easy to use; only 18 per cent of the respondents thought they were easy to apply.

The actual level of participation in previous revision exercises was quite low; 14 per cent of the non-professional respondents knew of someone who took part.

Information

Both the questionnaire and focused group discussions asked about the best ways of sharing information on standards and the revision process. Of non-professional respondents, 38 per cent indicated that the most effective sources of information were the workplace and schools, but *barazas* (village gatherings) and working groups were seen as the most effective channels. There was very little enthusiasm for women's groups and other methods of passing on information, such as exhibitions, church meetings and seminars. Those with greater awareness of standards positively influenced the choice of information source and strategy.

When it came to the potential role of institutions, about half (47 per cent) of the respondents thought that local authorities were the most appropriate means of disseminating information, followed by schools and colleges. The majority of people did not identify public institutions as effective dissemination vehicles. The reason for this attitude could be linked to prejudices harboured against such institutions, especially relating to their inefficiency and corruption. The implication is that the credibility of public institutions should be rebuilt, because they have great potential for training and educational outreach.

The focused group discussion (FGD) results regarding information are also revealing. In the Soweto area in Kibera, an unplanned settlement close to Nairobi city centre, residents reported that they obtained information on housing through the youth centre. Among the various channels of communication, radio and newspapers were the most preferred. *Barazas* were also used to some extent.

In Kibera, the men's group preferred the following methods for disseminating information on building standards:

- (political) party offices
- chief's *baraza*
- demonstration centres
- posters
- use of local community organizations
- seminars to train leaders who will later educate the people
- radio
- schools (lessons to be introduced in upper primary schools)
- visits by organizations dealing with housing for the community
- places of worship.

The women's group felt that the most effective way of passing on information about housing standards was through the schools, by training/teaching children at primary level. They also liked:

- newspapers
- television
- churches
- training seminars.

Women's groups were the most preferred option of the children's group, as they disseminate information quickly. Their other preferences were:

- demonstrations
- radio
- friends
- posters
- television
- schools and colleges
- invitation of groups that are aware of housing standards to conduct training sessions
- chief's *baraza*
- youth groups to train parents and other people who are not aware
- teachers in schools
- churches.

The self-help group preferred:

- chief's/district officer's *barazas*
- party offices
- community/local organizations/groups
- seminars
- television
- radio
- posters
- schools/colleges.

The professionals felt that there was adequate capacity to inform (46 per cent) and that existing information strategies are adequate (62 per cent). It is not surprising that they considered working groups and women's groups as ineffective means of dissemination, although 48 per cent agreed that the *baraza* was an effective tool. They felt that the state and local authorities would play an important role in the process of change. Specific suggestions made by professionals include:

- involving professional associations, NGOs, CBOs and private sector groups
- establishing and using a column in the ALGAK journal
- organizing regular seminars and workshops.
- influencing building practice through appropriate design
- establishing district regulatory teams and involving district land officers who administer leases.

It seems that professionals are more concerned with technical competence and in maintaining professional standards and have fairly limited views on information issues.

A user survey carried out in 1999 in Nakuru indicated that in that particular town there was heightened awareness among professionals and artisans. Among professionals, 73 per cent were aware of the revised by-laws, as were 80 per cent of builders. This positive trend was corroborated by an independent evaluation of the Enabling Housing Project undertaken in March 1999. The evaluation team wrote:

The entire process has contributed greatly to the development and transfer of skills ... On the part of the community, there was evidently a great deal of pride emanating from their new-found knowledge and skills. The knowledge that they could interact with the MCN [Municipal Council of Nakuru] and discuss their problems gave them added confidence to articulate their needs and problems without fear.

Swazuri 1999

Dissemination can therefore not only enhance awareness and skills, but also encourage people's own efforts to fight homelessness and poverty.

By late 1997 Code '95 was common currency among shelter professionals and activists, especially those in civil society. An inclusive committee (66 members) known as the Nairobi Informal Settlements Co-ordinating Committee met regularly to develop ideas for dealing with Nairobi's informal settlements. A Development Strategy was produced in October 1997 that highlighted the fact that 'the introduction of appropriate planning, shelter, and infrastructure standards is essential to enable the low-income majority of the population to improve their living environment'. The strategy document goes on to note that Nairobi City Council is in the process of adopting the revised building standards, but warns that Code '95 is an interim measure and a more comprehensive review of planning, infrastructure and building standards is still required. The strategy has since been adopted as a policy document by the city council and the Nairobi Provincial Monitoring Unit and has been disseminated among development partners to ensure the co-ordination of efforts.

Participatory house type design

A simplified building code enables the cost-effective and efficient use of materials and building methods. However, it neither guides the builder on spatial arrangement, nor on the efficient use of the site, nor on the appearance of the finished product. Therefore architectural services that are accessible and affordable to the people play an important role in effective strategies to provide shelter. Part of the aim of the dissemination effort in Nakuru was to demonstrate the ability of first involving the consumer in the house design process, and then equipping artisans, technicians, and draughtsmen with the education and skills to prepare designs for simple single-storey buildings. While this might seem an obvious step to take, it was in fact rather innovative and even risky. The architectural profession enjoys statutory protection in Kenya, and any attempt to encroach on its closely guarded territory is likely to encounter resistance. In this particular case, MCN was sympathetic and it was possible to hold several training sessions and, with the help of a university lecturer in architecture, to develop a dossier of community-inspired designs. These designs are based on extensive analysis of user requirements in various settlements. Many of the settlements are former white-owned commercial farms that were acquired by land-buying companies and co-operatives, so the plots are relatively large (varying from 15m × 45m to 30m × 90m) with poor infrastructure. Zero-grazing animals is common on the larger plots, while building rooms for letting is universal practice.

Client concerns revolve around a few main issues:

- the size of the house (the six-door house is a favourite model – see Box 8)
- sanitation
- site planning
- possibilities of extending the house, either now or in the future
- use of durable materials
- shop/residential combinations.

Box 8   Ezekiel Ndung'u: The six-door baron

Ezekiel owns and lives on plot No.79 in Kwa Rhoda, Nakuru. This site has no title, measures 32m × 61m, is serviced by a 12m road, has a water supply but no municipal sewer, and a power supply and telephone are within easy reach. There are six blocks of existing buildings, with the two blocks to the east housing commercial activities opening on to the street. All the buildings are of timber walls with galvanized iron sheet roofs except the owner's house, which has stone walls. There is a pit latrine block and a compost pit.

Ezekiel wanted a design for six rental rooms based on the common concept of six doors (*milango sita*), with an overall size of 10.8m × 7.2m. The construction materials should be as cheap and decent as possible; however, he prefers the stabilized soil blocks that he saw during his visit to the Mathare 4A Project in Nairobi. The new blocks needed to be placed conveniently between existing buildings. He asked that consideration be given to providing a new latrine block to cater for the increased population.

Source: Yahya et al. 1999

Thus the designer must be able to satisfy the requirements of the landlord, tenant, shopkeeper, dairy farmer and developer on one plot. Further details on the methodology used are provided in Appendix 4.

In facilitating the participatory architectural design of 22 demonstration houses, the project was designed to illustrate that, given the right conditions, community-based housing agents are best-placed to articulate their design preferences in the planning of housing development schemes. Well documented and disseminated, this shift from expert-driven to CBO-facilitated housing design is likely to contribute to more community-responsive models in the implementation of affordable housing programmes. Above all, the project output continues to provide evidence that, with a simplified approval process and the use of appropriate building technologies, low-income urban communities are able to gain access to decent, affordable and legal housing.

Lessons and impacts

Knowledge and technical capacity have improved since the housing standards review process began two decades ago, but does that mean that the review process would be easier and less costly now? The answer is probably no, as new problems have emerged about which little understanding has developed. Issues such as HIV, stress-related diseases, nutrition, pollution, toxic wastes, large-scale evictions, safety and crime were either unknown or not then considered worthy of serious attention. Even methods of analysing problems and finding solutions have changed.

Learning from the review process

If the 1980 study were undertaken today, the approach would be completely different, with greater emphasis on participatory methods, computer simulations and the links between shelter standards and poverty reduction. Review efforts need to be backed up by sound and consistent research, such as that provided by the University of Nairobi's Housing Research and Development Unit. The following lessons are worth noting:

- Housing standards should be reviewed on a continual basis. The review process is a cycle, which follows a pattern of stress–awakening–revise–implement–monitor–new stress and then starts again.
- The review process is a collaborative effort, hence the temptation to form task groups, inter-ministerial committees, consultative fora, steering committees, and other forms of collective decision-making structures; and the need for continual workshops, seminars and consultations, all of which consume time and money.
- The review process needs to be driven by a core of committed and knowledgeable reformers.
- Genuine concerns about health and potential hazards must be addressed in a professional manner, as they are likely to evoke emotional reactions and move the debate into the political arena.
- Donors must contribute more than money. They can guide policy orientation, supplement technical expertise and internationalize revision efforts. For example, UNCHS capitalized on the World Bank's efforts by inviting the GoK's consultant to Stockholm for an expert group meeting, recognizing Kenya's pioneering experience in this area.
- NGOs such as ITDG and Shelter Forum (SF) can play a catalytic role in moving the process forward and in strengthening the dissemination efforts. In fact, without such support governments cannot do much; but are such efforts sustainable?
- Reform creates its own momentum; once the basic steps have been taken it is possible to push for progress.
- Housing standards' revision fits in nicely with political rhetoric about improving people's living conditions and with the development agenda of poverty reduction. Both politicians and donors see it as a worthy cause, which is good for activists.

Who should be given the credit? This question is important for public officials, who often feel ignored and undervalued. While consultants and NGOs are paid specifically for their work, the Director of Housing and the Chief Health Officer have to be content with professional satisfaction, being those who initiated and directed the whole process.

The Enabling Housing Standards and Procedures Project (EHSP), an international project undertaken by ITDG, is designed to stimulate the active involvement of low-income housing agents in the standards development and review process, with the aim of enabling those on a low income to gain access to legal housing in urban areas, using more appropriate designs, materials and technologies. The EHSP and its sister project, the Integrated Urban Housing Project (IUHP), have had a noticeable effect, at both national and local levels.

At the national level, the Ministry of Local Authorities was persuaded to relaunch Code '95 three years after it was gazetted to give it greater publicity and recognition among the local authorities and other partners. The Ministry has informed all 167 local authorities about Code '95, and estimates that 50 per cent of local authorities have adopted it.

At the local level, the project managed to involve local low-income housing agents (landlords, artisans, etc.) in the standards development and review process. As a result, MCN introduced flexibility in the building plans approval process, and 50 building plans were approved at one time in advance.

On the ground, the project efforts had an impact in Kwa Rhoda and other neighbourhoods in Nakuru by increasing housing stock, creating potential for increased income by landlords and artisans, improving living conditions, facilitating the mobilization of local resources, and demonstrating new building technologies, such as stabilized soil blocks and ferro-cement.

Poverty impact

Cost comparisons between the developed units and conventional buildings show that the project has contributed directly to a 30 per cent reduction in building costs. Low-income households are now able to mobilize resources for decent and officially sanctioned housing: within the first year, 24.5 per cent of the trained housing agents began constructing affordable houses. In effect, during this pilot phase, firm foundations have been laid to enable low-income groups to gain access to decent and affordable housing. The work has also brought to the fore the challenge of dealing with the poorest people in society.

There is a marked appreciation of the revised by-laws and affordable building technologies by personnel in MCN. By September 1998, the 22 houses approved by the council had designs that specified the use of rammed earth, stabilized soil blocks and ferro-cement walling – alternative materials that had never before been approved by the local authority. CBO representatives are increasingly playing a pivotal role in encouraging members to apply for approval and pay the stipulated council fees. In Kwa Rhoda, for example, six demonstration houses have so far been constructed, and the number of people waiting to produce stabilized soil blocks is increasing. These people, who have owned plots in the area for more than ten years, felt the best houses they could put up were mud-and-wattle structures.

Empowerment

As indicated above, the participation of CBO representatives in group meetings, exchange visits and training workshops organized by ITDG and Shelter Forum at the local and national levels has increased knowledge and confidence in the design and construction of affordable housing technologies. Participants at such events share the lessons that they have learned, and the initiatives undertaken by CBOs following such events include sharing information on the revised by-laws (42.1 per cent), starting affordable house construction (24.6 per cent) and organizing community-based groups to plan and save for house construction. The training workshops have enabled the participants to:

- identify sites for the construction of demonstration houses
- select 12 community-based artisans to participate in workshops on the design and construction of appropriate building technologies.

CBO members such as Kwa Rhoda, Mwariki and the newly registered Artisans Group have on their own initiative approached Nakuru Municipal Council and paid the necessary fees to have designs approved. Above all, the exposure to information on housing technologies and meaningful dialogue with partner agencies has enabled CBOs and artisans to suggest closer interaction with key partners such as Localizing Agenda 21, NACHU and PRIDE-Kenya.

Gender impact

The national workshop on housing standards held in March 1998 recognized the roles played by different gender groups in housing development and management. Specifically, the event underscored the value for stakeholders in human settlements development to conduct gender analyses of housing needs in order to build on the skills of women, men and young people (Agevi 1998: 29).

The survey conducted among the agents and users involved in the pilot project provides some insights into the project's impacts on women and men. Of the users (men and women), 80 per cent are convinced that women can now afford to build houses, while 37.5 per cent of the female adult respondents interviewed plan to find the money to construct houses in the coming months. Of special significance, three women's groups in Mwariki, Kwa Rhoda and Bondeni have established merry-go-round savings and credit schemes for their members' house construction enterprises.

Project teams have proactively involved both women and men in the planning and implementation of initiatives. During the consultative design of the demonstration housing units, for example, the designers ensured that the preferences of both women and men were registered. The stakeholders' workshop attracted a total of 16 men and 14 women, while the CBOs exchange visit team to Nairobi and Kajiado comprised five women and six men. The emphasis on equity in providing technical support in the construction of demonstration houses is important; out of the six houses constructed or under construction, three belong to women, two are jointly owned, and one is a man's.

The project acknowledged that one shortcoming is the inability to select and train young female designers and artisans. One key activity in future should encompass awareness building on gender equity in technology development and the identification of young women to participate in an artisanal skills development programme.

Impact on marginalized groups

Pilot project work has generated considerable interest from marginalized and dispossessed individuals. In the period March to September 1998, for example, project teams received and processed technical enquiries and applications from three widows and two victims of ethnic clashes. These people own plots within Kwa Rhoda, but have not had the information or the means to construct decent and affordable housing. They are now able to mobilize resources for house construction. The pilot project recognizes, however, the broader and growing challenge of actively involving the landless and poorer segments of the population in the housing development initiatives.

In February 1998, the EHSP project organized a three-day workshop that brought together 19 Nakuru-based designers, consisting largely of 'professionally marginalized' groups in the building industry: the tracers, draughtsmen and self-made designers. One result of this event was the raising of the participants' awareness and the development of their skills on the revised by-laws and associated building designs. The 22 housing designs mentioned earlier were in part the result of the efforts of six of the trained 'para-designers'. The workshop acknowledged the importance of this cadre and strongly recommended that strategies be designed to legitimize their role.

Most artisans in Nakuru have always worked on their own, with little or no collective activity. As a result, they are vulnerable to unfavourable working conditions and low wages, and their already limited access to technical information and production equipment is made worse. A survey among small-scale artisans confirms this statement. Because of the project's support in strengthening their group, there is increased confidence and self-esteem among the trained artisans. One example has been in the production of the stabilized soil blocks and the construction of affordable housing units, where the artisans have been very vocal in identifying and reporting quality-control problems when they have arisen. During the July 1998 official launching of the demonstration housing units, and also at Shelter Forum's Annual Event, the artisans were able to articulate clearly their needs and promote the project's vision and methodology.

Sustainability

The housing agents interviewed recognize three key factors essential to project sustainability: long-lasting and easy-to-maintain technology (70 per cent), committed partners (10 per cent) and cost sharing by community groups (10 per cent). In terms of technical sustainability, 63 per cent of the housing agents contend that the responsibility for training more artisans should fall progressively on the trained artisans. Among the priority plans for the future, the CBO members are very much aware that the onus for managing house development efforts will be their primary responsibility. The future responsibilities of the CBOs are, in order of priority:

- disseminating information on the revised by-laws and ABTs (35 per cent)
- fundraising (22 per cent)
- mobilizing group members to organize house construction (22 per cent).

The project's awareness building and training activities have enhanced the CBOs' skills in the design, planning and organization of house improvement programmes. On their own initiative, one group, the Kwa Rhoda Neighbourhood, has mobilized members' savings and purchased several stabilized soil block pressing machines. Using their own artisans, the group is currently producing blocks for members and has already developed a strategy to generate income through the production of the blocks for members and new customers.

Many of the above achievements have been recorded by partner agencies, principally by MCN, CBOs and the trained artisans. There has been a remarkable transformation of the MCN's Town Engineer's Department, which interacts with, and responds to, the needs of the housing developers in low-income settlement areas. Furthermore, the council's commitment to keep the momentum of the revised by-laws alive is still very evident in its on-going policy of approving housing designs within 30 days. This facilitation from council officers provides an enabling environment for housing agents in low-income areas to participate in affordable housing schemes beyond pilot project intervention.

Environmental impacts

Environmental sanitation issues in the designated areas have been the mandate of Localizing Agenda 21 (LA21), a key partner with whom ITDG has maintained close working relations. Within Kwa Rhoda, Kaptembwo and Mwariki, LA21 has days set aside for improving the areas' drainage and cleanliness. In practice local committees mobilize residents to conduct clean-up campaigns. LA21 has also trained CBO members on solid waste management and sanitation. In the agreements with housing agents, ITDG is emphasizing the design and costing of latrines and soak-pits as integral to the construction of demonstration houses. (Initially, costing was limited to the main house. The average cost of a latrine is KSh15 000 and soak pits between KSh5000 and KSh10 000.)

The 1998 project review meeting noted with concern the new challenge posed by the holes left when soil is removed in the process of SSB production (dubbed 'SSB mini-craters'). Team members suggested building awareness among housing agents about a variety of rehabilitation options, for example using the holes as soak-pits or latrines, or simply refilling them.

Project teams have also expressed concern at the lack of tree-planting activities around the houses. Tree nurseries have been identified and consultations have begun with the Town Engineers' Department, WWF and religious organizations to promote appropriate tree planting in the designated areas. As part of the process of exploring options in urban agriculture, ITDG has linked the CBOs with a research team from the University of Nairobi.

One unique feature of the demonstration houses being developed in Nakuru is that the technologies being used have been tested by ITDG in its Maasai Housing Project. In this way tried and tested technologies are transferred from rural to urban areas.

Feedback from stakeholders

The residents of the low-income settlements in Nakuru acknowledged the role of ITDG in capacity building and appreciated the EHSP project activities. One of the project participants is renting out rooms that he built using SSB technology, which he says is affordable, durable and of a better standard than the walls of his former house. The technology has generated interest among residents in the area and beyond. Indeed, many visitors come to learn from the demonstration houses. Some describe the technology as clever, appropriate and encouraging. As a result of the project, one resident reported that community participation has been enhanced and that the community has accepted SSB technology. Many people have learned new skills and acquired new knowledge. One resident listed the technology's strong points:

- raw materials are easily available
- no transport is required, thus no transport cost is incurred
- provides employment and income
- the units have uniform shape and texture which are good qualities for finishing materials
- SSBs have a higher density than concrete blocks but they are easy to handle; they are smooth and thus friendly to the hands
- they are environmentally friendly
- less cement is needed; they encourage the use of indigenous materials and the simplified soil selection can be carried out by anyone.

The stakeholders expressed concern, however, about the pace of the construction programme, noting that a delay (caused by plan approval bottlenecks and scarcity of funds to purchase materials) was actually lowering members' morale. Although the plan approval process is better, there is still room for further improvement.

Some residents complained about the poor availability of soil for SSBs and about financial constraints. They asked for support to be increased to complete the units under construction before replication began in other neighbourhoods.

The residents recommended that the process of selecting building applicants be participatory and that CBOs be involved in the process. They also called for the revised building by-laws to be translated into local languages for ease of adoption. Though there were numerous documents on the project, partners complained about the lack of dissemination, highlighting a need for consistent feedback to partners and checks as to the accuracy of reporting. The participants requested a proper comparative costing guide on the available alternative building technologies, which was to include construction time, building lifespan, materials, labour costs and maintenance costs. Costing was also a key and sometimes contentious issue for MCN officers.

Some of the residents recommended that:

- CBOs should disseminate information on housing
- more artisans should be trained
- the MCN should provide services/maintain cleanliness
- sanitary provisions should be standardized, especially in high-density housing schemes
- co-operation should take place with other agencies to formulate an appropriate urban infrastructure programme
- banks and co-operatives should finance low-cost housing and promote savings and loans for artisans
- GoK should provide technical support, including the training of artisans on a broader basis
- women and young people should be included in the projects.

Partnerships and participation

It is clear that the process of revising housing standards and related regulations involves many individuals and institutions. They have to work together to achieve a common goal. Through partnerships they can pool resources, learn from one another, and offer mutual support and encouragement. They may or may not be bound by a legal arrangement. Nonetheless mutual trust is a prerequisite for success. Each member of the partnership is expected to have his or her own objectives in respect of what they want to get out of the relationship.

Who are the partners?

Although partnerships are a means to an end, they have lately come to be regarded as a desirable goal in their own right because of their enormous potential for empowerment and for enhancing social capital. As a result, 'partner' has taken on a broader definition and new methods of analysing and nurturing partnerships have developed. Depending on the task at hand, there could be several combinations of partnering, varying, for instance, from the fleeting relationship between a materials supplier and builder, to the more enduring co-operation between advocacy groups and government or between a borrower and a mortgage institution.

The traditional partners in the shelter sector were government, consumers and delivery agents such as local authorities, national housing boards and contractors. Today the circle is wider, and includes NGOs, donors, private developers and researchers. The NGO directory lists 28 Kenyan NGOs as being active in housing, urban development, and water supply and sanitation. Table 3.2 shows, for example, the collaborative activities and partnership web stretching across the shelter delivery scene in Nakuru, a Kenyan town with a population of 350 000. One lesson that has emerged from the project is that it is too tempting to think of partners only as institutions and organized groups, forgetting that the ultimate collaborator, supporter and instigator of social development is the individual, whether a civic leader, NGO official or citizen seeking shelter for him or herself and their dependants.

Table 3.2   Collaborative activities

Stage	Activities	Partners
Changing the law	• Identifying shortcomings • Learning from others • Code review	Government, researchers, consultants, legal advisers, legislators, donors, NGOs, activists
Sharing knowledge	• Dissemination and training • Technology assessment	CBOs, NGOs, LAs, media, schools, training institutions, professionals, artisans
Enforcement	• Simplifying procedures • Streamlining oversight • Tightening enforcement	LA, security forces, builders, CBOs, NGOs, landlords
Distributing inputs	• Developing new designs • Developing new materials • Making land available • Services distribution • Providing mortgages	CBOs, LA, private sector, utilities, NGOs, finance houses, savings associations, materials merchants
Building	• Materials supplies • Construction • Renovations/extensions	Manufacturers, suppliers, artisans, builders, LA, individuals, NGOs, CBOs

Challenging relationships

Relationships are not without problems. All partners have their own motives. Politicians will want to reap political benefits from any support they give to a project. It is the project manager's job to accommodate these desires in the best way. Moreover, partners have different strengths, endowments and working methods. NGOs are often frustrated by donor red tape. For example: they expect a proposal to be processed in days, even though in some organizations that process can take months, if not years. While projects and collaborative efforts usually start with raised expectations on all sides, as time passes attitudes can change. If there are delays or delivery problems partners will lose faith, commitment will fail, and loyalty diminish. The question then is how can partners share in both the success and the challenges, bask in the credit for triumphs, as well as shoulder the blame for failures?

Investing in partnerships

One of the most important contributions to partnership building is information sharing and training. Post-1995 dissemination efforts in Nakuru spearheaded by the municipal council and ITDG concentrated on local level and grassroots training. Table 3.3 lists formal training sessions and exchange visits, split by gender. One of the visits was to a demonstration site 250km away in Maasai-land where training in the use of local materials was underway. Thus, quite apart from the technology dissemination aspects, the participants could benefit from exposure to a different environment and climatic region. More men attend these events than women for a variety of reasons, including bias in the selection process, educational achievement differentials, male prominence among artisans and technicians, and the difficulty for women of being away from the home.

Table 3.3 Attendance at training events by gender

Training session	Male		Female	
	Number	Percentage	Number	Percentage
Stakeholders' workshop	20	58	14	42
Designers' workshop	17	70	7	30
Artisans' workshop	14	82	3	17
Launching of project	43	52	29	48
Exchange visits	7	63	4	37
National workshop on standards	5	71	2	29
Group meetings	27	44	34	56
Site visits	59	55	48	45
Shelter Forum Annual Event	4	80	1	20

The Government of Kenya has a stated interest in establishing relationships with private organizations and local communities in order to provide the national goal of decent housing for all. While opening a national workshop on housing standards in March 1998 in Nairobi, the then Minister for Local Authorities, Professor Sam Ongeri, asked the workshop to review the progress made by partners in pilot-testing the revised standards and procedures and to develop a strategy and partnership for the review, dissemination and implementation of revised standards (Agevi 1998). He said:

I also call upon all stakeholders, especially developers, financiers, and community-based organizations to work with us to ensure that as many people as possible benefit from the new regulations. Through our joint efforts, we must find ways of creating the capacity and revenue base in the local authorities necessary for managing the rapid growth being experienced. Professionals for their part, especially architects, engineers, and town planners, ought to answer the needs of the poor and the low-income families ...

The government will therefore establish a permanent board to review and update the Building Code on a continuous basis. Working in collaboration with government departments, research institutions, and the private sector, the Building By-laws Review Board will be able to guide the industry on all matters relating to the building industry.

The workshop's conclusion identified a number of possible commitments by various stakeholders (see Box 9). The Architectural Association of Kenya was singled out because of its influential position (hence the call to 'guard against dictating solutions to communities') and its eagerness to fight against poverty.

Box 9   Partnership workshop conclusions

The Partnership workshop (Nairobi, March 1998) successfully fulfilled the intended objectives as evidenced in the proceedings. The major highlights of the workshop included:

- the re-launching of the Local Government (Adoptive By-laws) (Building) Amendment Order, 1995 by the Minister of Local Authorities
- the proclamation of the adoption of the Informal Settlements Development Strategy by Nairobi District Development Committee
- the identification of practical challenges, experiences and achievements in Nakuru Municipal Council regarding revised building standards and regulations
- the commitment of partners to support and implement the strategy of revision, dissemination and application of building standards and procedures in physical projects as follows:

The government commitments

- to improve/upgrade the informal settlements/slums
- to recognize and support the role of other partners in the revision and enforcement of building by-laws and regulations
- to grant moratoriums on demolitions of informal settlements, by working closely with the Nairobi Informal Settlements Co-ordination Committee
- to support further legislation, and share experiences with other regions in collaboration with UNCHS/Habitat, especially in the areas of technology, legislation and capacity building

Local authorities' commitments

- to revise, adopt and implement appropriate building standards and planning regulations through pilot projects
- to create an enabling environment to speed up plan approval processes
- to engage in aggressive capacity-building and information dissemination programmes

Parliamentarians' commitments

The parliamentarians' commitments agreed in June 1996 in Istanbul, Turkey, that is:
- to contribute actively towards Habitat Agenda implementation
- to disseminate Habitat Agenda information and increase regional and international co-operation
- to promote legislation that supports affordable shelter development

Commitments of the Architectural Association of Kenya

- to establish building information centres to provide free or low-cost technical services to the needy
- to continue to demand a total halt to the demolition of informal settlements
- to ensure that professionals guard against dictating solutions to communities
- to act as public watchdog on matters pertaining to illegal settlements and collapsing structures
- to solicit cheap funding for use in improving living conditions in informal settlements

Private sector commitments, including CBOs and NGOs

- to provide community training and information dissemination
- to provide technical advice, finance, materials production and innovations
- to support research work on appropriate technologies
- to pilot-test revised standards

Commitments of ITDG Kenya

- to formulate and develop gender-sensitive, sustainable solutions and options that are acceptable, accessible and affordable to the majority of the population
- to support standards that can be implemented and replicated through the implementation and monitoring of pilot housing programmes in partnership with others
- to document and share relevant experiences in the field of housing standards and procedures from within and outside Kenya

Source: Agevi 1998: 36-37

Conclusions and future directions

The Kenyan experience in by-law revision has provided two decades from which lessons can be drawn. It is clear that while major revisions are undertaken at the national level, implementation is very much a local affair. In the final analysis, it is a relationship between the regulating authority, typically the municipal council, and the builder, as was evident in Nakuru, where the municipality took special measures to ensure that the revised code was quickly disseminated and adopted. In the national arena, it is obvious that massive investment in terms of funds, expertise (both national and international) and time will not guarantee success unless it is accompanied by political commitment and constant goading by concerned activists and reformers. Writing a technically competent code is only half the battle; it is also necessary to win over the minds of those who actually build the housing.

Dissemination of project experience has shown us that participating communities and institutions need clear goals and roles. It is also useful to work within a time frame, because delays cost money and reduce commitment. Information and training packages for various community groups and stakeholders are important, and a good communications strategy is essential. Clear technical standards, including safety, environmental and sanitation requirements are at the heart of projects. Indeed, infrastructure is taken for granted as a municipal obligation. The division of responsibilities is one area that still requires much work; detailed costings, possibly using the life-cycle approach, are needed. Cost information is usually rudimentary and grossly inadequate.

The revised building code for low-income housing in 1995 was a landmark event in Kenya's struggle to cater for the housing needs of its six million urban residents. In spite of its succinctness, the document remained largely unused for the following two years because of inadequate awareness of its progressive provisions. It was a government document rather than a people's document. The fact that it had taken dozens of professionals and as many years to make the revisions only added to their inaccessible nature. Vigorous efforts by various stakeholders to coerce local authorities into adopting the revised code did produce some positive results, but what was lacking was a systematic evaluation of how the revision had been undertaken, the extent of people's participation, the dissemination efforts made, and the response of industry players to the policy change. A survey carried out by ITDG in 1997 produced useful information on these issues. The survey highlighted the need for proactive and imaginative intervention by concerned individuals and groups to help municipalities to popularize the new code.

A pilot project in Nakuru, designed and implemented by ITDG in collaboration with the municipality and community groups, helped poor people to gain access to affordable technologies; helped to simplify plan approval procedures in the town hall; to introduce improved sanitation; to promote house building and ownership among women; to widen the pool of design capacity in local communities; and to strengthen the organizational and management capacity of CBOs. One important activity was the repackaging of the new provisions into more friendly and comprehensible formats for training and awareness-building purposes. Such activities need single-minded commitment by a few individuals who can guide the whole process and find innovative ways of overcoming obstacles.

Future directions

Code '95 was a major step forward, but it was in fact the beginning of a new struggle to have the proposals adopted and implemented throughout the country. This task has proved to be more challenging than the actual technical or legal reform, which means that much effort and thought must be given to the marketing of changes in housing and urban development standards. Although much has been written about participation and dissemination, the concepts and accompanying techniques are far from refined; they are still developing. Thus the improvement of participatory methods is a challenge which, in Kenya at least, ought to be taken up seriously. The preferred methods of information exchange still depend on face-to-face contact, such as information sharing in schools, places of worship, party offices, and *barazas*.

Given the extent to which the Kenyan review process benefited from considerable external support, how can future efforts be localized? Donor support, though useful, has its limits. National capacity to resource and sustain housing standards monitoring and review on a continuing basis is essential. New methods of financing the process ought to be developed, bearing in mind that government budgets are declining. If progress is to be made in this area, then costs must be cut and new funding sources found. A rigorous economic and financial appraisal could help crystallize the issues.

Attention must also be paid to the need to develop appropriate standards for those services and activities that people use outside their house, such as open spaces, streets and footpaths, schools, health centres, and so on. While planning standards do exist and are used extensively, making them compatible with the emerging dwelling standards is far from satisfactory. Informal settlements need guidelines, based on realistic standards for improvement and rehabilitation, as a prelude to tenure regularization. Quite apart from land servicing standards, land titling criteria also need further investigation and simplification.

The next challenge is to devolve the regulation function to local communities. While isolated instances where this approach has worked do exist, what is missing is a critical mass of experience that will enable practice to be institutionalized and working methods and rules to be developed. Does the much-vaunted private sector have a role? Finally, it is easy to forget that standards revision must be built on a solid foundation of scientific research. The challenge then is how to use poorly resourced research facilities and personnel to the best advantage.

4
LESSONS FROM ZIMBABWE

Introduction

Under British rule Zimbabwe was known as Southern Rhodesia. Though the name and the colours of the national flag have changed, many of the laws governing the built environment have remained the same. Before independence in 1980 many mass rental housing schemes were built, mainly with government funding, in municipalities and state townships. These schemes account for nearly half the current housing stock and comprise mainly semi-detached one-room bachelor and two- to four-bedroom family housing, built either of cement blocks or concrete prefabricated panels and asbestos roofing on 200m² plots. Black people were not given title to housing or permanent urban residence, so all housing stock provision and consumption was on a rental basis.

Official reports by the Director of Physical Planning and Ministerial Commissions show that the standards and housing practices of this period were greatly influenced by, and adapted from, South African ideas and practices. Consistent with colonial policies and practices of the day, review processes were technocratic and did not consult low-income consumers. The development and implementation of housing policies involved only planners, engineers and housing administrators in the Housing Services Branch and the Department of Physical Planning of the Ministry of Local Government and Housing (MLGH).

The failure of government policy to involve end users and builders in forming housing delivery policy is highlighted by the continued prescription of unaffordable minimum standards and procedures for building, which has resulted in many people remaining homeless or living in illegal, 'substandard' housing. The failure to develop review systems to make housing standards responsive to the economic realities of the people and to housing markets has contributed greatly to the overcrowding of the existing housing stock. Illegal housing developments, homelessness and under-performing housing delivery systems are evident in all of Zimbabwe's urban areas.

After independence in 1980, public sector provision of housing units for people on low incomes ceased and government support was redirected to 'sites and services' and 'self-help building'. This strategy was pursued in an attempt to meet the increasing demand for housing. Unfortunately, public sector provision of serviced land was inadequate because of systematic failures in the acquisition, subdivision, servicing and registration of urban plots. In 1980 Harare had 5500 serviced plots delivered. This rate has since decreased to 1500 per year, while the housing waiting list has increased at a rate of 10 000 units per year and currently stands at over 100 000 (Mubvami 1999).

In the years between the International Year for the Homeless (1987) and Habitat II (1996), major changes in housing policies in developing countries focused on improving the performance of housing delivery systems. Partnerships between the public and private sectors, NGOs, donor agencies and communities are now viewed as essential and the concepts governing them have seen a shift in roles. The private sector and civil society are now taking on an increasingly significant role in housing delivery and project implementation, while central and local governments are beginning to consider, and occasionally engage in, enabling partnerships and frameworks.

However, these enabling frameworks and partnerships for enhanced housing delivery are unlikely to increase access to legal housing for the majority in Zimbabwe unless standards review systems are put in place. They are also unlikely to change the situation if people continue to perceive housing standards and procedures as impediments to their self-build housing initiatives. More importantly, unless standards review systems cease to be technocratic, one-off activities, building standards will continue to be poorly perceived and often ignored. This situation can be improved, however, if housing practitioners and governments initiate the process of establishing standards review systems and processes that are more responsive and sensitive to people's needs. What would be the essential characteristics of a review system that can make standards responsive to stakeholders and the majority of the population?

This chapter presents research and project experience from Zimbabwe which has aimed to develop innovative approaches in managing housing standards and in setting up standards review systems. The key issues that emerged and will be explored in more depth are that:

- access to legal housing could be improved if it were universally recognized that effective standards review processes and procedures are important
- standards would be appreciated if the people concerned participated in their review
- unless standards review systems are participatory, it is impossible to ensure that new standards meet people's means, needs and priorities and are generally understood
- housing delivery performance and access to legal housing in cities can be increased if new standards are responsive to changes in economic circumstances and housing market trends
- raising awareness of new standards depends upon how information on building standards and procedures is disseminated to all stakeholders as an integral aspect of review processes.

Project research carried out in Zimbabwe from 1996 to 1999 aimed to answer the following key questions:

- How have reviews of building standards and procedures been undertaken in the past, and to what extent have they been effective in enabling access to, and delivery of, legal housing?
- How is information on revised building standards and review procedures disseminated to all parties?
- How effective have past review processes been in increasing awareness, understanding and use of building standards?
- How are current standards and review procedures perceived by consumers and what lessons can we learn?
- What essential characteristics should a standards review system possess?

This chapter has been organized into five main sections. After the introductory remarks, the second section explains briefly the background to housing policy in Zimbabwe and reviews past revisions of housing standards. The third section presents the findings of research data from surveys conducted to assess the perception of revised standards and review processes in selected housing schemes in the towns of Harare, Bulawayo, Mutare and Gweru. The fourth section considers training issues in developing frameworks for review systems. The final section deals with approaches to influencing official and popular thinking, and is followed by a summary of the lessons learned.

The review process

Providing adequate housing for Zimbabwe's 13 million inhabitants is a formidable task. Along with unemployment, poverty and homelessness, declining living standards and deteriorating access to socio-economic infrastructure and services, insufficient develop-ment of urban low-income housing ('low income' in Zimbabwe refers to people earning less than Z$1200 (US$80) per month in 1997–8) is one of the nation's most serious problems. It is estimated that about 35 per cent of the population is urban, concentrated in 22 towns of varying size around the country. The large- and medium-sized urban centres are Harare (estimated population 1 200 000), Chitungwiza (800 000), Bulawayo (600 000), Gweru (280 000), Mutare (270 000), Kwekwe (250 000), Masvingo (240 000), Chinhoyi (230 000), and Marondera (220 000).

Official policies on housing in Zimbabwe, especially on minimum housing standards, squatter settlements, rent control and housing provision, reflect those of other African coun-tries that attained independence much earlier than Zimbabwe. In spite of efforts by the Ministry of Local Government and National Housing (MLGNH) to formulate low-income housing policies and strategies since independence in 1980, there is little evidence to show that experience in other African countries such as Kenya, Nigeria and Ghana has been taken into account, particularly in the area of setting enabling minimum housing standards. High standards have been maintained and enforced, not reviewed to respond to changing economic circumstances or new building technologies. The housing problem has grown as urbanization has increased, resulting in more homelessness, which is reflected in growing waiting lists, overcrowding in existing housing areas, and the unaffordability of official housing standards.

Many people believe that because of the high standards and the failure to review them adequately, the opportunity has been lost to provide adequate shelter for all, despite Zimbabwe's high level of urban infrastructure and its relatively well-developed financial institutions and technical expertise.

Housing standards review practices from 1980 to 1998

Two major reviews of housing standards were undertaken by the government, in 1982 and 1992. The subject of these revisions is given in the table in Appendix 5, along with commen-tary on the attributes of each standard in terms of accessibility and affordability.

At independence the transformation and improvement of urban housing was at the top of the new government's agenda. Housing standards were raised drastically, and new building procedures were introduced. Title ownership of housing was introduced, which meant that black people could own houses and reside permanently in towns. Plot sizes were revised upwards from 200m^2 to a standard minimum size of 300m^2, and the minimum size of dwelling that had to be complete before the plot could be occupied was a detached four-room core unit complete with running water, toilet system, and tar road frontage. Housing schemes had to be fully serviced with social and physical infrastructure. The pre-1980 rental stock was converted and upgraded for home ownership. The government and municipalities also reviewed Zimbabwe's housing delivery system and procedures in line with practices and experiences in other developing countries. New concepts and practices emerged: home ownership, core-housing, aided self-help, site and services, cost recovery and donor funding were introduced. Consistent with technocratic practices in many countries, government officers rarely consulted the consumer in introducing these changes.

Although the revision of pre-independence standards increased access to legal home ownership for black people and upgraded the existing housing stock, the new standards were unrealistic because the mandatory minima were unaffordable and unsustainable, as international donor advisers such as USAID and the World Bank pointed out.

In line with post-independence expectations for change, improvement of urban living conditions, and social justice, the review process conducted by the Ministry of Public Construction and National Housing (the predecessor to the MLGNH) in 1981 was undertaken in a spirit of radical change, but with little consideration for the urban poor. There is no indication that consultation occurred with primary stakeholders nor that inclusive review systems and procedures were ever the objective. The resulting standards were in use between 1981 and 1992. During this time the demand for housing increased dramatically and the cost of building escalated, while real incomes declined because of inflation. The impact of these revisions made the standards unaffordable, which severely constrained the housing delivery process, despite subsidized housing finance packages provided jointly by government and donor agencies. Though standards were evidently a bottleneck and calls for downward revision were growing, it took a very long time for the government to respond. A further review was not carried out until 1992, by which time many housing opportunities had been lost.

During the period from 1981 to 1992 a number of local researchers produced reports and publications on low-income housing in Zimbabwe highlighting the magnitude of the national housing problem and outlining how appropriate standards could help alleviate the situation. Three papers focused specifically on the review and performance of planning and housing standards (Mafico 1989, 1991 and Musandu-Nyamayaro 1993). They stressed the need to review procedures and processes in order to facilitate the delivery of low-income housing. The key point the researchers make is that, in the context of Zimbabwe's unstable financial and employment markets, it is counterproductive to hold housing standards static and apply them rigidly. The papers advocate more affordable standards but stop short of putting the review systems under the spotlight, as ITDG's research seeks to. When the second major review of low-income housing standards was eventually undertaken in 1992, the despondency evident among home seekers, building societies, and other stakeholders in the low-income housing sector gave way to relief and rejuvenated initiatives, as a number of constraints were removed. As a result of the new initiatives, such as site and services housing approaches, a wide range of housing schemes were developed by both local authorities and private developers around the major urban areas. These included the Budiriro and Kuwadzana 3 schemes in Harare, Chikanga scheme in Mutare, Mkoba extension scheme in Gweru, and Nkulumane in Bulawayo. Beneficiaries of these schemes were allowed to occupy serviced stands and then to build at their own pace as resources became available.

An analysis of the major housing standards reviews of 1981 and 1992 shows that both were ad hoc responses to a crisis situation that had been developing for some time. There was no effort to develop a framework to institutionalize systematic, participatory review of standards. Each review was a one-off reaction to unlock bottlenecks made apparent by mounting criticism of the unaffordable and unresponsive building standards and procedures. But it is counterproductive to hold standards static for ten years in fast-changing, unstable macro- and micro-economic contexts. More suited to these contexts and circumstances are standards review systems and frameworks that are inclusive, continuously reviewed, and responsive to the dynamism of the situation.

Prevalent perceptions and attitudes

The efforts to investigate key concerns adopted the 1992 review as a benchmark of how revision was carried out, how standards are perceived, and whether they have improved delivery and access to housing. It was felt to be essential to understand users' perceptions and feelings about existing standards as a starting point in the search for suitable ways to establish the review systems and procedures of the future. Assisted self-build is now the dominant mode of house construction, so what assumes major importance for standards policy formulation is information and indicators on the nature of relations between users and the building standards and the review system. The research questionnaire sought to gather responses and indicators on:

- the level of awareness of standards
- sources that created awareness
- expected sources of information
- necessity and usefulness of housing standards
- potential contributions by stakeholders to the review process
- the effectiveness and affordability of revised standards
- means of dissemination of information
- perceptions of housing application procedures and building inspection stages

The sample surveyed 400 respondents from seven residential areas in Zimbabwe's largest towns, Harare, Chitungwiza, Kwekwe, Gweru, Bulawayo, Marondera, and Mutare.

Awareness and sources of information on housing standards

The survey findings on the extent of awareness of current housing standards among low-income housing consumers and housing administrators are summarized in Table 4.1. Of the 400 people interviewed, 9 per cent were aware of the revised housing standards. The remaining 364 respondents (91 per cent) are completely ignorant of the standards revised in 1992. They do not know why the standards were revised nor do they know the new materials and technology permitted as a result of the revision. And now that they do know about them, there is no avenue through which potential housing beneficiaries or delivery agents can express their views on the revised standards. Though people knew that the local authority is the standards inspection and enforcement authority, all 400 respondents showed lack of awareness of how and when standards are reviewed.

Regarding sources of information on revised standards, respondents say that local authorities and contractors are the main sources of such information. Since there are no readily available information packages, beneficiaries only learn about aspects of standards from building inspectors and contractors during the construction of their dwellings. This finding reflects the critical role of local authorities and contractors in the provision of information relating to the construction of housing. Local authorities are responsible for enforcing standards, while contractors have to comply with the established standards and procedures in order to get their buildings inspected and approved. Both groups know the revised standards, and are in a good position to disseminate information to house builders.

The analysis of awareness levels according to sample areas covered by the survey revealed that awareness is generally higher in the smaller urban settlements of Marondera (23 per cent), Mutare (13 per cent), Kwekwe (10 per cent), and Gweru (10 per cent) than in the larger towns. Bulawayo has the lowest level of awareness of revised standards among consumers at 1.7 per cent, followed by Harare and Chitungwiza at 2.3 per cent and 2.6 per cent respectively. Perhaps this reflects closer and more regular interaction between consumers and government authorities in smaller urban centres.

Table 4.1   Awareness of housing standards (n = 400)

Neighbourhood	Awareness		Sources of awareness					
	Yes	No	Council	MPCNH	Contractor	Neighbour	Press	Books
Harare	16	156		4	4		5	3
Chitungwiza	1	37			1			
Kwekwe	3	27			1			2
Gweru	3	27	1			2		
Bulawayo	1	59			1			
Marondera	7	23	5		2			
Mutare	5	35	3					2
Total	36	364	9	4	9	2	5	7
% represented	9	91	2.2	1	2.2	0.5	1.3	1.8

Notes: MPCNH = Ministry of Public Construction and National Housing; this has now been combined with the Ministry of Local Government and National Housing to create the Ministry of Local Government and National Housing (MLGNH).

Source: Field survey interviews

The survey also assessed the level of awareness of revised standards among local administrators, architects and engineers involved in housing provision. These local authority professionals indicated that they were aware of the revised standards but did not participate in, nor make suggestions for, their revision. They only learned about the revised standards by means of directive circulars from the Ministry of Local Government and National Housing (MLGNH). There is limited or no commitment from professionals employed by local authorities to promote any of the new materials, technologies or practices now permitted by the revised standards. This situation will certainly not be redressed by failing to consult those professionals during the formulation of legislation that they will be expected to implement.

Notwithstanding the high level of ignorance about existing standards, it was thought important to establish the extent to which consumers knew where to get information on revised standards if they wanted it, and how to suggest ways to improve existing standards. Responses were sought from consumers who had indicated ignorance about current standards (see Table 4.2), and from the professionals who had not been involved in the review of standards.

Table 4.2   Consumers' sources of information on revised housing standards (n = 364)

Neighbourhood	Consumers' expected source of information						
	No idea	Council	MPCNH	Building society	Contractor	Co-operative	Total
Harare	25	56	46	14	2	13	156
Chitungwiza	14	4	17			2	37
Kwekwe		20	5		2		27
Gweru	2	5	13	2	5		27
Bulawayo	41	17		1			59
Marondera	2	21					23
Mutare	7	24	3		1		35
Total	91	147	84	17	10	15	364
Percentage	25	40.4	23.1	4.7	2.7	4.1	100

Notes: MPCNH is the Ministry of Public Construction and National Housing; it has now been combined with the Ministry of Local Government and National Housing to create the Ministry of Local Government and National Housing (MLGNH).

Source: Field survey interviews on consumers

The surveys showed that 25 per cent of the people interviewed had absolutely no idea where they could get information on standards, while about 40 per cent expect local authorities to provide it. The central ministry (now MLGNH), building societies, contractors, and housing co-operatives are also expected to disseminate information on standards to consumers. There is clearly no defined, systematic means of making information on standards available, nor for enabling consumers and professionals to feed back their opinions on current or future standards. This results in limited appreciation of the current standards and of the housing products that are legally sanctioned.

The recommendation that emerged from these findings is that there is a need for local authorities to prepare information packages and set up open review systems at neighbourhood housing offices. Such a development would enable consumers to provide feedback based on their experience of implementing the standards, as well as about the associated cost implications and their experiences of living in the resultant housing. It was also suggested during the survey that a higher level of awareness would increase debate and promote knowledge of newly approved, more affordable, building technologies. Such a framework could form a sound basis for the continuous updating and development of standards that people know about and identify with, and provide more appropriate choices to people on low incomes.

Professionals such as planners, engineers, and housing administrators employed by local authorities learned of the 1992 revised standards through ministerial directive circulars distributed by the central government. Their counterparts in private practice, building societies, and housing aid agencies do not receive these circulars, however. Often, they only hear about revisions in the press and then have to try to get copies of the directives.

Are housing standards necessary and useful?

Since standards and review procedures that are known, understood and appreciated as necessary and useful by the beneficiaries are more likely to be responsive to needs and subsequently adopted, it was considered important to understand the prevalent perceptions of the necessity for standards. People in the seven towns were asked whether standards are necessary and useful and why. The results are given in Table 4.3.

Table 4.3 Necessity and usefulness of standards (n = 400)

Area	Are standards useful?		Reasons why standards are useful						
	Yes	No	Durability	Safety	Privacy	Social harmony	Public health	Aesthetics	Control
Harare	153	19	54	44	2	26	22	70	43
Chitungwiza	18	20	5			1		1	11
Kwekwe	30		14	18		7	6	6	12
Gweru	29	1	4	10		8		9	6
Bulawayo	59	1	13	21	1	16	4	14	16
Marondera	29	1	6	14		9	2	11	9
Mutare	39	1	19	16	2	8	2	16	16
Total	357	43	115	123	5	75	36	127	113
Percentage	89.3	10.7	28.8	30.8	1.3	18.8	9.0	31.8	28.3

Note: % on reasons given on why standards are useful exceeds 100 per cent because many respondents gave more than one reason.

Source: Field survey interviews on consumers.

Most people, 89 per cent, supported the view that housing standards are useful. According to the respondents, standards are important because they:

• enhance the aesthetic value of housing as a consumer good (31.8 per cent)
• guarantee the safety of houses built (30.8 per cent)

- ensure the durability of houses and thus protect consumers from shoddy work (28.8 per cent)
- enable local authorities to enforce control on activities of contractors and builders and thus protect consumers from being 'ripped off' (28.3 per cent)
- ensure peace and social harmony among neighbours (18.8 per cent). As several respondents remarked, 'standards minimize differences between houses built in one neighbourhood and, as a result, reduce or eliminate jealousy among neighbours'.
- promote and protect public health and so improve the living environment (9 per cent)
- ensure privacy at household level (1.3 per cent).

Table 4.3 also shows that nearly 11 per cent of respondents are not in favour of the enforcement of housing standards, and were sceptical about the value of housing standards not because standards are intrinsically bad but rather because of weaknesses in the manner in which they are applied and enforced. It was argued, for example, that more often than not standards have the unintended effect of making housing unaffordable, particularly for low-income groups. Furthermore, they argued that standards and building by-laws, particularly the building inspection procedures, give an opportunity to enforcement agencies and officials (such as building inspectors) to extract bribes from builders and contractors. This problem needs to be addressed through initiatives to enhance the values and integrity of systems and practices in urban local authorities in Zimbabwe.

Potential stakeholder contributions

The survey revealed that very limited consultation took place between the government and other stakeholders in the housing sector during the review of housing standards in 1981 and 1992. The key stakeholders in the housing delivery process who might usefully have been consulted include consumers, local authorities, donors, housing co-operatives, research and design institutions, NGOs, builders and contractors, building societies and professionals (architects, engineers, planners, etc.). The reviews of standards carried out in 1981 and 1992 appear to have been limited to the officials in the ministries in charge of housing. Asked whether they would have participated in the standards review process if they had been invited, all professionals and 89.3 per cent of consumers covered by the survey said yes.

The research aimed to establish why respondents wanted to participate in the review of housing standards. The main reasons cited were to:

- share our experiences and influence policymaking on housing standards and delivery (11 per cent)
- allow us to give our opinions and objections and decide on that which affects us (50 per cent)
- be consulted, as a basic right, on such important matters that affect our lives (51 per cent)
- advise policymakers on such important issues like acquisition of land for housing development and plot sizes (40 per cent)
- advise on cost-effective ways of servicing land and also on space optimization (45 per cent)
- share ideas on promotion and use of alternative building technologies (30 per cent)
- contribute to building designs (14 per cent).

The above analysis suggests that participation and the establishment of review procedures is likely to foster individual and community empowerment while improving access to housing.

But how can this participation be encouraged? There needs to be a shift away from centralized ownership and determination of housing standards, review systems and procedures to local ownership and control. Approaches to setting and reviewing standards should change as well: instead of being highly technocratic and prescriptive, they must be demand-responsive and participatory. However, a minority believe that not everybody can make a meaningful contribution, that lay opinion tends to be ignored and that the cost of housing is rising irrespective of the level of participation, and these views should not be dismissed.

Research and design organizations such as ITDG Zimbabwe and the Scientific and Industrial Research Development Centre have a considerable stake in developing alternative and affordable building materials such as SSBs and micro-concrete roofing tiles (MCRs). These institutions, and others, would have been able to make a useful contribution to the revision process because of their extensive practical experience of building demonstration housing units in Harare, Bulawayo, Chitungwiza, Mutare and training centres around the country.

The reasons given by those who said they would not participate in standards reviews (11 per cent), even if they were invited, were as follows:

- lack the necessary expertise to contribute meaningfully to the development of standards (4 per cent)
- even if they participate, their views and suggestions would be disregarded by officials (10 per cent)
- the cost of housing will continue to rise whether they participate or not (11 per cent).

The survey wanted to know what consumers and institutions felt were the main issues, and which issues they would want to change if they participated in reviews. These key issues were identified as house designs, plot sizes and building materials.

First, consumers and professionals are keen to be involved in the standards review process so that a wide range of designs is incorporated into standards. Current housing standards are considered restrictive in terms of building designs, resulting in monotonous housing estates and the approved designs are not always the most cost effective. Second, there is a strongly held view among consumers, institutions and professionals that they should be consulted about plot sizes and optimization of space in housing development projects. While the reduction of minimum plot size from 300 to 150m^2 under the 1992 revised standards was a welcome development, there is a strong feeling that the minimum plot size should be 200m^2 rather than 150m^2. A plot of 150m^2 is considered too small to accommodate a four-roomed house and leave some space for other activities and facilities considered essential by households, including ground for growing vegetables, a play area for children and car parking. It must be pointed out that this view may be biased by the fact that some of the respondents covered by the survey are in the middle-income category. Households that truly belong to the low-income category are unlikely to ask for a parking space. Consumers who make such demands are in fact middle-income households who find themselves occupying low-income housing estates because of 'down raiding', which has become a significant problem in Zimbabwe in recent years as a result of demand for housing exceeding supply.

Finally, consumers, architects, engineers, contractors and producers of building materials feel strongly that if they participate in the review they would be able to increase the choice of acceptable building materials in urban housing projects. There is a wide range of alternative and less expensive building materials that would improve the delivery and affordability of housing. The use of such alternative materials is restricted, however, either because they are relatively unknown or because their use is discouraged or prohibited by existing standards.

This analysis suggests that people's participation in, or contribution to, this decision-making process and its local ownership will result in more enabling and sustainable housing standards and delivery systems. The first challenge in this process is for central and local governments to create a framework for officials to work in partnership with communities. The second is to develop processes that enable communities to give informed views and choices on standards. Table 4.4 presents a summary of issues that survey respondents felt both consumers and professionals could effectively work on, if they were involved in the housing standards review process.

Table 4.4   Potential areas of contribution by institutions, professionals and consumers

Agent	Areas on which contributions would be made			
	Plot sizes	Housing plans and designs	Space optimization	Use of cost-effective building materials
LA officials:				
Architects	C	C	C	C
Engineers	C	C	C	C
Planning	C	C	C	N
Contractors/builders	N	N	N	C
Building material producers	N	N	N	C
Consumers	C	C	C	C

Notes: 'C' means agent would be willing and able to make effective contributions; 'N' means agent would not be able to make an effective contribution on that issue.

Source: Survey interviews

Effectiveness and affordability of revised housing standards

No readily available assessment of the effectiveness and affordability of the revised standards has been made since they were released in 1992. ITDG's project study therefore sought to establish consumer perceptions of the impact of revised standards on housing delivery and affordability. The predominant view expressed by consumers (75 per cent) and professionals (95 per cent) was that the current revised standards have achieved little in terms of improving the delivery of low-income housing. The rate of delivery of new housing stock has continued to lag behind the rate of growth of demand for additional housing units. The rate of increase of house construction costs has continued to outstrip the growth of wages and salaries, particularly in low- and middle-income groups. It was pointed out that high inflation, prevalent in Zimbabwe during the 1990s, has tended to offset any potential gains that the new standards might have created. The cost of building materials and labour has increased sharply, thereby minimizing some of the benefits of the new standards, such as reduced plot sizes.

Approximately 8 per cent of consumers interviewed actually lamented the introduction of revised standards. The revised standards had had no significant positive impact on delivery and affordability of housing and yet some of the building technologies introduced are perceived to have reduced the quality of housing. For example, 95 per cent of the beneficiaries of the Kuwadzana extension housing scheme (which uses steel frame walls) think that steel-frame houses are neither durable nor safe. They complained of excessive noise from the walls at night from the steel contracting. At the time of the survey one house had been completely demolished and was being replaced by a brick house. Approximately 25 per cent of consumers covered by the survey said they would destroy the steel-frame houses and then build with bricks if they had the resources to do so. There is also a strong feeling that the reduction of plot sizes is worsening population density in low-income housing estates.

Information dissemination and facilitation procedures

Local authority employees said that the national dissemination of information on standards is the responsibility of government ministries, which should send relevant circulars to all interested parties. Local authorities should then take a leading role in disseminating such information to consumers in their areas. Consumers said that relevant government ministries and local authorities should disseminate information on standards. The means of dissemination suggested by respondents include newspapers (25 per cent), pamphlets and posters (20 per cent), public meetings (40 per cent), and electronic media (29 per cent). Research and design institutions that produce and promote alternative building materials and building technologies also have an important role to play. One of the most effective ways of promoting new technologies is by building demonstration housing units and helping housing co-operatives and provincial vocational training institutions to train people in their production and use.

The procedures followed by consumers in applying for housing have a strong bearing on the efficiency of the housing delivery process. Out of a sample of 400 consumers interviewed, 87 per cent are aware of the procedures to be followed. Of these consumers, 20 per cent considered the housing application procedures to be straightforward because application forms are brief and easy to fill in. The other 80 per cent considered housing application procedures to be lengthy and cumbersome and a number of reasons were given in support of this view:

- Corruption is evident among officials of local authorities in the processing of applications and allocation of housing plots. Queue-jumping is common practice for those able to bribe their way through the bureaucracy, while those who wait their turn for allocation may not be seen for ten years or more.
- The time lag between submitting an application and getting called for a plot allocation interview was considered to be too long, with the result that many people without houses are discouraged from registering on the housing waiting list. No one knows when he or she will be called for an interview, and, when a plot is eventually allocated, the individual may not have the financial resources to build. It was therefore suggested that local authorities should provide advance warning on impending plot allocations to enable prospective beneficiaries to mobilize resources for house construction. Because of the uncertainty surrounding plot allocation, the majority of prospective homeowners have resigned themselves to being lifetime tenants because they regard applying for housing as a waste of time.

- Housing application procedures are considered to be cumbersome because of the lack of co-ordination between local authorities and building societies. This problem has sometimes led to queue jumping when people who are not on the application list of a local authority have been allocated plots developed under schemes sponsored by building societies.

When asked for ideas and suggestions on how housing application procedures could be improved for the benefit of consumers, respondents made the following points, summarized in Table 4.5:

- increase the delivery of residential plots by local authorities to reduce the housing waiting list
- decentralize applications from ministerial head offices to district offices
- eliminate corruption in the housing application and allocation system
- co-ordinate the activities of local authorities and building societies in order to avoid confusion (and possible corruption) in the allocation of plots.

Table 4.5   Suggestions for improving application procedures (n=400)

Area	Number of respondents	Suggestions made to improve application procedures			
		Increase supply of residential plots	Decentralize applications	Stamp out corruption in application and allocation system	Co-ordinate between local authorities and building societies
Harare	172	145	28	88	94
Chitungwiza	38	34	21	30	20
Kwekwe	30	24	22	25	18
Gweru	30	25	21	20	10
Bulawayo	60	55	45	50	23
Marondera	30	25	13	27	12
Mutare	40	36	10	25	15
Total	400	344	160	265	192
Percentage	100	86	40	66.3	48

Note: The total percentage of suggestions made exceeds 100 because many respondents gave more than one suggestion.

Source: Survey interviews

Building control inspections and their relevance

Local authorities' house construction control stages comprise inspections at the following stages:

- setting and pegging
- trenching
- foundation
- wall plate level
- roof level
- plumbing and fittings
- final certification stage.

The research aimed to establish whether beneficiaries understood clearly the reasons behind the building control stages and their attitude to those controls. Questions were also asked to find what improvements needed to be made to the control process. In this regard, 60 per cent said they did not know the reasons behind the enforcement of building control stages. Consequently, most beneficiaries view building control stages merely as a bureaucratic requirement imposed by local authorities. It was suggested that local authorities should do more to disseminate information on the value of building control. The remaining 40 per cent who understood and appreciated the need for building control stages stated that it is necessary in order to protect consumers against bad practice by contractors and builders, for example, through the use of cheap and unsuitable building materials, and that the controls ensure production of quality housing that is durable and safe for occupation.

The overriding concern of respondents with existing building control practices was that the process is too slow. It is not unusual for project completion dates to be missed because of delays in the inspection of completed stages. These delays are the result of a shortage of building inspectors, inadequate transport and incidents of corruption among inspectors. It was alleged that some inspectors use the shortage of transport as an excuse not to carry out inspections on time, but when monetary inducement is offered the transport problem ceases to be an issue.

Summary of research findings

Reviews are currently undertaken by ad hoc task forces comprised of government officials. Both the 1981 and 1992 standards were reviewed by a committee of a few select individuals drawn from MPCNH and other government departments considered relevant. Other key stakeholders in the housing development process, such as local authorities, consumers, producers of low-cost building materials, building societies, small contractors and builders have so far not been invited to participate in review processes.

It is the non-involvement of key stakeholders that accounts for the slow pace of implementation, the lack of innovation and the absence of debate on alternative and cost-effective housing technologies. It is plausible to conclude that the negligible rate of adoption of alternative low-cost building materials such as SSBs is to a large extent the result of misconceptions about the value of this material on the part of builders/contractors, consumers, building societies and so on. Inclusion of such materials in regulatory instruments would help to counter misconceptions and support those wishing to produce and employ them.

The survey findings suggest that an effective standards review process must include the following elements:

- *Participation* Processes must be as participatory as possible, ensuring that all key stakeholders in housing delivery have some involvement in standards formulation. The formation of strong, representative residents' associations is essential and the selection of participants must be based on their ability to make a positive contribution.

- *Contextual relevance*   The review must relate to context as much as possible and thus take into account the local economic, cultural, and social environment. It is irrelevant and meaningless to develop standards that are not affordable by, or popular with, the majority of people.
- *Continual processes*   The review must follow a process approach rather than be a one-off activity, so that standards are always relevant to the changing context within which they are implemented.
- *Sufficient institutional capacity*   There is need for clear review institutions, procedures and schedules to ensure clarity about who spearheads and who participates in the process. At a workshop held to discuss the findings of the field study, participants recommended that a National Standards Review Board be created consisting of MLGNH staff and representatives of donors, building societies, professionals, local authorities, contractors, building material producers and NGOs. In addition, they also recommended that local review committees be set up in each urban centre, housed under the respective local authority.
- *Adequate dissemination*   Dissemination of information on reviewed standards and alternative technologies is crucial. Responsibility for dissemination needs to be clearly established, as does the institutional capacity to carry it out. The proposed National Standards Review Board could assume such a role.
- *Practical demonstration*   Public demonstrations are essential to enable beneficiaries to measure the performance of new or revised standards. Demonstration raises awareness and provides proof of the technical feasibility of new standards and is particularly useful in the case of new building technologies.
- *Simplified procedures*   Housing application procedures need to be simplified and made more transparent in order to speed up the process of housing delivery. It is necessary to bring authority closer to the people by having building permits approved at district office rather than at head office, thereby increasing local accountability. In this way the incidence of corruption in the issue of permits and inspection of buildings could be substantially reduced.

Although professionals and their institutional employers are generally aware of the revised standards, especially new plot sizes and occupation procedures, they have no understanding of new building materials and technologies that are now permitted, such as SSBs, MCR, and steel-framed structures. Professionals were not included in the 1981 or 1992 reviews and generally view standards as being imposed from above, and hence are often lukewarm about adopting them. In general, there is a widespread view among both consumers of low-income housing, professionals and institutions involved in the development of low-income housing that the revised standards have had limited impact. Nevertheless, standards are generally considered to be necessary because they enhance the value of housing stock and ensure that houses are structurally safe for occupation.

Consumers indicated that they consider housing application procedures to be bureaucratic with burdensome requirements, and often involve corrupt practices in plot allocation and building control.

On the basis of the research findings and conclusions derived from them, subsequent project activities have aimed to increase awareness of revised standards and procedures, especially among low-income households, to disseminate information on standards, and to influence officials to further revise standards and procedures in order to make them more accessible.

Documentation and dissemination of revised standards

The findings of the survey, carried out in selected urban areas from September to December 1996, have been presented in the previous section. These findings were shared and discussed with project beneficiaries and other stakeholders at a national workshop held in Harare in March 1997.

Two key recommendations emerged from this first workshop. First, it was recommended that a handbook outlining the revised standards and procedures be prepared and disseminated to low-income households via local authorities in order to increase awareness of standards and procedures among low-income households and thus improve their access to decent and affordable housing. Second, it was recommended that the project facilitate the creation of a national review board. The function of the board would be to carry out regular reviews of standards and procedures in a participatory manner.

Verbal support for initiatives is more forthcoming than action, but platforms such as national seminars enable activists to continue to apply pressure on the stakeholders concerned to act on promises made publicly. The Civic Forum on Housing has been pursuing the issue of forming a national review board, for example. Creating such a board will take a lot of resources and involve collaboration by a wide range of stakeholders whose persistent determined efforts will be required to see it through to fruition. The board has not yet been established.

In response to the first recommendation, a handbook on standards and procedures was produced and disseminated to all local authorities and was subsequently distributed by them. Both local authorities and low-income households find the handbook useful, as it explains the basic facts about prevailing standards and procedures to home seekers (see Box 10). The burden of explaining legal requirements and processes lies with local authorities. The information contained in the booklet initially replaces the need for face-to-face meetings, freeing up housing officers to concentrate their efforts on other duties. There have been several requests to translate the handbook into the two national languages in order to widen its reach and local relevance.

In addition to the locally relevant information resources, it was felt important to share the project experiences in Zimbabwe with wider, international audiences. Contributions to international journals and publications are important in raising the level of debate among academics, politicians, professionals and policymakers, thereby keeping the challenging subject of housing standards and their impact on the lives of the urban poor on the development agenda. It is also hoped that such debate will stimulate other researchers to embark on associated research to take the debate further, highlight pockets of good practice, and facilitate international learning.

Box 10   Popularizing information to increase understanding and accessibility

The initiative to produce simple information about the regulations and procedural requirements to access land and build affordable housing arose from a national seminar organized as a project activity.

The handbook uses straightforward language and illustrations to answer many questions that people normally ask local authority officers about the procedures that have to be followed, and why these procedures exist, as well as the various building controls stages and the regulatory requirements for various design aspects of the housing product.

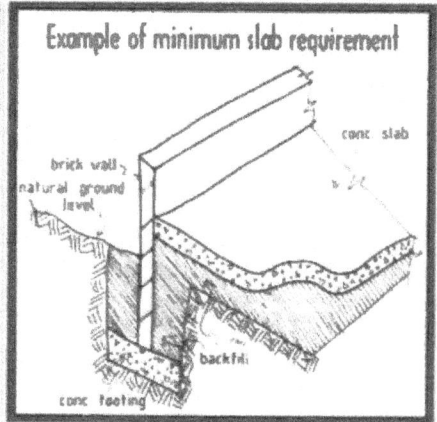

Cartoons and illustrations are used to explore common misconceptions and to answer questions that people may have about their applications, the procedures and specific technical issues relating to house construction.

Source: Mugova and Musandu-Nyamayaro 1998

Demonstration of revised standards in practice

ITDG's initial project target was to design and construct 50 houses with people in order to demonstrate in a realistic setting the new designs and building technologies permitted under the revised standards. The assumption made in project planning was that local people would be readily persuaded of the value in building such houses, therefore the project did not try to raise the resources to support actual construction. It soon became apparent that, for a number of reasons, such a high level of construction activity would not be forthcoming within the timeframe of the research project.

The adoption of new designs and technologies has inherent risks. Poor and marginalized people are least able to carry risks or absorb the costs of failure associated with such risks. The reluctance of building societies to provide mortgages to low-income groups, particularly on non-conventional structures, exacerbated this situation. Because of these problems, it was

Photo 8   This household has saved money by using newly approved building technologies in the construction of their home in Chitungwiza.

decided to concentrate efforts on working with a few selected households in low-income communities to build demonstration houses where innovative designs and revised standards would be applied. Three houses were built, one in Chitungwiza and two in Epworth, both peri-urban settlements located about 25km from Harare.

The construction of these structures has started to have some positive effects. There are few exact copies of the houses, although one family in Chitungwiza has tried to replicate the demonstration house, building their own home using the same technologies and designs. At least forty other households are currently involved in the production of innovative building materials, which they intend to use for their self-build initiatives. A further two houses have been built in Marondera, a smaller urban centre to the east of Harare. In response, a housing co-operative consisting of 120 members has already indicated interest in reproducing the designs and technologies. These exciting developments will help to demonstrate the potential impact of the revised standards.

Creating an enabling regulatory environment and enhancing local building materials production are significant steps, given the real barrier that access to affordable materials represents to low-income, self-help builders. Local materials production and informal construction practices have the potential to add value, generate income and develop local technological capacity – all important factors in reducing urban poverty (Tipple 1999). Given the declining value of the Zimbabwean dollar and the escalating costs of imported materials, any reduction in costs is helpful.

Not every experience of using cost-effective materials and technologies has been successful in Zimbabwe. Problems have been encountered in a number of large-scale housing schemes targeted at the low-income sector, including the use of Terra-block and timber houses in Mutare and steel-framed housing in Kuwadzana, Harare. The technologies applied in these projects have not been replicated on a wide scale and it is doubtful they ever will be, for a variety of reasons. In Mutare, a Terra-block house was built in Dangamvura in 1990. The house developed very serious cracks and had to be replastered several times, mainly because of poor supervision and workmanship during production. Today, the house is used as a workshop by a co-operative because most people consider it to be unsafe. Steel-framed houses in Kuwadzana have attracted some of the strongest criticism, as the walls are thin and people feel they are not strong enough. One study revealed that water seeps into some of the houses because they have been built in inappropriate places, in areas with high water tables. Some complaints result from the belief – and social aspirations – that walling should only be made from fired bricks.

Such negative experience of using non-conventional technologies inevitably results in a bad reputation in the marketplace, and users, builders and local authority professionals become reluctant to experiment with any new material. Project experience highlighted the need for carefully organized access to facilitate production processes. SSB production depends upon access to a block press, for example. When innovative practices are introduced, it is important to ensure proper training of skills and close supervision in order to maintain high product quality. Notwithstanding the real and perceived problems encountered in introducing new building technologies on to the market, the beneficiaries of demonstration houses built with SSBs by the project have positive attitudes to their homes:

- the house is easy to extend
- the bricks look good and you do not have to render the walls
- the blocks are easy to chase out for electrical conduits compared to conventional bricks.

Studies show that SSB technology significantly reduces the cost of construction compared with conventional clay bricks. The total cost of the four-roomed demonstration house constructed in Chitungwiza was Z$108 000 at 1997 prices. Two years later, with the building index having shot up by about 75 per cent, the house costs about Z$189 000; similar conventionally built four-roomed core houses were constructed at an average materials' cost of Z$200 000 per unit in mid-1999. The addition of labour costs would increase this figure by 25 per cent to Z$250 000. Given the cost of constructing a four-roomed house, acceptance of incremental construction is crucial in increasing access for low-income people. All local authorities have accepted this and all the self-help housing schemes follow this practice. USAID housing programme adviser, Mr Eliah Tafangombe, illustrated the benefits of the incremental construction approach by citing the example of projects implemented in Bulawayo, Zimbabwe's second largest city (see Box 11).

The cost of a house is determined in part by the plot size, the price of which is, in turn, related to the services that are provided for that land, for example the road frontage, sewerage and water infrastructure and connections. The larger the plot, the more expensive the services will be. Since the cost of the services is included in the price of the land, land costs are often the initial stumbling block for low-income homeseekers. The reduction of land costs therefore becomes very important in facilitating access to housing. Plot size has been a critical issue in both of the revision exercises; the most recent reduction to allow minimum plots of 150m^2 is clearly a step in the right direction. In Mutare, in the Hobhouse 1 and 2 schemes, residential plots were being sold in June 1999 for Z$87.75/m^2 which means a 150m^2 plot cost Z$13 162. Of the 20 000 people on the Mutare housing waiting list, 16 000 earn between Z$500 and Z$3 000 per month, making even the smaller 150m^2 'stands' unaffordable.

In Marondera, people face similar problems of affordability. The new residential area in Rutendo has mixed plot sizes, some below 150m^2; serviced land is selling for Z$105/m^2, so a 150 m^2 plot costs Z$15 750, added to which will be a Z$3000 service charge, the total cost of the

> **Box 11   Benefits of an incremental housing development approach**
>
> The regional housing adviser for USAID, who is based in Harare, holds some strong views about the efficiency of the incremental housing development approach in increasing access for low-income households to affordable housing. His confidence in this approach has grown because of the impressive results achieved in the Nkulumane housing development scheme implemented in Bulawayo, the second largest city in Zimbabwe.
>
> The project was started with beneficiaries taking on mortgages provided jointly by building societies, the government of Zimbabwe, and USAID. Beneficiaries were allocated plots ranging in size from 200m² to 300 m² and left with options to develop their own house plans and build at their own pace. Some five years later, the results of the scheme are truly phenomenal. Starting from humble single-room core structures, households have made huge investments in the development of their houses over the years. Today the scheme is characterized by well-built and well-maintained five- to six-roomed houses in a large range of designs and materials. None of these features would have existed if homeseekers had been told to build using predetermined designs or 'supply and fix' contractors.

minimum plot then amounting to Z$18 750. The 200m² plot, which is the size favoured by most local authorities, costs Z$21 000 before service charges. Low-income household members in Marondera prefer the smaller plots because they are cheaper, suggesting that people prefer buying plots within their means rather than overstretching themselves. A study carried out in Marondera–Cherutombo by Plan Inc. in 1999, where plots are 150m², indicates that size is not plot owners' only concern: equally important is access to secure, legally validated land ownership that enables them to sublet, even on a 100m² plot, thereby generating income. The other issues of concern to home seekers are the cost of the plot, availability of financial resources to build, availability and cost of building materials, house plans and designs and the time it takes to have them approved, and bureaucratic procedures in inspection and approval of various stages of construction (Mugova and Musandu-Nyamayaro 1999).

Impacts of revised standards and lessons learnt

In order to counter the project's lack of construction, it was decided to look at the link between revised standards and affordability, and a user survey was undertaken. The survey sampled two sets of users – those who built houses prior to the 1992 revision and those who built after it – and made a comparative assessment of pre-and post–1992 housing schemes. The study sought to determine the level of satisfaction users had with the houses provided, and to highlight the impact of the new housing standards on affordability. The research was undertaken in Harare in the low-income areas of Kuwadzana Extension, Kuwadzana NSSA, Budiriro 5, Dzivarasekwa Extension, Dzivarasekwa Co-operative, Kambuzuma, Highfields Flats, Chitungwiza Founders and Chitungwiza Ministry of Local Government and National Housing. The key findings and interpretations of the survey were as follows:

- *Stand sizes* Most (86 per cent) of the plots allocated before 1992 measured an average of 300m^2. Approximately 47 per cent of the respondents felt that this was too small for gardening or extending their houses. Among the post-1992 sample, 60 per cent of respondents did not know the size of their plots, which ranged from 150m^2 to 400m^2. Residential space was clearly also used for business purposes, such as poultry rearing. The 150m^2 plots were considered too small by respondents who owned cars.
- *Waiting time* Almost half (45 per cent) of pre-1992 homeowners moved on to their plots before the main house was built; only 32 per cent moved after the whole structure was complete. The majority of people felt that early occupation was an advantage as it reduced the burden of double rentals, ensured the security of materials being stored on site and made supervision of the construction process easier. Most homeowners who built post-1992 were on the housing waiting lists longer than the pre-1992 homeowners, an indication that urban local authorities found it increasingly difficult to provide sufficient serviced plots as demand rose. Only 5 per cent of the post-1992 respondents moved on to their plots before completion of construction, mainly because most of the projects were being constructed by developers rather than through self-help.
- *Revisions made* Appendix 5 provides a summary of the key issues that emerged from the comparative study. The study concluded that some of the new materials are not popular with the poor. It also noted that most people had still not taken advantage of the new building lines (or plot coverage), nor were they increasing their use of alternative and cheaper building materials allowed by the 1992 revision standards in urban housing projects. One explanation could be that most housing schemes were constructed by the MPCNH without any input from beneficiaries on design and material usage.
- *Understanding and simplifying procedures* The handbook described in Box 10 provides useful information to prospective home seekers on plot allocation procedures and construction options. A total of 3000 handbooks were produced and are circulated to users by local authorities and other project partners, such as the Civic Forum on Housing. The influence of this publication remains anecdotal. In Marondera it was reported that the handbook helped to limit the time housing officers spent explaining procedures and reduced the number of trips that home seekers had to make to obtain advice (in one case, over 90 trips were recorded). Home seekers are also helped because they are better able to understand procedural requirements and no longer have to employ a middleman in the process of building approval. The handbook has therefore filled an information gap, benefiting both users and enforcers of by-laws. The potential impact of information resources such as the handbook has been realized by a number of organizations. The Civic Forum has an information pack and is introducing posters as a step towards further simplifying and disseminating the information contained in the pack.

Despite these efforts, official council bureaucracy remains a problem. Initially the project hoped to help local authorities to reduce the time it takes to process housing applications by about 30 per cent. However, this wish has not been fulfilled, although important efforts continue to be made by many local authorities. For example, Harare City Council has tried to reduce the time it takes to get a plan approved by creating a unit within the housing department consisting of engineers, architects, and surveyors. This unit is responsible for approving development plans for low-income housing and is supposed to make approvals with little delay, a worthy idea that has yet to yield significant results because of institutional resistance. The officials concerned aim to make approvals within one month, but currently recognize that this goal is not always achievable and therefore recommend that people call or visit to pursue any applications that have not received approval after one month.

Four workshops were held between 1996 and 1999 to share project research findings and experiences and to obtain feedback from primary and secondary stakeholders. The workshops have proved a valuable means of exchanging information and of discussing standards and procedures. A broad spectrum of participants were involved in all of the workshops, representing policymakers, low-income and marginalized groups, academics, housing co-operatives and donor agencies with an active interest in the housing sector. Face-to-face interaction is clearly one of the benefits of such workshops, as are the resultant recommendations on the way in which to make standards and procedures more enabling and participatory in future. Project evaluators felt that the decentralization of such dissemination activities would help to increase the project's influence.

- *Influencing the policy agenda* One of the project's objectives was to influence official thinking on any review of standards and procedures. Officials interviewed said that the project has altered their thinking on the regulation of low-income housing. The Department of Physical Planning is revising minimum allowable plot sizes from 150m^2 to 100m^2, and officials admit that project initiatives have played a part in this process. In carrying out the revision, the department will adopt a participatory approach: a major study will be undertaken to consult with the intended beneficiaries. In their view the involvement of users and other stakeholders will ensure that new standards are accepted and sustained. The move towards allocation of smaller plots by local authorities is significant in increasing the number of legal dwellings. The divergence between the opinions of professionals and politicians remains apparent; the former are convinced of the need to adopt a flexible, realistic approach, while the latter remain governed by political pressure to maintain the highest possible standards. The consultative study envisaged is perceived as a useful tool in avoiding political fighting that surrounds the revision of regulatory frameworks.

This innovative thinking is, however, currently constrained by political influence and interference. The results from such a study will be critical in convincing politicians who still argue against further 'downward revision'. Other stakeholders, including local authorities and donor agencies, are agreed on the need to constantly revise standards and make them more enabling. For example, USAID indicated that standards in use in Zimbabwe are very high compared with other developing countries and support the idea of incremental construction (see Box 11). To reach agreement, it will be necessary now to address, or bring on board, the various fora of urban local authorities, including the Directors of Housing and the Town Engineer's Forum. Often the personnel in local authorities who are aware of the need to review standards are fairly low ranking and at times too timid to take recommendations to their bosses. It is also important to include local politicians, such as councillors, in the process. They are the people on the ground who can influence thinking in local authority organizations.

- *Alternative technological practices* The poor performance of alternative technologies in some housing schemes has clearly had a negative impact on the reputation of some cost-effective housing options. The demonstration houses have, however, had a positive effect in terms of raising the level of awareness of innovative materials and designs permitted under the revised legislation. The demonstration houses in Chitungwiza and Epworth have been visited by prospective homeowners from other towns, and SSB technology is growing in popularity. These negative and positive experiences offer important insights into the way in which new technologies should be introduced to ensure wider acceptance and replication. It is critical for users and other secondary stakeholders to be widely consulted during the whole technology transfer and adaptation process to make sure that their resources, needs and priorities are respected in making technology choices. Consultation is essential to convince users of the technical efficiency, financial viability and desirability of new building techniques. The acceptance of innovative and more affordable building materials as alternatives in urban housing projects is an important step in increasing access to legal urban housing.

Key lessons to emerge from project initiatives in Zimbabwe

Partnerships are critical in creating effective and successful policy dialogue and influencing the national housing agenda. It was only possible for ITDG to affect policy dialogue by working in partnership with other development agencies, including Plan International, Housing People of Zimbabwe, Habitat for Humanity and the Civic Forum on Housing. It is essential to continue lobbying government and local authorities to further revise standards and procedures if the needs of low-income households are to be supported. Those seeking to change policy will need to make continual efforts on a long-term basis. These efforts must go beyond meetings with key officials and target politicians engaged in decision-making at local, national and international levels.

It is evident that innovative building technologies, such as SSBs, allowed by revised standards can have a significant impact in making affordable and legal housing accessible in urban areas. Locally produced materials are an effective means of overcoming the overwhelming shortage of construction materials, adding value locally, and especially supporting self-help construction projects.

Revisions allowing smaller plot sizes have helped low-income families to benefit from land ownership and, subsequently, from better quality housing. Housing standards revisions currently include consideration of housing technologies and plot sizes only; the integral nature of housing and the services connected to it mean future revisions should also consider standards governing infrastructure and service provision.

5
OVERRIDING ISSUES

Introduction

By far the biggest shelter challenge in the developing world is the extraordinary growth of informal settlements. It is the one phenomenon that should define the scope and direction of future attempts to reform regulatory frameworks, because without addressing that particular concern other efforts to improve the housing conditions for the majority of people will have a diminished effect. Making poor people's housing affordable and accessible, and ridding it of the stigma of illegality, has great potential to enlarge the urban economy and integrate illicit settlements into mainstream urban life.

This chapter will highlight those issues that are likely to dominate the housing standards debate in the foreseeable future, as indicated by project experience, commissioned case studies and review of the available literature. At an international project workshop in June 1999 marking the end of the Enabling Housing Standards and Procedures Project, the participants analysed case studies from a number of countries and identified key issues (see Box 12) that merited further debate and action (Schilderman 1999). Another conference soon after at the Institution of Civil Engineers in London emphasized the need to recognize the complexities and the potential of informal development, while at the same time discarding the colonial heritage in urban development standards. The liberation of urban development codes is therefore a matter of serious concern among reformers and practitioners, who often feel frustrated by inappropriate planning and design criteria.

Developing countries cannot afford the standards they have legislated to uphold, as their need for housing far outweighs the available resources. Investment in housing does create wealth, and the pace of asset creation across all income brackets can be accelerated by widening the standards band. Reviewing standards and setting them at more affordable levels increases the range of available choices and unlocks those talents that lie dormant. Relevant and affordable standards could result in more and better houses and in greater economic activity through materials production, financial services, small-scale production enterprises, retail trade, maintenance functions and so on. Indeed, this is the rationale behind urban improvement programmes. The regulatory threshold therefore becomes an issue. What are the costs and benefits of regulation? What is the minimum desirable level of regulation?

It is evident that when buildings are costed, the costs of regulation only appear incidentally, if at all, because they are taken for granted and some are met by society as a whole through taxation. Building permit fees are usually nominal and in no way reflect the true cost of administering the control system. Cost is often used as an argument to reduce regulation, especially in the face of pressures to minimize production costs. All the same, certain types of regulation are on the increase: 'Citizens in many countries express a desire for more regulation in areas such as environmental protection, public health, and safety standards. Rising incomes partly explain the increased interest; as consumers become wealthier, they demand more amenities such as cleaner air and water and better sanitation' (Guasch and Hahn 1999). Is that why the élite in the poorer countries demand higher standards and stricter enforcement irrespective of the needs of poor people?

Packaging standards

Issues surrounding the way in which standards are presented and disseminated are a significant aspect of the housing standards debate. The diversity of information and the different types of audience point to the need for a correspondingly diverse range of languages, media and channels of distribution. Clearly, information resources are often lacking, leading to a correspondingly low level of awareness about what standards are and what they mean in practice.

> Politicians may announce efforts to reduce housing costs but frequently this is only lip service ... while changes in the building codes lead to rises in the cost of housing. The 'silence' in the housing conflict represents the lack of public awareness of these code changes and their effect on housing costs. Because of their complexity and dryness, building codes are not newsworthy subjects.
>
> Goldberg 1990

Box 12   Key issues

At an international workshop on housing standards held in Rugby, England in June 1999 the existing literature was reviewed and fifteen case studies were presented. During the case studies, workshop participants kept note of key issues which needed further attention or debate. These can be grouped under five broad headings:

Definition and scope

Defining the terms and concepts
Defining indicators
Criteria such as affordability, flexibility, local relevance
Broadening the scope, from housing to mixed uses and neighbourhoods

Dissemination

Learning from each other worldwide
Overcoming reluctance, raising awareness
Marketing of standards, etc.
Coalitions and partnerships to push for change

Review process

Initiators and champions
Participation
Keeping the issue alive
Overcoming the resistance to change
Review methodologies

Implementation and enforcement

Financing and implementing the process
Enforcement and control

People

Building professionals and artisans
Gender
Partnerships
Capacity building and education

Source: Schilderman 1999

A large amount of technical, social, financial and process information is required to build a house to optimum standards. The One Million Houses Programme in Sri Lanka clearly recognized this fact and used several tools for sharing and managing information, including household files, workshops, on-site training and support (Sirivardana 1999). Information and education campaigns in Sri Lanka were made much easier by the high literacy rate (estimated at 90 per cent). Families had updated information for their day-to-day use. Householder files contained documents such as growth charts of households, building plans, cost estimates and municipal rates receipts. These records were supplemented by an official support system, which maintained a personalized and accurate information base. Information was considered an integral part of the Community Action Planning process, which sought to produce a consensus document, based on a carefully prepared and organized community workshop. As part of implementation a series of issue-based workshops lasting half a day or one whole day were held. Issues that came up often included:

- the formation of community development councils (CDCs)
- community action plan formulation
- community building guidelines
- housing loans and information
- community contract system
- maintenance of common services
- support of women's enterprises
- market links and people's fairs
- community monitoring and evaluation
- the role of urban local authorities.

Both people who were waiting to be allocated a plot of land and those who had begun building needed information on a variety of topics, including:

- the procedure to be followed when obtaining an allocation of land
- the steps to be taken when building a house
- (for applicants and builders) the reasons why inspectors insist steps, stages and materials requirements must be followed
- the requirement that each stage of construction must be approved before proceeding.

In Jamaica, the Association for Settlement and Commercial Enterprise for National Development (ASCEND), a coalition of the private and public sectors and NGOs, directed its efforts to addressing issues of shelter for people living below the poverty line. 'In 1996, ASCEND produced a series of manuals aimed at supporting the planning and development of low-income settlements, including a *Starter Standards Manual* (for incremental housing) and an *Affordable Types Manual* (for self-builders). ASCEND has helped to raise awareness of the critical importance of affordable standards in housing delivery, and its manuals have been developed in a process of fairly wide consultation' (McHardy 1998).

Box 13   ASCEND initiatives in Jamaica

ASCEND emerged in Jamaica in 1993 and was legally registered in 1994 as a non-profit-making company. Formed to address the issues of providing shelter for those on the breadline, ASCEND is a national coalition of the private, public, and non-governmental sectors including professional bodies. Five committees have been established to deal with the areas that the organization regards as critical:

- Physical planning and development
- Quality of life committee (community development and empowerment)
- Economic and financial aspects
- Legal aspects
- Public education and communications

These subcommittees are the policymaking and programme arm of ASCEND. They are responsible for developing the proposals that will operationalize strategies. This will take the form of policies, programmes or projects, including the provision of training and professional expertise in the preparation of manuals. These manuals will be revised based on the feedback in the implementation process.

In 1996 ASCEND produced a series of manuals to help in the planning and development of low-income settlements in Jamaica, including a *Starter Standards Manual*, a *Community Development Manual*, *Affordable House Types Manual*, *Beneficiaries Policy Manual* and a *Beneficiary Selection Policies Manual*.

The purpose of *Starter Standards* is to ensure that low-income communities develop rationally, making efficient use of community and external resources to create better conditions for themselves.

The first steps in preparing *Starter Standards* involved detailed discussions with all relevant government agencies in collaboration with the professional associations through the Professional Societies Association of Jamaica. The manual has since gone through several stages in which local and overseas consultants have drawn up the guidelines for starter standards. This process of review is ongoing and therefore the finalization of the manual is still in progress.

An unrelated guide to the shelter units has been developed. A manual of over sixty small house designs for owner-builders has been prepared. These designs meet the legal requirements and can be personalized by the owners.

Source: McHardy 1998

Language and media

Existing documentation is couched in technical terms, if not jargon, as it is the style thought to be essential in legal documents. Regulations use technical language and must be precise in order to ensure accurate and consistent interpretation in cases of litigation. Lack of clarity means that acts cannot be enforced for the purposes for which they were intended. Strange language can result when foreign texts are adapted and/or translated to suit local requirements. To illustrate the point, *What is a Drain? The Kenyan Building Code* (The Government Printer 1968:9–10) says, 'drain' means 'any drain used for the drainage of one building only, or of premises within the same cartilage and made merely for the purpose of communicating therefrom with a receptacle for drainage, or with a sewer into which the drainage of two or more buildings or premises occupied by different persons is conveyed'. Then there is a separate definition of 'sewer' and forty-four different clauses dealing with standards for drainage, 'sanitary conveniences' and sewers. There are many similar examples of obfuscation in the document.

While there is a real need for accuracy, codes are rarely translated into layman's language. This inaccessibility has inspired some countries to rewrite their codes to present them in a clear and concise way, sometimes using illustrations. (An example from Kenya is presented in Appendix 3.) Some industrialized countries realized the need for greater clarity, and only as recently as the 1980s acted to provide more accessible documentation by separating the law, as stated in the regulations, from 'deemed-to-satisfy' clauses. The purpose of such clauses is to help designers and builders interpret performance standards by presenting suitable technical options. The numerous laws concerning buildings and related matters in the UK were very confusing. The legislation was revised in 1984 to become one act with 135 sections and 7 schedules. In 1985 the Secretary of State introduced the building regulations, which consisted of a manual containing the regulations and linking them to 13 booklets of approved documents that showed ways in which the requirements could be satisfied (Barritt 1995:3).

Similar efforts were made in the revision process of 1982 in Kenya when the task force with the remit to review housing standards was also commissioned to provide 'recommendations ... illustrated in a manual showing clear and simple examples of construction and infrastructure details' (UNCHS 1985:34). These reports appear to have been published and distributed mainly through the efforts of NGOs. There are many people involved in revising standards, while literacy levels among the beneficiaries, councillors, engineers, architects, politicians and builders vary enormously. To effectively reach all of these people would take considerable funds and resourcefulness. Numerous media have to be used, for example:

- ITDG Zimbabwe produced a booklet that was delivered to all municipal councils.
- The Danish Building Defects Fund has a database of existing housing defects.
- France helped Vietnam to revise its regulations, which included an element of training.
- Design competitions were organized by housing authorities in China, and a demonstration village was built.

Sometimes only formal means of communication are produced and widely issued, for example announcements made by central government in newspapers and gazettes promulgating the revised by-laws. Ministry circulars sometimes inform council employees about revised regulations, which is one source of information made available to construction professionals, as was the case in Zimbabwe (see Chapter 4). In many countries new policy measures are announced in a government gazette, which is widely distributed and carries some weight. These formal notifications are important, but a lack of in-depth support materials can lower the quality of alternative building materials production, as was the case with SSB construction in West Africa, where the only source of information available was the published results of laboratory testing, which for most people were inaccessible (Aka 1996:2).

Information systems are notoriously difficult and expensive to establish. New technology is generally thought to be essential for any system. The high costs of computers are gradually coming down and could soon come within reach of the budgets of developing country municipalities. Initiatives in Mexico to improve local government information services were supported by external funds and technical services, as it was thought worthwhile to develop the capacity to manage information about existing resources and settlements. If external funds are not always available, affordable information systems must be designed and installed.

The Andhra Pradesh Primary Education Project (APPEP) in India and the ILD (Instituto para la Libertad y Democracia – the Institute for Freedom and Democracy) initiative in Peru both highlight the significance of ownership of information. Through participatory processes, engaging the target beneficiaries in information gathering and analysis, users are assured of the origins and accuracy of data collected and will tend to benefit from a sense of ownership of it. Owning the information will ensure that any information pertinent to local realities and needs will be retained and not rejected as irrelevant material sent down from above. This principle lies behind the methodology pursued by CRATerre-EAG in preparing the Pan-African standards for compressed earth blocks (CEBs) for example.

Peruvian initiatives to revise building standards incorporated a variety of activities as part of a carefully planned dissemination strategy. The former National Housing Research and Normalization Institute (ININVI) recognized the need to create awareness at different levels: among public servants, professionals, academics, specialist technicians and instructors, and self-help builders.

The ILD information system (see Figure 6) was built on the idea of simplified and people-friendly approaches, eliminating duplication, reducing costs, and relying on readily available documentation to validate information. For example, notarized public deeds have been substituted by easy-to-complete printed forms, and notarized building certificates have been replaced by printed forms and photographs (Institute for Freedom and Democracy 1991:1–5). Other interesting examples include:

- The Regional Centre for Research on Human Settlements in Indonesia produced fourteen survey sheets to help people make informed choices about housing technologies and designs (ESCAP 1979:27).

- The Building Research Unit in Tanzania was responsible for producing technical guidelines to help improve low-cost houses and to disseminate to a wider public the contents of the Township Rules 1980.
- In the UK, building control officers are currently grappling with the problem of providing access to buildings for people with disabilities. This revision was scheduled to take effect in October 1999, but some parts applied earlier. One officer commented: 'It's so hard to read; we get a few leaflets saying how it should be applied – I think I'll just use these' (interview with a DOE officer 1999). Other resources exist in the form of guidelines, such as those produced by the National Housing Federation, which 'draws on the experience and expertise of the Federation's members as well as a wide range of existing good practice material' (Cotton 1998:VIII). Guidance is not only offered to support professionals in their caring duty, but also to the general public via more succinct leaflets.
- Guidelines in the USA clearly explain the purpose of the regulations as well as the content and technical aspects of constructing each building element. Propagation material goes so far as to tackle gender issues by 'encouraging' women to build the best they can since the building code does not give preference to men.
- The Ministry for Local Government and Lands of the Gambia produces information leaflets explaining development, building permits (how to obtain them and from whom), what to do in the case of permission being denied, and what to do once it is obtained. The final sections cover what happens in the case of contraventions (Laws and Regulations Information leaflets).

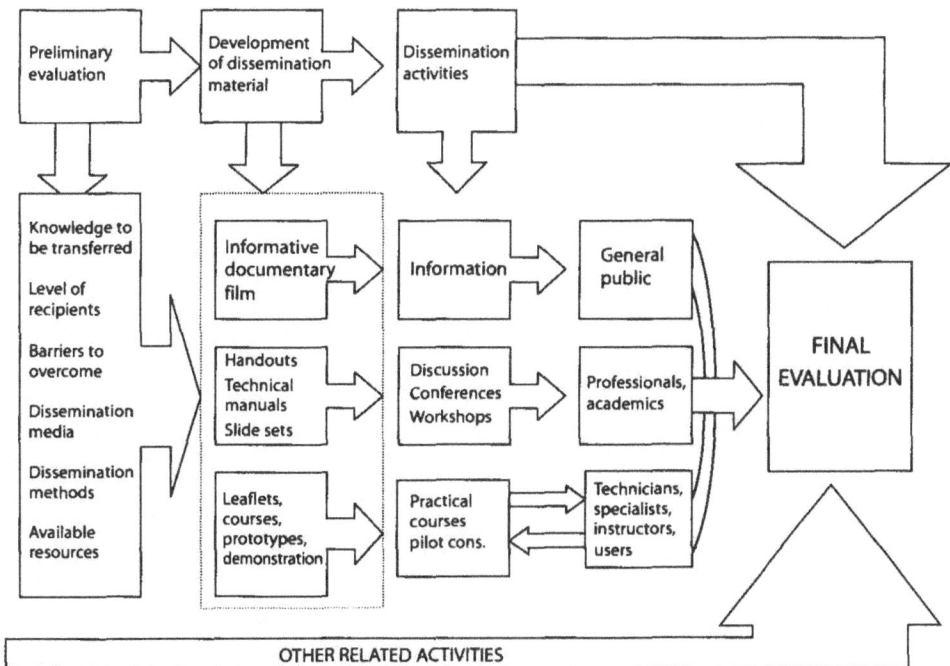

Figure 6   Dissemination methodology used in Peru

Source: Diaz 1984

Some countries have developed very refined dissemination methods. Canada, for instance, has an impressive dossier of promotion materials on many aspects of housing and urban development standards, produced mainly by the Central Mortgage and Housing Corporation in the two national languages, English and French.

The secret of successful dissemination is information. A comprehensive and well-managed database can:

- help review codes
- help focus on the review process
- improve the flow of information
- enhance co-ordination efforts
- help create transparency in standards administration and revision
- improve dialogue between officials, users, civil society and private operators
- support monitoring and enforcement efforts.

Adequate information and good communications help to establish meaningful partnerships and collaborative programmes. Changing attitudes in the finance sector can be accomplished by astute packaging. The mortgage lender is less interested in technical specifications of construction materials and techniques and more in official certification of title to the property, compliance with the planning and building regulations, and houses that keep their market value. Thus revised standards must result in houses that can be sold. The lack of money is a major impediment to providing housing to those on a low income. However, suitably packaged standards can help to unlock the vast financial resources of institutions looking for viable investment opportunities.

Standard designs can be one way of interpreting regulations and demonstrating clearly what they mean in practice. There is an argument that says design standardization leads to loss of creativity and diversity in the built environment, but type plans do offer useful guidance and can greatly facilitate the process of obtaining planning and/or building permission. Block approval of type designs has been shown to work in Nakuru, Kenya, in Dar Es Salaam, Tanzania (Tanzania Housing Bank 1978), and in Jamaica, where an NGO produced several documents, including design manuals, to help the housing process targeted at people in the community (see Box 13).

While many millions of people provide their own housing solutions, very few have the benefit of any technical training. Even those who do have experience to draw on, such as artisans, will be unable to use new techniques according to regulations unless they have had the opportunity to study and understand them.

It is essential to demonstrate how to use revised or new standards, especially where the materials and techniques are new and unfamiliar to the population concerned. A national workshop in Burundi recommended that public sector buildings be constructed using newly regularized local materials (Baransaka 1996), while the APPEP erected 29 school buildings in order to convince teachers, parents, community leaders, engineers and politicians that cost-effective technologies could increase access to educational facilities at an affordable cost. Given the scale of investment required in housing, people are unlikely to experiment with unknown technologies even if they are approved. Demonstration clearly enables people to see for themselves what the result will be. Even though housing projects and programmes usually allow for some demonstration, there is little capacity to offer technical support to people on low incomes as a matter of course.

Informal enforcement

When a series of earthquakes hit Turkey in mid-August 1999 and killed nearly twenty thousand people while maiming, displacing and traumatizing many more, building contractors and municipal authorities bore the brunt of people's wrath for failing to enforce building regulations. The country's Prime Minister admitted on television (all the major international channels repeated his statement many times) that many deaths had been caused by poor quality construction and neglect of elementary precautions needed for earthquake-prone areas. Developers know they are being watched more carefully, and not just by public officials. Informal enforcement can take the form of either direct management and enforcement of a regulatory regime by local communities, or alternatively it could manifest itself in the form of strict monitoring by community groups backed by political pressure. Various permutations of these two models are possible. The role, scope and potential of informal enforcement have lately been receiving attention from other researchers. Richard E. Messick (1999) notes that the informal enforcement mechanisms that have drawn the most attention are reputation-based systems that permit merchants to trade in the absence of a court system that could ensure contract performance. He gives examples of informal enforcement agents in the form of credit information bureaux, consumer testing laboratories, better business bureaux, and other entities that provide seals of approval or quality guarantees. One reason why informal enforcement is popular is that it is less expensive and faster than official channels. The issue then is how these beneficial and pragmatic ways of doing business can be integrated into the established administrative mechanisms. Can the management of housing standards take advantage of these approaches? Lessons from literature and field observations indicate the importance of the following eight requirements in an auto-regulatory regime:

- an overall framework of basic values and yardsticks (e.g. relating to health and safety), including the recognition of property rights
- identity with clear or implicit objectives. This statement does not necessarily mean that communities would be homogeneous, as they are by nature complex; in a low-income settlement there would be people who are landlords, tenants, guests, squatters, servants, indigenes, strangers and many other categories.
- some sense of understanding with the authorities, who often need to be sympathetic and willing to bend the rules in the spirit of facilitating development. 'Standards stretching' should be seen by the authorities as a legitimate tactic.
- a collection of rewards based on reputation and status. Building a beautiful home elevates the owner in the eyes of his neighbour, hence the lure of processed and imported materials, and of glossy finishes (glazed tiles, cement plaster, oil paints) over the more traditional textured finishes.
- a system of appropriate measures to penalize errant members, accompanied by swift and inexpensive dispute resolution mechanisms
- a dynamic and vibrant local economy that enables people to build, alter, extend, demolish and improve their properties all the time. Stagnation and decline cannot support regulation since people's energies must be directed elsewhere
- readiness to copy, learn and adapt new building methods and materials. By absorbing new techniques a community is able to test its regulatory abilities and maintain the neighbourhood's variety and vitality.
- a corps of innovators, risk-takers and leaders who are willing to take upon themselves the leadership of the group or community concerned in regulating the built environment. In

both Africa and Asia there are whole communities that are governed by spiritual leaders. They could be regarded as mini-states or local authorities with their own building and development rules, for example in Tuba in Senegal.

The scope of community-based regulation is wide, and it could control land subdivision and allocation, the laying of infrastructure, site planning, choice of house types and building materials, and even type of occupancy. Devolved regulation could have the 'negative' effect of segregating communities along ethnic or tribal lines, however, if the dominant group can keep out members of other groups through prejudice or sanctions.

When it is too late

When three thousand people were made homeless by a fire at an unplanned settlement called Maweni in the Kenyan coastal tourist resort of Malindi in 1996, the *Daily Nation* carried the headline 'Strict Byelaws, Not Fire Engines, Will Save Lives'. The paper reported that at a fundraising meeting organized for the victims the Minister for Energy 'warned that even if the local council had the most efficient fire brigade, the fire would have left behind the same amount of losses'. Because 'the area lacked access roads, was congested, and most construc-tions were on top of water supply pipes and under power lines ... Perhaps the greatest chal-lenge facing the Malindi Municipal Council's planning department is enforcement of by-laws on future projects to ensure that access roads are respected and water connection joints are left intact'. This is only one local example of the numerous types of disasters affecting people and houses every year all over the world. Earth tremors, volcanic eruptions, hurricanes, floods and conflicts are reported every day in the international media. When world leaders met in Istanbul for Habitat II in 1996 they urged governments, local authorities and all interested parties to 'develop, adopt, and enforce appropriate norms and by-laws for land-use, building, and planning standards that are based on professionally established hazard and vulnerability assessments' (UNCHS 1997:97). This is one of the thirty-two recommendations by the conference for the purpose of disaster prevention, mitigation, and rehabilitation. Such exhortations are necessary because most countries are not as well prepared as, say, Japan or the USA. The Taiwanese government was quick to blame contrac-tors when 3000 people died during an earthquake in September 1999, just a month after the disaster in Turkey. The BBC reported (World Service on 26 September 1999) 'flagrant viola-tions [of building regulations] amounting to criminal negligence'. Disastrous events always produce knee-jerk reactions about standards, but higher standards are meaningless unless resources are allocated to enable people to observe them.

The housing needs of refugees and internally displaced people are normally treated as a special case. Yet, as of 1995, there were 14.5 million refugees and asylum seekers and 21.6 million internally displaced people worldwide (IFRC 1996). Conflict has become such a permanent feature of the world scene that a distinct body of knowledge is emerging on how to deliver basic shelter quickly and cheaply under very difficult security and environmental conditions (personal interview with Praful Soni, UNHCR architect, October 1995). African experience extends to building shelter for displaced persons in Rwanda, Kenya, Tanzania and Sierra Leone. In all such cases approved codes are put aside and architects, engineers, planners and logistics experts concentrate on preventing disease, sustaining life and protecting children. Camps can be very large, accommodating tens of thousands of people.

The devastation of the surrounding countryside is therefore often a problem, but pres-sures to resettle are so huge and immediate that little thought can be given to such environmental nuances. Once the refugees have gone home and camps are abandoned, the local population are left with vast disfigured landscapes. The result is increased scarcity of local building materials such as timber, thatch, yarn, skins, bark and other natural fabrics that are so important to indigenous technologies. Changes in local climate and drainage patterns also affect dwelling location and durability. Unfortunately, little attention has been given to developing rehabilitation standards.

Climate change is likely to affect population movements, availability of construction materials, water resource levels, and the structural integrity of waterfront properties. Not only will vector-borne diseases such as malaria (60 per cent of the earth's surface inhabited by people is expected to become a malaria-prone zone very soon) become more common in the South, but the spread of pests that attack timber, thatch and other building materials, such as white ants, could have a severe impact on housing economics. The discovery of termites in southern England (*Chartered Surveyor Monthly* 1999) sent shock waves through British maintenance professionals, who hope it was an isolated and temporary infestation.

Transnational influences on local choices

Efforts to devolve and localize regulatory authority must take into account the countervailing forces of national and transnational influences. Local measures can acquire additional validity and legitimacy by borrowing external ideas, support and resources. Local mortgage markets could tap into global financial markets provided there are adequate safeguards to protect borrowers in a poor country from the uncontrollable fluctuations in liquidity, interest rates, exchange rates, and other financial parameters. Producers of building products and pre-fabricated components have much larger opportunities for marketing their products, helped by international credits and guarantees. Industrialized countries have put in place elaborate export financing mechanisms to support the manufacturers and producers of processed materials.

Other aspects that are relevant to housing standards and living conditions at the local level include the:

- incorporation of international experiences and best practices in attempts by enterprising architects to design housing projects on the principles of green architecture. Elements of waste recycling, maximum use of renewable energy, on-plot food production, use of natural and local materials, and digitization of some control functions in the house can be combined to build a universal home, as it were. Such 'eco-houses' are largely experimental in nature, and examples range from single homes to whole communities.
- increasing uniformity of professional standards and quality control measures. Materials testing laboratories, national standards institutions, manufacturers, designers and contractors are all striving towards uniformity and conformance. This trend is probably most advanced in Europe, where the European Union has established, or supports, a variety of institutions to promote trade and the exchange of expertise between member countries.
- privatization and international ownership of infrastructure. As water, power, telephone and transport companies in the developing countries become privatized and the share of foreign ownership increases, the standards of provision are likely to change to suit the profit objectives and management style of the new owners. Providing cheap or free water from standpipes in unplanned settlements may no longer be viable.

- growth in world trade. Although trade in building materials is only a minor proportion of total world trade, it has nonetheless benefited from general growth. Cement, sanitary ware, electrical goods, paints and construction steel are being shipped from China, India, Brazil, Iran, South Africa and other newly industrialized countries. Wide variations in quality and prices are evident because of different production costs and export subsidies in the countries of origin.
- pollution resulting from foreign direct investment. Poor people are the most likely to suffer from polluting industries and the dumping of hazardous wastes. 'In a globalizing economy, the increasing occurrence of trans-boundary pollution and the transfer across national borders and regions of technologies hazardous to the environment can represent a serious threat to the environmental conditions of human settlements and the health of their inhabitants. Governments should therefore co-operate to develop further international legal mechanisms to implement Principle 13 of the Rio Declaration regarding liability and compensation for adverse effects of environmental damage caused by activities within their jurisdiction or control to areas beyond their jurisdiction' (UNCHS 1997:84).

Collaborative efforts

The growth of privatization and the diminishing role of government affects all walks of life. Commerce and civil society are assuming greater roles in ordering and facilitating urban development. In China enforcement is partially undertaken by private companies (designers, contractors, consultants, and so on) who are required to undergo training courses to familiarize themselves with new standards. A lot of emphasis is placed on training and accreditation. At the same time members of the public have the right to expose actions that contravene approved standards. A similar trend is evident in Africa. In Senegal 'the Government is pushing hard for the private sector to get more involved in the activities of ISN [the Senegalese Institute for Normalization]' (Diagne 1998:13).

The concept of development facilitation has been given legislative backing in South Africa through the Development Facilitation Act (Act 67 of 1995) which attempts to move away from the traditional development control legislation by providing a more positive and supportive environment for those who wish to build. Facilitation can be provided through institutional and infrastructural investment, land distribution, and the propagation of skills and new technologies. All these activities would benefit from private sector participation. Regulation and co-ordination would nonetheless be necessary to protect the weak, curb waste and corruption, and ensure compliance with national policy priorities. The South African Development Facilitation Act 1995 is a fast-track approach to development that:

- bypasses existing apartheid legislation
- initiates development planning through land development objectives set by municipalities or provincial governments
- resolves conflicts rapidly at provincial level
- provides for a fundamental review of the planning system to be undertaken by a Development Planning Commission.

The legislation is backed by a range of policy instruments in an Urban Development Framework (RSA 1997) which includes:

- undoing the apartheid city

- planning for higher densities
- reform of the urban land and planning system
- improving urban transportation
- environmental management
- a Municipal Infrastructure Investment Framework
- a National Housing Programme featuring a housing subsidy scheme, mortgage indemnity fund, and a national housing finance corporation
- promoting urban and local economic development
- partnership arrangements and clarified roles for government and local authorities.

South Africa regards a definitive policy framework as essential, and while not all countries may have the resources and the expertise to produce an urban development policy, it is nonetheless important that as much thought as possible is given to future needs and priorities. Apart from its role in resource mobilization, the South African private sector also operates a dynamic standards review regime through the Agrément system administered jointly with the Council for Scientific and Industrial Research (see Box 4, page 53).

Summary

Enabling standards are the key to unlocking the recognition, goodwill and resources needed for the purpose. The foundation for a new development paradigm appears to be the ability to mobilize the resources, ingenuity, knowledge and solidarity available in informal settlements. These efforts can be helped by two sets of approaches. First, it is important to create partnerships with a variety of community groups and other interested parties such as professional societies, builders, materials manufacturers and civil society. Such alliances can be formal or informal, but their main roles should be overcoming resistance to change in the packaging and dissemination of new standards, raising the profile of housing and appropriate building codes as a major social and economic issue, and ensuring effective monitoring and enforcement. All this calls for imaginative use of the media and other information tools.

Second, experience has shown that, by working together, the various parties raise their collective capacity to solve problems and meet new challenges. A variety of training methods have been developed to enable the individual household to contribute effectively to the overall process of improving housing conditions and the urban environment.

6
GETTING FUTURE STANDARDS RIGHT

The quest for order

Though houses provide shelter from the elements and space to live in, they can be dangerous places if not properly built. The danger is increased when large numbers of inhabitants crowd into cities, towns, villages and other forms of compact living space and engage in a wide variety of economic and production activities, consume resources and produce all sorts of waste. Sheer numbers dictate that rules must be established and observed to regulate the use of space (especially land), water, natural light and other endowments; to control the deployment of weak and combustible materials; and to prevent the spread of disease. Disposing of human waste in a village of five hundred people is already quite difficult; there are a hundred cities in the world with more than five *million* inhabitants.

Three billion people live in urban areas, and while urbanization is continuing apace. The very concept of the home and what it embodies is changing. The failure of governments to cater for their citizens' basic needs means that at least 600 million people in urban areas worldwide live in life- and health-threatening conditions. Poor people throughout the world have to cope with substandard housing and homelessness. Improving the situation calls not only for increased spending on basic services such as water supply, sanitation and roads, but also for suitable policies to tackle the causes of such widespread deprivation. When it comes to housing, recent comparative studies show wide variations in quality between countries with equivalent per capita incomes, indicating that non-economic factors have a strong influence on how people live, and that yardsticks of housing adequacy and acceptability are to some extent culture specific.

The fact that a sizeable proportion of urban residents (observers quote figures as high as 60 per cent) live in unplanned and spontaneous settlements, where people build without any form of official authorization, has prompted the argument that regulation is superfluous, and at best an impediment to investment and development. There are nonetheless strong arguments to the contrary. The case for standards is based on the need for organization and quality management criteria; economy in the use of materials; the capacity to innovate and deploy better construction methods; and the overriding goal of ensuring safety. Defining all these requirements in terms of rights and obligations invariably calls for a legalistic and highly technical approach that is not always easy to understand. Codes and regulations seem remote from the people, especially poor people who are in greatest need of assistance and guidance. For example, finding land on which to build is made extremely difficult by the intricate planning, subdivision, surveying, registration and transfer rules that are normally found in several statutes and rarely in one comprehensive document. A number of government offices – ostentatiously called 'institutions' by experts – are involved. Nevertheless, someone has to guarantee security of tenure for orderly development to take place. The same limiting factors apply to building materials, as the freedom to cut costs, speed up the building process, or enhance appearance must be constrained by the need to ensure safety, durability and the good health of the occupants. People's curiosity uncovers new building materials, finishes and components almost daily, with the result that cherished rules soon become obsolete and need to be modified and new rules have to be made.

Indeed, the focus of this book has been the methodology for revising housing standards and related legislation. Although there is no evidence that a standard method will have success, a picture has emerged on a set of principles that need to be observed to ensure a successful outcome. These principles will be discussed later in this chapter. It has also emerged that administrative systems affect the management of existing regulations as well as the change process, as manifested in bureaucratic procedures and attendant costs. What is a rule or regulation in one country could well be a statute or act of parliament in another. Standardized definitions do not exist.

The heterogeneous approach is partially explained by history. Early civilizations developed distinct rules for builders, the earliest recorded evidence being the rules and plans for the construction of Beijing several centuries before Christ. Other regulatory regimes emerged later in various parts of the world, each with its own cultural peculiarities. While the Chinese were obsessed with maintaining harmony with nature and higher powers, and the Romans placed great emphasis on structural robustness and safety, the colonials went to great lengths to design housing standards that they felt were appropriate to the respective needs and status of the rulers and the indigenous people. Housing standards for natives were in the form of building rules for temporary buildings, common in the former British colonies. For the former the standards were a carbon copy of British, French, German or Portuguese enactments. With increasing levels of international co-operation in the second half of the twentieth century we see cross-cultural traffic in innovations accompanied by the increasing influence of aid-giving countries and agencies have played a larger role. Aid for urban development and housing is normally accompanied by conditions relating to the types of standards to be used, thus establishing a link between technical specifications and sound financial practices. Within countries, however, financial institutions are generally conservative, being concerned mainly with safeguarding their wealth and, to a lesser extent, with security of tenure and structural durability.

Change instigators

An attempt has been made to analyse those factors, agents and forces that motivate housing standards revision. International policies and trends have been found to have a strong influence on national decisions. Not only was the colonial world driven by decisions made in metropolitan capitals, but even in the second half of the twentieth century we find strong influences emanating first from the major world and regional groupings, like the United Nations system, the European Union, and the former Soviet Union, and second from the major intellectual centres, universities, and research institutions in the North. The Habitat I conference in Vancouver was a landmark event as it focused world attention on human settlements and housing problems and resulted in the formation of UNCHS, which was

Photo 9   This housing in Villa el Salvador, Lima, reveals the continuous process of improvement – a process that must be taken into account when making regulations.

concerned with promoting appropriate housing standards in all member states. Countries did pay attention, if only by including the topic in national housing policies and debates. The World Bank was at about the same time developing an extensive urban development programme whose main objective was to promote home ownership and access to basic services among the poor by means of sites and services and squatter upgrading projects. The adjustment of housing infrastructure standards to suit these objectives was an integral part of the programme. Countries like Kenya, Tanzania, Senegal, India and Indonesia were frontrunners. The Kenyan revision exercise, first mooted in the mid-1970s, was of this genre. Two decades after Habitat I, the City Summit repeated calls for governments to design and enact building codes and planning regulations that are affordable, durable and sustainable. National plans of action had been prepared by most countries, and the issue of housing and infrastructure standards received serious attention in many of these documents. In all these proceedings, UNCHS has been enjoying the support of other agencies in the United Nations system including WHO, UNESCO, UNICEF, and the World Bank, each of which has its own agenda.

The above and other international efforts were buttressed and given intellectual legitimacy by scholars who undertook field research in the 1960s and 1970s, first in South America and then in Asia and Africa. Their main contributions were to argue the case for the recognition of spontaneous settlements as viable communities with great potential for improvement and economic development and to demonstrate that humble unauthorized structures can be improved step by step and transformed into decent houses and real estate investments. Indeed, incremental processes are a crucial factor in cost-effective housing delivery; increased access to shelter can only be facilitated when recognition of the people-driven processes guides formal policy, investment and practice. The principle of starting from a base of minimal standards needs wider acceptance and facilitation. Long-term support is essential, and interventions should be far-sighted and not confined to project cycles.

Within nations one of the most important catalysts for change is the fear of disease spreading in urban areas. There is widespread awareness of the link – either real or perceived – between health and overcrowding, lack of ventilation and hazardous materials. Because of its scientific credentials the health lobby tends to wield a great deal of influence on policymaking. Devastating consequences are also to be expected from fire or building collapse, and the prevention of these two eventualities is also seen as a major concern. In fact, a cyclical pattern can be observed, with regulations being bent with the approval of the authorities until people lose their lives in a major fire or collapsed building, when the rules are tightened again. Regulatory authorities have to walk a tightrope between reality and ideal situations, especially in circumstances where for economic and humanitarian reasons poor people must be housed so that they can participate in the urban economy. It is thus also in the private sector's interest to have a working regulatory regime that commands the confidence of the majority. Developers, designers and building materials' manufacturers push for faster plan approval procedures and less expensive standards; they sit on review boards and standards institutes committees. Financial institutions and insurance companies can exert pressure against the use of unstable and non-durable materials.

Political influence on housing standards works in several directions. While leaders aspire to improved living conditions and decent housing for the people, they have to fight for budgetary allocations and realistic standards that can produce as many houses as possible. For example, Kenya's president appointed a task force in the mid-1980s to develop and refine proposals already made on standards for low-income housing, but when the report was presented it took several years before the proposals were enacted. The reason was partly inter-ministerial rivalries and partly a reluctance to institute a more relaxed regulatory framework in a situation where there was already extensive unauthorized construction. Thus the tension between easing and tightening controls weighs heavily on politicians and policymakers. Likewise, successful efforts to reduce plot sizes in Zimbabwe subsequently came to nothing for political reasons. Nations like to maintain an image of progress, modernity and compassion, values used as a measure of government's achievements that find expression in the built environment.

Changes are also often initiated by the users themselves, who locate, build, service or extend their houses in ways that force the authorities to recognize the new realities and change the rules accordingly. Those users living in disaster-prone areas need to help to be prepared and to fortify structures against collapse. Furthermore, in the rich countries there is pressure to incorporate advances in technology and to harmonize standards across boundaries in the interest of free trade.

Revision method and content

Evidence from both the literature and the case studies indicates that revising housing standards is a lengthy process. The players include government departments, local authorities, the professions, builders, private sector interests and users. Technical tests ought to be accompanied by wide-ranging consultations and precise documentation. Allocation of legal responsibility for building failure is an important consideration; for example, in some countries insurance cover must be arranged by the building owner and the contractor.

Because of the cost, time considerations and political implications, comprehensive revisions involving all aspects of housing standards are rare. Usually the focus is on specific areas of improvement and on existing frameworks. For standards relevant to low-income housing the revisions could concentrate on all or some of the following aspects:

- minimum room sizes, allowing multiple function rooms and reduced circulation space
- minimum of two rooms to allow for subletting and extension
- reduction or complete omission of finishes and non-essential fittings, with allowance for future provision
- allowance for local, traditional and less expensive materials
- more economical layouts, smaller plots and cheaper options of services, including water supply, drainage and sanitation
- faster building permit approval procedures.

Facilitating the use of local materials such as mud bricks, thatch, timber and lime can help reduce costs and should be among the more important objectives of the revision process. While a variety of standards can be developed based on physical/geographic, sectoral, historical or elective criteria, a useful underlying principle, which is gaining credence and popularity, is the performance standards approach. This approach allows for a wide range of materials and technical solutions to be used as long as they meet functional requirements. Recent innovations include extra-legal frameworks, land sharing, community land trusts, relaxation in land and infrastructure requirements, earth-based products for wall and roof construction, lime and other natural binders, and the approval of new materials and building components through the agrément system. Enforcement innovations include self-regulation, local control and informal enforcement.

Nearly all innovations should be consistent with the principle of incrementality, while gender concerns should assume increasing importance, not so much in standards formulation but in related activities such as training, capacity building, house/plot allocation procedures, and neighbourhood planning. Land allocation and tenure regularization efforts should be directed towards achieving equity in distributing wealth-enhancing assets between men and women.

What has been the impact, if any, of these innovations? Although there have been hardly any definitive studies and evaluations, it is generally agreed among housing professionals and researchers that the effects include increases to the housing stock, reductions in construction and procedural costs, creation of income-earning opportunities, and improved access to credit for those who would otherwise be excluded.

To summarize, there is a set of principles that ought to guide code revision efforts. These principles are:

- *Relevance* Revisions should be relevant to national environmental and economic circumstances and deeply rooted in local cultures and living habits.
- *Cost reduction* Changes must result in cost reductions so that adequate and affordable shelter is made available for the majority of the population.
- *Focus* Changes should focus on enlarging the housing stock and improving the housing conditions of poor people, including those living in unplanned settlements.
- *Participation* The revision process should be participatory and based on contributions from all sectors in the housing delivery process.

- *Flexibility* Requirements should allow for flexible interpretation, enabling a variety of materials and technical solutions to be used and innovations to be incorporated.
- *Access* Revised legislation should be well drafted, easily accessible, and widely disseminated.
- *Incrementality* Incremental improvement of the title, dwelling and its surroundings should be promoted.
- *Procedures* Plan approval procedures should be fast, free from corruption, and inexpensive for the builder.

Learning from experience

Extensive field investigations of housing standards administration and revisions in Kenya and Zimbabwe have provided insights into the issues at stake when attempts are made to transform a largely colonial regulatory framework into an enabling and supportive set of codes and procedures. Plot sizes happened to be a significant issue in both countries, probably a reflection of the high value placed on that commodity. In both countries the vestiges of the colonial administrative style manifested themselves in the exclusive nature of the code revision process. There was little participation. As a result the people were very slow to adopt the revised rules and new technologies. Other important findings are as follows:

- While major revisions are undertaken at the national level, implementation is largely a local affair – a relationship between the regulating authority and the builder.
- Massive investment by way of funds, international expertise, and time will not ensure success unless accompanied by political commitment and continual goading by concerned activists and reformers.
- A clear and comprehensive communications strategy is essential for marketing changes to codes and regulations. New provisions need to be packaged into friendly and comprehensible formats to build awareness.
- Partnerships have lately come to be regarded as a desirable goal in their own right because of their enormous potential for empowerment and enhancement of social capital.
- Participatory and dissemination techniques are still far from being perfect, but great progress is being made and new methods are emerging.
- Donor support, though useful, has its limits; efforts must be made to develop national capacity to finance, staff and sustain housing standards monitoring and review on a continuing basis.
- The standards revision process should not confine its attention to the house and its contents but should also take into account those spaces and activities taking place immediately outside the house and at the neighbourhood level. It is important to take a holistic approach.
- Self-regulation and informal enforcement can make a difference, but more thought needs to be put into developing relevant techniques.
- A solid foundation of scientific research is essential for building sound standards revision systems.
- Innovative building techniques and materials allowed by revised standards can significantly improve accessibility by the poor and low-income households to decent and legal housing.

While proposing more relaxed standards and devolved regulation, we ought to remember that as people get richer they demand more regulation in environmental protection, public health and safety, all desirable aims that will continue to be a major concern of governments and local authorities for a long time to come.

It can be done

Will the living conditions of the urban poor in developing countries improve in the future? What will the regulatory frameworks of the future look like? Will there be more or less regulation? Who will regulate whom? What will be the main areas of focus for building codes and planning regulations? Current indicators based on this analysis indicate that an overriding concern is to secure the legality and recognition, first of those structures and devices that poor people can afford, and second of innovative designs and schemes that defy traditional notions of what a dwelling should be like or how services should be provided. As urban lifestyles become more complex, both for the rich and poor, so the design and management of standards will have to be more flexible.

The home as workplace is as valid a demand in an unplanned settlement as it is in a well-to-do neighbourhood. City planners should design control mechanisms that will support urban agriculture and other economic activities that help sustain the livelihoods of the poor. Water collection and distribution, sanitation and energy are other areas in which enabling standards of provision can be developed to suit particular communities.

In the first place, therefore, the need for innovation is paramount. It extends over all the key areas of urban development and organization. By far the most important deficit area in terms of resources and ideas is land. When city officials in Delhi allowed minimum plot sizes of 9m^2 it must have been after a great deal of soul-searching, technical research, social pressures and political manoeuvring. In many other developing countries there are similar and equally bold moves to make land more accessible. In the unplanned settlements there is unlimited scope for developing suitable standards for title regularization, land development, and infrastructure provision, a task that will doubtless take several decades. Advances in water treatment supply technology, waste disposal, transportation, and communications will lighten the burden of meeting desirable minimum standards of servicing. Information science promises to facilitate code management, enforcement, cost recovery and revenue collection. Indeed, the monitoring of standards and code compliance is set to benefit immensely from improved communications and information technology to the extent that decentralized regulatory structures (e.g. at the community, neighbourhood or village level) could become a reality without compromising technical quality criteria such as accuracy, integrity, timeliness, coverage and compatibility with other area monitoring systems. A wide array of electronic devices are already available for doing that, and more are being developed, all of which will help to make an inexpensive building control information system a viable proposition. Improved monitoring and procedural methods can help make the building control system more transparent and less prone to corruption. Unfortunately the management of housing standards has been tarnished by corruption in many countries and removing that blemish must be a matter of high priority. Necessary measures include education, surveillance, adequate penalties and tightening the rules and codes of ethics governing construction industry professionals.

Second, local authorities and governments ought to realize that housing standards and the accompanying legislation need to be subject to constant review in order to keep abreast of changes in living habits, technology and economic imperatives. The challenge, therefore, is to design and establish competent and well-resourced institutions for carrying out those revisions, taking into account the fundamental need for participation, information, training and other aspects of involvement and empowerment. There will be an ever-increasing need for changes to be generated from below and for sensitivity towards the wants of the majority.

Third, the challenge is to widen the scope of the struggle to get housing standards right. The dwelling's surroundings also deserve attention, and in future more attention will need to be focused on site planning standards, social infrastructure, and urban environmental standards. Yardsticks and relevant criteria will have to be developed to ensure that adequately housed people are also working people. Efforts to make housing standards relevant and affordable will come to nothing unless they are buttressed by economic development programmes that generate jobs and raise income levels. Materials requirements should be adopted to promote the production and use of local materials, including natural materials. A bigger and more varied package will enable swaps to be done between different elements; for instance lower building standards could be compensated for by superior servicing levels or more outdoor space could offset smaller rooms. This idea could be developed further into collective and area-wide criteria such as ambient standards, which seek to apply the performance specification concept to whole dwellings and clusters. After all, the basic requirement of a dwelling is that it should be livable, durable, legally owned and affordable.

Fourth, building legislation applicable to low-income housing should not only be comprehensive but also clear, accessible and enforceable. Whether to have a single all-encompassing document or a series of enactments will to a large extent depend on country circumstances. But a prerequisite is the ability of legislation to incorporate rules and regulations specific to local requirements, to recognize the role of 'customary' law, and to integrate informal enforcement mechanisms. These requirements, coupled with the need for periodic reviews, pose a great, though not unsurmountable, challenge to legal draftsmen, who are being increasingly called upon to temper harsh legalese with more friendly language. Efforts to make justice more accessible must include attempts to make legal provisions governing the right to build easily comprehensible even to the illiterate.

Finally, collaborative efforts between nations need to be stepped up to facilitate knowledge and technology transfer; to enlarge resource flows in the form of trade, aid, investment and financial transactions; to exchange expertise in the prevention, and control of, fire, floods, earthquakes and other hazards; to push for a more caring international regime; and to enhance research efforts and capabilities. At the regional level it is desirable to develop databases of suitable standards and institutional frameworks as well as models and best practices which nations and individual communities could adapt to their own needs. It is only through such exploration, learning and adaptation that we can hope to tackle the housing needs of the billion people who live in destitution in shantytowns and unauthorized structures. Housing standards, double or otherwise, are a powerful tool in the global struggle against urban poverty.

Appendix 1
The four dominant models of building control

This Appendix expands upon the definitions and concepts discussed in Chapter 1. It is divided into three sections: definitions; four models; and regulations in Francophone Africa.

Definitions

General Definitions

Act (or Ordinance)

A statutory governmental enactment, authoritative decree, law or regulation to control physical development of the built environment, which can only be amended through legislature.

By-law

Statutory and similar to Act but enacted by a subsidiary legislative authority, such as a municipal council. The term 'building by-laws' means local, not national, building regulations.

Building regulations (or rules)

A set of detailed controls for the construction of buildings. They expand upon Acts, but on their own are statutory. These detailed rules may therefore address such elements as site conditions and use, water quality, means of access, natural lighting, ventilation, fire resistance, lighting and earthquake protection of buildings. Both regulations and rules are administrative edicts drafted for the purpose of implementing a particular policy or strategy. For instance, domestic sanitation in Kenya is regulated through the Drainage and Sanitation Rules proclaimed by the Minister of Health under public health legislation.

Building codes

A set of practical, technical and administrative rules and requirements for the construction of buildings. Building codes are not statutory, unless made so in the regulations. In most instances, regulatory and mandatory issues are contained in the regulations, whereas the codes support the regulations with technical requirements and details.

Codes of practice

A set of technical guides, which are not statutory, for good design and construction. They are either published separately or as part of building codes. Codes of practice for design will typically deal with loads (dead, live, wind), materials (masonry, timber, concrete, steel), elements (foundations, walls, floors), and special structures.

Decrees

In the absence of a parliamentary system of government, laws are made through decrees. In some African countries building and planning decrees made in colonial times are still in force as they have not been updated.

Legislation

Building legislation encompasses all legal instruments for controlling building operations. It normally takes the form of one more acts of parliament or legislature, for example a Building Act or Housing and Urban Development Act.

Standards

Covering the physical characteristics, materials, components and buildings and how they will be deemed satisfactory for use in the given context. They regulate design by specifying such items as room size, distance from adjacent buildings, types of material and construction techniques. There are also standards for specific materials such as cement, steel, aggregate, timber, paint and so on that specify types, qualities and means of quality testing. Standards, to which codes and regulations often refer, are normally published separately.

Specifications

Sometimes called construction or technical specifications, they refer, like standards, to certain stipulated requirements under which the construction of elements (foundation, walls) will be deemed satisfactory. They are statutory and are published separately from codes and regulations.

Definitions adopted by the European Union (EU)

Regulation

Building regulations are documents containing requirements for buildings laid down by an official body (parliament, the government or the responsible authority) to ensure the safety, hygiene, stability and level of amenity compatible with environmental and social requirements during the construction and throughout the lifetime of the building.

Standards

Building standards are documents chiefly stating the essential properties of building, building components and building products, including their dimensions, characteristics, and performance. Frequently, standards also contain information about how these properties can be verified. In general, building standards are related to building regulations by virtue of the fact that the properties stated satisfy requirements in the regulations, and it is for this reason that reference is often made to standards in regulations.

Four models

Traditionally, building codes have restricted themselves to the safety of structures. The earliest recorded code, that enacted by King Hammurabi of Babylon, simply stated that every house should not collapse. Building codes range from those that cover an entire nation to those designed for a specific region. Four models of building regulations have evolved through history, all within the cultural and legal framework of their places of origin. These four models are commonly classified as Anglo-Saxon, German-Nordic, Napoleonic and planned economy. Although the regulations vary from country to country, they are similar in their basic structure. Four components are common to all the models: Legislative (acts, ordinances, by-laws); technical (regulations, rules, codes); enforcement (administrative procedures); and support (complementary reinforcement facilities).

The *Anglo-Saxon model* is followed in the United Kingdom, except London, and in many English-speaking countries. The legislative body issues a building law and local governments are responsible for its interpretation into building codes. This model assumes the availability of competent and incorruptible public officials in local building departments and does not guarantee territorial uniformity among codes. The Anglo-Saxon model does not clearly define who bears responsibility for mistakes committed by a builder.

The *German-Nordic* model is followed in the Federal Republic of Germany, Scandinavia, the Netherlands, Austria, Switzerland and London. The legislative body issues a building law and the central government is responsible for its interpretation into building codes. Public departments covering the entire country control compliance with the codes and assist builders with their interpretation. This system, like the Anglo-Saxon model, presupposes an adequate supply of competent public servants in the many building departments required for code implementation throughout the country. This approach does not clearly attribute responsibility when builders make mistakes.

France, Belgium and many other French-speaking countries adhere to the *Napoleonic model*, which does not involve any formal building codes. Master plans and other policy instruments governing development are statutory and contain standards regarding health, safety and other matters of public concern. Compliance with these instruments is checked by public departments, a process that often involves complicated legal procedures. The other aspects of building quality such as stability, durability and other technical issues are the responsibility of the builder. Known as the 'decadal guarantee', this responsibility requires the builder to guarantee that the building will function well, in terms of its structural and other essential components, over a ten-year period. Responsibility is limited to two years for less critical aspects of the building such as surface finishes. This approach has produced an insurance system whereby builders insure themselves against any errors, and the technical insurance companies enforce quality control over construction. The criteria are publicized by independent research organizations. Compliance then does not rely on any publicly enacted codes or regulations. The disadvantages of this system include lack of clarity on matters related to health and layout and its slowness, which has often been attributed to the public administrators in charge of granting building permits rather than to the system itself, which is relatively free of bureaucracy.

In the *planned-economy model*, the state is given the task of planning, building and transforming the built environment. There are no codes, but there is standardization in the form of technologies accepted by builders, planners, engineers and architects. This centralized approach implies that the system is comprehensive in that issues concerning stability, durability, thermal properties and health will have been considered during the development of the standardized technologies.

The main disadvantage of existing building control mechanisms, irrespective of the base model, is that low-income settlements are completely ignored. In many African cities, over 60 per cent of the urban population lives in squatter settlements. Rural settlements are usually not subject to the formal rules. By excluding the bulk of the population, building regulations are failing in their objectives of promoting safety and health in construction.

Regulations in Francophone Africa

Legal basis and control mechanisms

African countries have generally adopted both the approach to building regulations and the specific standards of the four models based on historical ties. Francophone countries have tended to use the Napoleonic model. The by-laws and codes of the Belgian Congo (1959) are used in Rwanda. In Senegal the *Code de L'Urbanisme*, based on the Napoleonic model, is the legal mechanism regulating construction. In the various Francophone countries, the legal basis, organizational structure and control system are similar to those described earlier in the Napoleonic model, and share its strengths and weaknesses. Some countries, such as Cameroon, which uses both the Napoleonic and Anglo-Saxon models, have adopted more than one approach, largely a result, again, of past historical influences.

Institutions

As in Anglophone Africa, there is a network of largely public institutions responsible for building control. The ministries of housing and public works, together with the municipal authorities, oversee the legislative, technical and enforcement components of the regulations. These public bodies are usually understaffed so that implementation and quality control are not very effective, despite the fact that the laws may be sufficient. Some countries, such as Rwanda and Cameroon, have all building regulations covered by a single act which, theoretically, should make regulation much simpler than in countries where there are overlapping acts.

National standards institutions are abundant, but there are very few local standards on building materials in practice, and European standards are generally adopted. Research institutions dealing with the construction industry, in particular local building materials, are also commonly found in the Francophone countries, but they do not directly address building legislation and their findings are rarely incorporated in regulatory instruments. While professional bodies exist, there are no formal procedures or qualifications for entering the field of practical construction.

Review Process

Owing to the involved legal procedures of the Napoleonic model, any review or amendment of even one technical issue can be a protracted and frustrating legal battle. Although research activities into building materials and their production are widespread and innovative, no comprehensive revision and subsequent implementation of building regulations seem to have taken place in the Francophone countries.

Appendix 2
The housing standards administration system in China

The housing standards administration system, relevant organizations and their responsibilities

The standards administration system is composed mainly of three organizations: the Department of Standards and Quotas of the Ministry of Construction (DSQMC); the Local Standardization Department (LSD); and the China Construction Standardization Institution (CECS). The relevant industrial departments of the state council are in charge of administration of the relevant industrial standards and codes. The LSD looks after the administration of the local construction standards. CECS, a non-governmental organization, is entrusted by the government with the administration of recommended standards. Some new organizations related to housing development issues have also been established when China made some reforms recently. The Housing Industrialization Office of the Ministry of Construction (HIOMC), for example, is a new organization – established in 1998 – focusing on housing industry development.

The Department of Standards and Quotas of the Ministry of Construction

Housing standards form part of construction standards. While the DSQMC is in charge of the comprehensive administration of construction standards, it also has special responsibilities for administering not only housing standards issues, such as developing national housing standards, but also industrial standards and guiding local standards.

The administration work on construction standards by the department mainly involves the implementation of laws, regulations, standards and policies relating to construction. The work includes:

- organizing the development of administrative laws and regulations and construction standardization
- developing administration systems and working plans
- organizing development and implementation of national standards on construction
- undertaking supervision and review work.

The Local Standardization Departments

The construction administration departments of a province, or the municipality directly under the central government in an autonomous region, can approve local construction standards; organizations with lower rank in construction administration do not have the authority to approve local standards. LSDs' responsibilities include implementing the strategies of construction standardization and formulating local standards that will apply in their locality.

A working group is established in order to develop a standard. After finishing the development work, an administration group will be set up to explain the standard and prepare for future revision work.

China Construction Standardization Institution

DSQMC and LSD are government bodies. With the economic reform process, China is gradually trying to move some responsibilities from government bodies to non-governmental bodies. In order to achieve this aim, some non-governmental organizations have been established, such as the CECS, which was created in 1979. It is composed of 36 technical committees and nine local construction standardizations institutions. More than 3000 professionals have joined the CECS. The basic responsibilities of this organization are:

- formulating recommended standards under the trust of the government
- organizing academic activities concerning construction standards
- publicizing the knowledge of construction standards
- editing the journal *Engineering Construction Standardization*
- providing suggestions relating to construction standards for government
- engaging in international academic activities for standardization
- providing technical consultation on construction standards.

The Housing Industrialization Office of the Ministry of Construction

The HIOMC, established in 1998, aims to:

- implement the principles and policies on housing construction and housing industrialization that are formulated by the state and the Ministry of Construction
- carry out the state's key scientific and technological industrial projects
- promote the process of housing industrialization
- establish and perfect the technology management system of housing industrialization
- increase the overall technology level in the modernization of China's housing industry.

The functions of HIOMC

HIOMC's main responsibilities are:

- to offer centralized management, co-ordination and guidance concerning the Pilot Project of the Urban Residential Area, the state Scientific and Technological Industrial Project for Affordable Housing in Urban and Rural Areas in 2000 and the Modernization Project of the Housing Industry of the Ministry of Construction
- to provide technological guidance for the construction of affordable housing in China
- guided by science and technology, to establish the technical system of housing construction; to bring forward technology proposals on housing industrialization; to promote phased development, intensified production and commercialized supply by the housing industry; to provide technological support for the research and establishment of the Chinese management system of housing construction
- to implement the technology policies on housing construction and housing industrialization formulated by the Ministry of Construction and the departments concerned

- to assist in fulfilling the specialized tasks on housing construction and the housing industry
- to establish an evaluation system for housing types and functions and a licensing system for housing products and components; to promote the implementation of these systems
- to put forward the technology development and demonstration ratification, and then to implement these projects. In accordance with market demand, to organize technology development for housing, its products and components
- to enhance information exchange on housing technologies, as well as international co-operation in science and technology.

Organization of HIOMC

HIOMC consists of three departments and a committee, namely the departments of administration, pilot and demonstration projects, and evaluation and licensing and a committee of consultant specialists.

Like HIOMC and Local Housing Industrialization Offices, government bodies in different regions and cities have also been established and are responsible for the same sort of issues as HIOMC, but on a local level. HIOMC is an important organization that now operates under the supervision of the Ministry of Construction, but it will be independent in the near future.

Appendix 3
Analysis of changes introduced by Code '95 in Kenya

Minimum standards

As a result of a 1990 seminar designed to begin a process of reviewing and reforming standards, a task force was set up, chaired by the Ministry of Lands and Housing. Progress was slow, until a lack of resources prompted members to take a field trip on their own doorstep. They went to local housing settlements, both formal and informal. This first-hand, eye-opening encounter with reality finally persuaded the entire team that what was needed was not scaled-down standards with prescribed materials, but minimum standards from which everyone could start.

Task force members felt the standards must be related to the performance of the materials used and should not exclude the rough and ready materials with which most people were building. They had to allow people to start with a very basic structure and to add to it whenever they had the inclination and the money. This alternative approach to the review, the 'bottom-up' model, identifies the lowest common denominator for health and safety, setting a framework within which improvements may be made over time.

The following pages are reproduced from a report of the Enabling Housing Standards and Procedures Project, and they show the main differences between the 1968 and 1995 by-laws in terms of room size, roof, ceiling, walls, water supply, cooking area, sanitary provisions, washing facilities and refuse provision.

CHANGES TO BY-LAWS AS THEY RELATE TO LOW-COST HOUSING

1968 ROOM SIZE 1995

216   Every habitable room shall have a superficial area of not less than 75 sq.ft. with a minimum width of 6ft. 6 in. and shall contain a minimum area of 40 sq. ft. for each person accommodated therein. In every dwelling there shall be constructed not less than one habitable room having a superficial floor area of not less than 120 sq.ft.

216   (1) A dwelling room shall have a minimum superficial area of 7.0 sq.m. for a single room occupancy and a minimum internal dimension of 2.1m. Provided that the number of persons to be accommodated in such rooms shall be calculated on the basis of 3.5 sq.m. per person.

(2) In case of a multi-purpose room occupancy, a habitable room shall have a minimum area of 10.5 sq.m.

(3) All habitable rooms in a domestic building shall be adequately ventilated

(4) Every habitable room in a dwelling supplied by electricity shall be provided with not less than one properly fixed power socket outlet. This shall be done in strict compliance with the Electric Power Act (Cap. 314) and the Electric Supply Act (Cap 315).

ISSUES
- Adequate but affordable space
- Multiple occupancy by not only couples but whole family
- Access to power supply
- Adequate natural ventilation and size of window

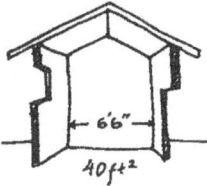

IMPACTS
The possibility of a whole family occupying a single room dwelling which is spacious, well ventilated and supplied with power. This recognizes the existing circumstances of the many families who cannot afford more than a room.

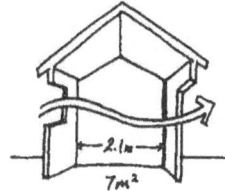

← 6'6" →

40ft²

← 2.1m →

7m²

ROOF

96.   The roof of a building shall be weatherproof.

97.   For roof coverings, the requirements of by-laws 96 of the By-laws shall be satisfied if constructed in accordance with the relevant rules specified in the fifth schedule to these By-laws. (Note: The fifth schedule is a detailed specification of allowable roof constructions)

225.   Roof covering materials shall be capable of resisting the penetration of weather elements. Roofs shall be properly constructed to support the load of the roof covering materials and to resist destruction by vermin, wind and corrosion.

ISSUES
- What materials are acceptable? e.g. Are thatch, shingles and metal sheeting acceptable in urban areas?
- What are the regional variations in climate and materials availability?
- How can new materials e.g. tiles be allowed?
- What are the comparative costs of different materials?
- Should asbestos be outlawed?

IMPACTS
◌ **Significant cost reductions**

◌ **More interesting and pleasant roof shapes due to use of varied coverings**

CHANGES TO BY-LAWS AS THEY RELATE TO LOW-COST HOUSING

1968   CEILING   1995

225 1. If a ceiling is provided the average height of a habitable room shall be not less than 7ft. 9 in. with a minimum height of 7ft. and the portion below 7ft.9in. must not exceed 25% of the floor area.

2. If a ceiling or similar insulation is not provided, the average height measured to the under side of the roof covering shall not be less than 8ft. 3in. with a minimum height of 7ft. 6in. and the portion below 8ft. 3in must not exceed 25% of the floor area.

3. Height in excess of 9ft. 3in shall not be included in calculating the average height.

225A. (1) If a ceiling is provided, the average height shall not be less than 2.35 m. with a minimum height of 2.15m. The area with a height less than 2.35 m. shall not exceed 25 per cent of the floor area.

(2) If no ceiling or similar under roof insulation is provided under a metal sheeted roof, the average height (measured to the underside of the roof covering) shall not be less than 2.50 m.with a minimum height of 2.30m. The area with a height less than 2.50m. shall not exceed 25 per cent of the floor area.

ISSUES

■ Is a ceiling absolutely necessary? Hence the "if"

■ Appropriate ceiling height for various climatic regions

■ Main function of ceiling. Is it insulation, protection from vermin/insects/snakes or good appearance ?

IMPACTS

■ Choice between ceiling or greater room height
■ Bias towards eliminating ceiling and using roof cover with high insulation values e.g. tiles (clay or cement)

WALLS

222A Party wall shall:-
(a) Have a minimum fire resistance of half an hour
(b) Be carried upto to the underside of the roof covering which shall be bedded onto the wall; and
(c) Extend to the external face of external walls

223 All internal walls shall be colour-washed with a hard-wearing material

222. Walls shall be capable of supporting the roof and resistant to vermin and dampness.

PARTY WALLS

222A. A party wall shall be constructed so that it is non-combustible and will restrict the spread of fire to adjoining property.

INTERNAL WALLS

223. All internal walls shall be smooth finished with an even surface.

ISSUES

■ Limited range of allowable materials
■ Cost
■ Foundation
■ Thickness: adequate to provide stability, weatherproofing, thermal and sound insulation
■ Fire resistance

IMPACTS

■ Substancial cost reduction (Mud,timber etc. can now be used)
■ Expanded aesthetic possibilities
■ Enlarged market for local/ traditional materials.

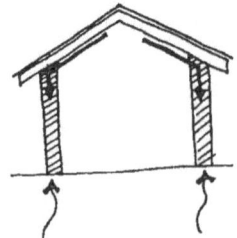

CHANGES TO BY–LAWS AS THEY RELATE TO LOW–COST HOUSING

1968 WATER SUPPLY 1995

226 The supply of water, shall be to the satisfaction of the council and if required, provision shall be made for water storage.

226 The supply of water, shall be to the satisfaction of the local authority and if required, provisions shall be made for water storage.

ISSUES
- How much water is adequate?
- What should be the source?
- What are the acceptable quality parameters?
- How much storage, if any, should be required?
- The basic assumption is that water will be provided by public water companies or municipal authorities at reasonable cost

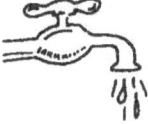

IMPACTS

COOKING AREA

218 1. Sufficient properly designed cooking areas shall be provided with suitable provision for the storage of food.

2. If the cooking area is in the form of a recess or verandah, it shall have a superficial area of not less than 24 sq.ft. with a minimum dimension of 3ft.6in.

3. If the cooking is proposed to be carried on inside a habitable room, the area of such room shall be increased to not less than 50 sq. ft. for each person accommodated therein.

4. If a kitchen is provided in a dwelling, it shall be of not less than 25 sq. ft. having a minimum dimension of not less than 4ft. 6in.

5. A flue shall be provided in every internal cooking space. Unless other satisfactory provision is made, the flue shall be constructed to have an internal unobstructed area of not less than 27 sq. in. and shall be constructed of suitable materials and terminated at a point of not less than 3ft. above the roof level adjacent thereto, or not less than 1ft. above level of the ridge of the roof.

218 Sufficiently properly designed cooking areas shall be provided with suitable provisions for the storage of food and with adequate ventilation.

ISSUES
- Adequate space
- Food storage
- Cooking inside rooms
- In house versus outside kitchens
- Natural ventilation and emission of gases and fumes

IMPACTS
- Cost reduction through voluntary elimination of flue
- Room for innovation in arrangement of facilities and ventilation

CHANGES TO BY-LAWS AS THEY RELATE TO LOW-COST HOUSING

1968   1995

SANITARY PROVISIONS

1968

217   1. A latrine and an ablution shall be provided either in separate compartments, in which case each compartment shall have minimum dimensions of 4ft. 6in. by 2ft 6in or in a combined compartment having a minimum are of 18sq.ft.

2. Where a combined compartment is provided separate provision for the washing of utensils shall be made to the satisfaction of the Council

3. The walls of any latrine or ablution, shall have a smooth and readily cleansed surface of a height of not less than 4ft. 6in. above the floor level and trowelled to a smooth finish, and the floor shall be likewise and laid to proper falls. The junction between the floor and the wall shall be formed with a cement cover of similar construction of radius not less than 1.5in.

4. For each family or group not exceeding six persons, there shall be provided one latrine and one ablution, or one combined water closet and ablution as required under paragraph (1) to this by-law

5. Unless the Council otherwise agrees, an ablution shall be fitted with a shower which shall be operated by an approved self-closing valve

6. A latrine or an ablution compartment shall have a floor constructed of cement concrete not less than 2in. in thickness.

7. If the pan is sunk into the floor it shall be encased in cement concrete not less than 3 in. in thickness.

ISSUES

- Flexibility in choice of materials and permutation of facilities
- Acceptable provision of washing for utensils
- Adequate waste water disposal
- Ease of maintaining cleanliness of walls and floor

1995

217   (1) All dwellings shall be provided with sufficient and properly constructed sanitary accommodation and washing facility.

(2) A latrine and washing facility shall be provided either in separate compartments in which case each compartment shall have a minimum dimensions of 1.35m. by 0.75m. or in combined compartment having a minimum area of 1.65 sq.m.

(3) Where a combined compartment is provided, a separate provision for the washing of utensils, shall be made to the satisfaction of the local authority.

(4) The floors of all latrines (or w.c.'s) shall be and showers constructed of a smooth water proof surface and laid to fall. The walls of each compartment shall be so constructed as to resist penetration of water up to a height of 0.5m. above finished floor level.

217A. Notwithstanding any provisions on sewage disposal provided in any other law:-

(a) short lengths of rigid-sewer pipes (concrete, clay, asbestos or cement) shall be joined with flexible water proof joints;

(b) flexible sewer pipes (U.PVC's) shall be joined and laid according to the manufacturers' instructions;

(c) all sewers and drains shall be carefully laid to ensure that the pipes are not broken or cracked. In particular flexible sewer pipes (U.PVC's) must be surrounded by carefully placed granular materials before the trenches are back filled;

(d) waste pipes from sinks, wash basins and similar appliances may discharge either, over or directly into a back inlet trapped gulley.

IMPACTS

- Cost reduction in wall construction (Wider choice of materials and finishes)
- Cheaper and more accessible drainage materials (Allowance for PVC drainage pipes, previously not considered)

CHANGES TO BY-LAWS AS THEY RELATE TO LOW-COST HOUSING

1968 — WASHING FACILITIES — 1995

219 1. Facilities shall be provided for washing clothes. The requirements for this by-law shall be satisfied if washing slabs or splash areas are constructed at the minimum rate of one per six persons of a minimum size of 3ft. by 2ft. or the slab and 3ft. by 3ft. for the splash area. The area for additional persons shall be increased by 1 sq.ft. for each additional person.

2. The floors shall be constructed of concrete 3in. thick, laid on a suitable foundation. They shall be trowelled to a hard wearing easily cleansed surface and Kerbed in such a manner to contain water.

3. The floor shall be laid to suitable falls and drained to an improved point of dispersal.

4. Unless the council otherwise agrees, each washing slab or splash provided shall be fitted with a 0.5in. stand pipe and bib cock connected direct to the water main. Additional stand pipes for communal use may be required by the Council.

219. All dwellings shall be provided with sufficient facilities for washing clothes and utensils and such facilities shall be adequately drained.

ISSUES
■ Detergents have replaced soap and thus changed washing habits
■ Plastic containers (buckets, basis, etc) make washing relatively mobile
■ Is a fixed washing slab and splash area necessary?
■ Alternative materials e.g. stone or brick should be allowed.

IMPACTS
Improved economy e.g kitchen sink can serve both functions i.e. washing utensils and clothes, so can a stone or plastic basin under a stand pipe.
(Flexibility in design, location and construction of washing facilities)

REFUSE

221 1. A concrete paved area constructed as provided for in by law 220 of these by-laws, shall be provided for every refuse bin.

2. The paved area, shall be surrounded on three sides by an approved kerb to contain the refuse spillage.

3. Not less than one refuse bin, shall be provided for each family unit or for every sixth persons accommodated.

221. Suitable provisions shall be made to accommodate sufficient refuse bins or other suitable receptacles on the plot.

ISSUES
■ Basic assumption is municipal collection and disposal
■ Protection of bin from dogs and children
■ Adequate provision for each family household

MUNICIPAL BINS

IMPACTS
Plastic bags are widely used, especially where collection is done by private contractors (Cheaper alternatives for disposal)

Source: Agevi and Yahya 1997

Appendix 4
Architects as facilitators

Deepening the impact of revised standards in a secondary town

Introduction

This is a summary of several reports and training materials prepared for ITDG Kenya and Nakuru Municipal Council for the purpose of disseminating the changes brought about by the revised building code (1995) in Kenya. The revisions had been specifically designed to make new materials and innovative technologies accessible to urban low-income households through the performance standards approach. Nakuru, a town of about 350 000 population situated 160km west of the capital Nairobi, was one of the first municipalities to adopt the new code, and the council went further to identify seven neighbourhoods in which the code should apply. These neighbourhoods consisted mainly of informal subdivisions, undertaken in the 1970s and 1980s, of former plantations and farms (sisal, wheat, maize) belonging to white settlers. To make Code '95 have a greater impact, it was necessary to use a combination of different approaches, including:

- identifying user needs and training requirements
- preparing training materials and holding a series of workshops and consultations for the major players such as designers, artisans, builders, and community leaders
- preparing prototype plans and supporting the construction of demonstration houses
- conducting design clinics.

The above activities were supplemented by periodic impact studies and evaluation reports. In such situations it is necessary to strike a balance between the information and technical requirements of the community on the one hand and the objectives set by external sponsors on the other. The key activities are briefly discussed below.

User needs analysis

The first step was to hold a series of meetings in February 1998 with the Municipal Engineer and his staff to understand the problems experienced by developers in having their plans approved. The following observations were made:

- Most planners and developers were not aware of the revised Code '95.
- Finance houses and insurance companies were not aware of Code '95.
- Most people still build illegally because: the plan approval process is too lengthy; building inspection fees are too high; they have accumulated payments to council (water, rates, etc); they are not aware of the regulations (most property owners are farmers in the outlying districts); they do not care.
- On average, plans take approximately six weeks to be approved from the date of submission.
- Plans for any building above four storeys have to be submitted by a registered architect.

- According to available statistics, an average of thirty building plans are submitted per month, a majority of these, say 60 per cent, are medium-cost proposals. Up to 95 per cent of the plans submitted are approved.
- Change of user applications are submitted to the Town Clerk, then the technical committee checks them and recommends/does not recommend them for approval.
- Extensions of leases are granted based on redevelopment proposals by the Commissioner of Lands. At the moment an application has to be made to the Commissioner, who in turn makes a recommendation to the Town Clerk.
- Subdivisions of plots are submitted to the Town Planning Committee after scrutiny by the Town Engineer's Department.
- All plans submitted to the council must bear the plot number and the name of the owner. Submission fees should be verified, and the user of the plot and the rates payments should be ascertained. The Water and Sewage Department, including the Public Health Department, should scrutinize the plans. The Town Engineer then recommends the plans for approval.
- The developer or his agent circulates the plans up to the stage of payment of submission fees.
- During the construction period inspections are carried out at foundation stage, DPC level, wall plate level, roof and completion stage.

The following designated settlement areas were visited:

- *Bondeni* A fully serviced settlement area whose titles are leasehold from the municipal council. The average plot size is 15m × 45m.
- *Lakeview* A private and freehold settlement, where the plot size ranges from 15m × 45m (675m^2) to 0.4 hectares (4000m^2). There is no water-borne sewer system, and pit latrines/septic tanks are the common means of sewage disposal. Lakeview has a very good security system operated by the community.
- *Mwariki* A settlement in excess of 40ha. owned by a land-buying company, on leasehold title from the Commissioner of Lands. Most plots measure 20m × 40m. There is power supply, water supply and some all-weather spine roads.
- *Lanet Hill/Karatina* These settlements, which lie to the east of the municipality, have average plot sizes measuring 20m × 40m. They originally belonged to land-buying companies and have leasehold titles from the commissioner of lands.

A meeting was also held with selected designers, which was an opportunity to ascertain the level of training and skills of the various designers, including:

- a building Inspector at the Town Engineers' office who has an Ordinary Diploma in Building and Civil Engineering conferred by the Mombasa Polytechnic
- a freelance designer with basic technical training only at technical school level
- a draughtsman in the Municipal Architect's office who has had on-the-job training in various organizations since 1971
- a Works Officer at the Town Engineers' office who has a Higher National Diploma in Building and Civil Engineering conferred by the Mombasa Polytechnic
- an Architectural Assistant in the Municipal Architect's office. He has had on-the-job training in various organizations since 1961
- an Architectural Assistant at the Ministry of Public Works and Housing with an Ordinary Diploma in Building and Civil Engineering conferred by the Kenya Polytechnic.

All the designers had basic communication skills in both English and Swahili. They were also competent in interpreting technical drawings.

These discussions helped the Design Team to decide in which direction the training and participatory design activities should go. Further discussions were held with plot owners, landlords, tenants and craftsmen selected at random in the various low-income settlements. The leader of the design team, who lectures in architecture, prepared notes of interviews with residents from Kwa Rhoda (8 residents), Kaptembwa (6 residents) and Mwariki (7 residents).

It emerged from these interviews that each plot owner has a unique set of problems. The plot is viewed in many different ways: as an investment; as a cushion against financial distress; as a business venture; as a source of status and reputation in the community; as an insatiable consumer of funds and effort; as a source of conflict with the authorities. Expectations vary considerably, but they generally include the ideal of a fully developed plot with permanent and impressive buildings with running water, proper sanitation, power and probably a telephone connection. Rooms for letting are mandatory, and some retail space if the owner is lucky.

Training materials were prepared, covering mainly house design, plan approval procedures, and a manual of appropriate building technologies with emphasis on locally available materials such as stone, earth, timber, corrugated iron sheets, shingles, clay tiles, and fibre-reinforced cement tiles. A workshop was then held at a local hotel where these solutions were presented and analysed by participants.

Design typologies

Based on the user needs analysis and the resultant design briefs, several design types were conceived, which can be seen in Figures 7, 8, 9 and 10. However, it should be noted that three main types of designs evolved, which are self-contained own houses, rental rooms and rental shops. There was one case where the user required semi-detached rental two-bedroomed houses. The rental rooms varied from single rooms, bed-sitters, and rooms with a cooking corner, to double rooms. The shops were normally attached to stores (rooms) that could be let out separately.

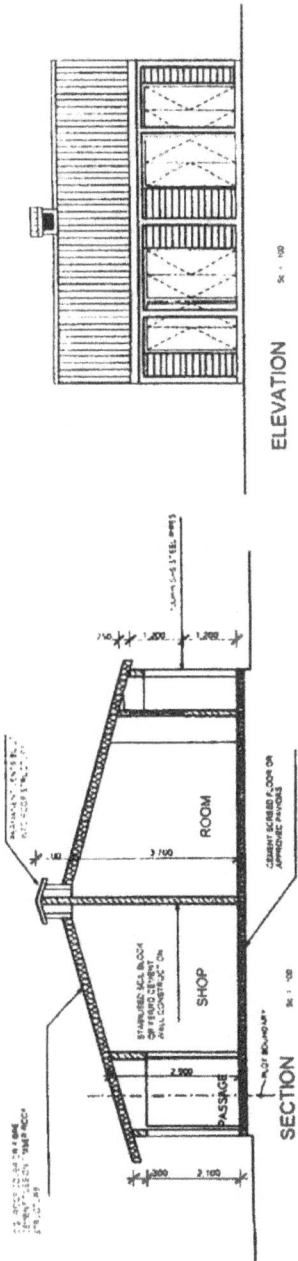

ELEVATION

SECTION

FLOOR PLAN

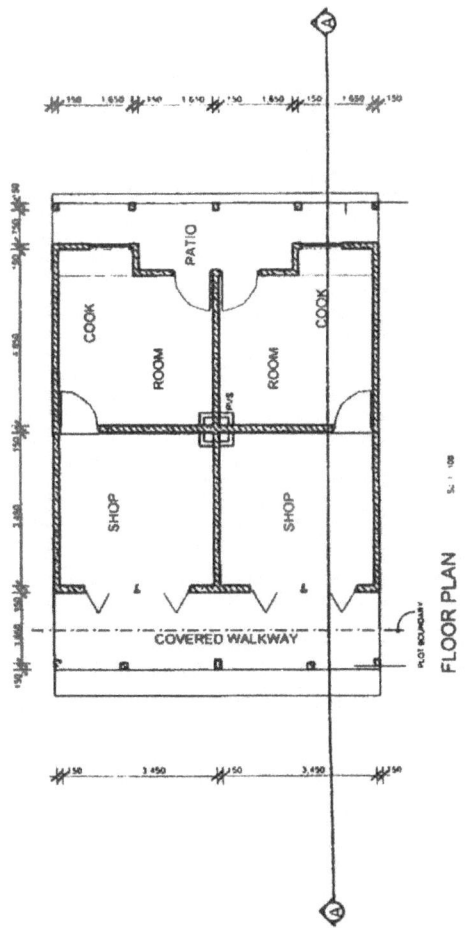

Figure 7 A block containing two shops with one room with cooking facilities attached

ELEVATION   Sc 1 100

SECTION   Sc 1 100

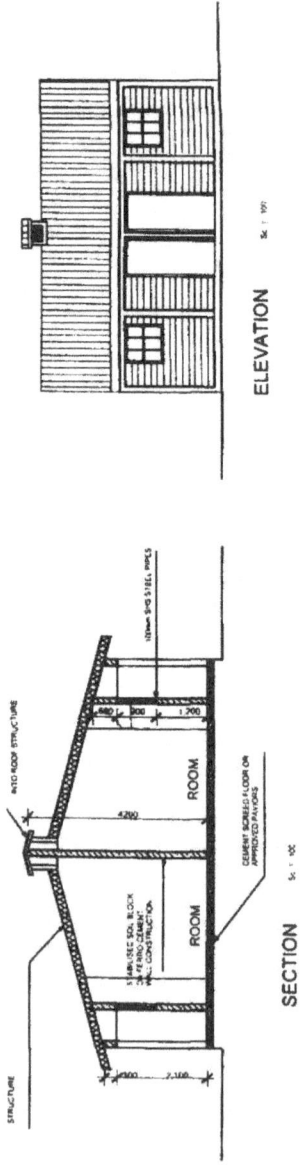

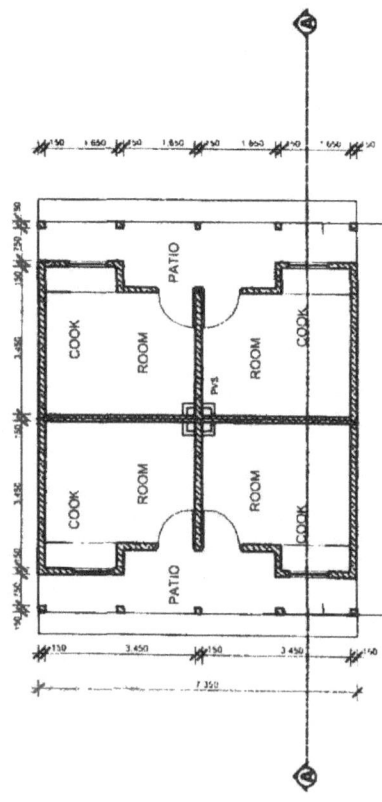

FLOOR PLAN   Sc 1 100

Figure 8   A block of four single rooms with cooking facilities

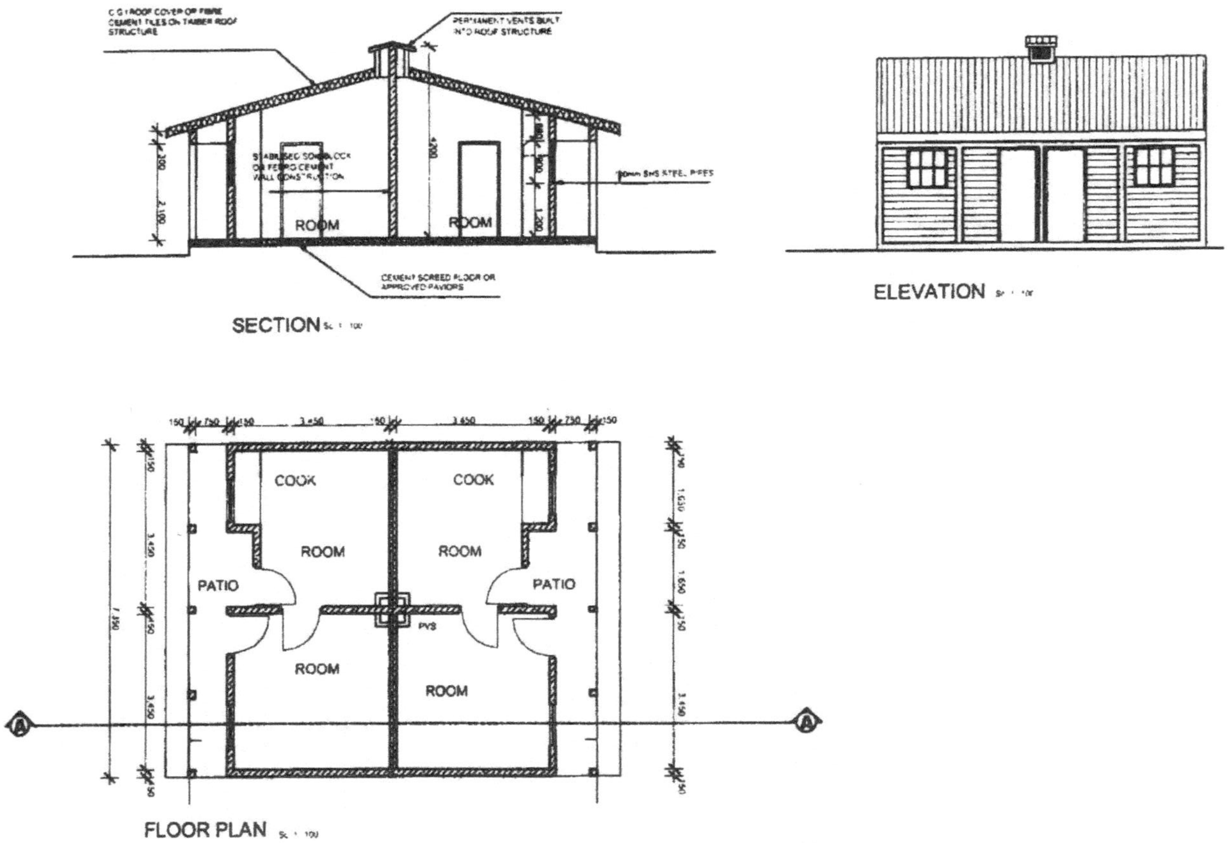

C.G.I. ROOF COVER OF FIBRE
CEMENT TILES ON TIMBER ROOF
STRUCTURE

PERMANENT VENTS BUILT
INTO ROOF STRUCTURE

38mm SHS STEEL PIPES

ROOM

ROOM

CEMENT SCREED FLOOR OR
APPROVED PAVIORS

S KIRTING SCREEN COCK
ON FED CEMENT
WALL CONSTRUCTION

SECTION sc 1 100

ELEVATION sc 1 100

FLOOR PLAN sc 1 100

PATIO

COOK

ROOM

PVB

ROOM

ROOM

COOK

ROOM

PATIO

Figure 9   A block of two double rooms with separate entrances for each room to enable subletting

ELEVATION

SECTION

FLOOR PLAN

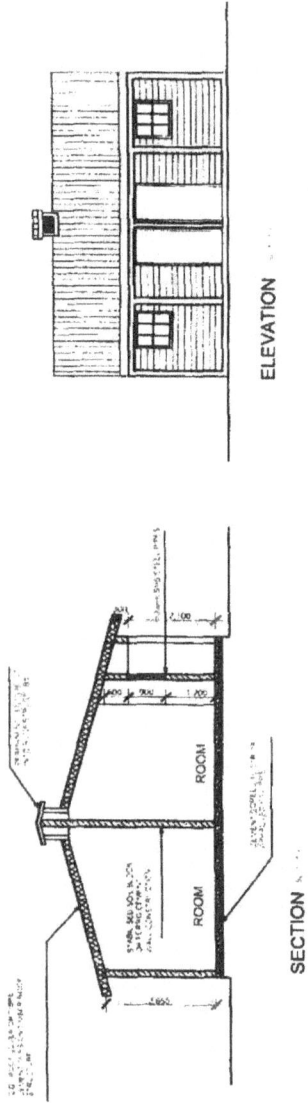

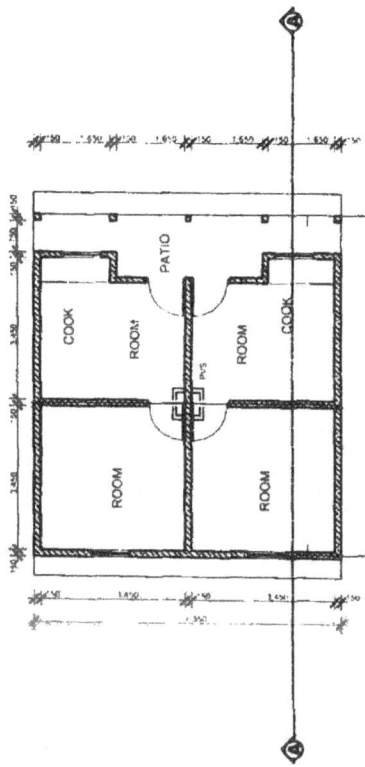

Figure 10 There was also demand for a double room unit that was side by side

Source: ITDG Kenya

Most users preferred to use stone and corrugated iron sheets, because they are the cheapest, readily available materials. Timber is readily available, but its use is limited as it is fairly expensive. In addition, most artisans are not familiar with timber, and find it cumbersome and uneconomical. Sisal is readily available in the Nakuru area for the manufacture of fibre cement tiles/sheets, products with a higher thermal performance than galvanized corrugated iron sheets. However, these materials are hardly used, and most users were not even aware of their existence. The use of stabilized soil blocks seems to have been inspired by a visit to Nairobi. Although the soil type in Nakuru may not be the best quality for SSBs, some people are currently experimenting with this material. This area is worth exploring; in fact, there are already structures that were built in the 1930s with walls of soil blocks reinforced with hay. Rammed earth construction is another area that can be investigated.

The sanitary conditions in Kwa Rhoda, Kaptembwa, and to a lesser degree Mwariki are deplorable. One step that can be taken is to make a regulation that a waste soak-pit must be constructed on each plot. In this way the current practice, where all waste water from plots flows on to the roads, so making the roads impassable, will be restricted. From a public health point of view it is recommended that pit latrines be constructed at the rate of 4 rooms (doors) per pit and 4 to 6 rooms per shower. The type of latrine with masonry walls to the pit that allows for seepage into the ground and can also be exhausted is recommended.

The control of the urban edge in most of the peri-urban areas presents a design problem in as far as the streetscapes are concerned. It may be necessary to have no building lines but make it mandatory that space be left free of any buildings at the entrance to each plot. It is also necessary to allow a certain percentage of plots, say 40 per cent, in these areas to be of mixed use, that is, commercial-cum-residential. Experience has shown that on nearly every plot, some kind of commercial activity seems to take place. It should be formalized by allowing mixed uses and so improve job opportunities. Another area that needs to be addressed is the demand for practising urban agriculture. Many users in the three areas of the study practised zero grazing and/or chicken rearing. To what degree should these practices be allowed and, if they were, should there be specific zones in any given settlement?

Design innovations include:

Creation of cross-ventilation in a single room   The traditional multi-purpose lettable single room presents problems of cross-ventilation, as it is accessed and lit from one side only. Working with the Nakuru-based design group, it was possible to design a room that affords cross-ventilation by introducing permanent vent/s on the opposite side of the window opening.

Creation of covered walkway   The traditional rooms have no overhang from the roof to give protection from the elements. By introducing a covered walkway, doors/windows and the walls are protected against weathering. The covered walkway can also double up as an outdoor cooking/sitting room.

Introduction of soak-pit per plot   The wastewater disposal from each site has a direct effect on the general drainage system of a given neighbourhood. The introduction of a soak-pit on every plot for wastewater disposal makes sure that there is little or no spillover to the street and helps to improve the sanitary conditions of the neighbourhood. The construction of proper sidewalk drains along all streets will take care of the street water run-off.

Masonry-walled pit latrine   The traditional pit latrine, particularly in the volcanic Nakuru soils, is susceptible to collapsing. By introducing the masonry-walled pit, it is possible to allow the sullage to drain into the ground.

Design clinics

With the aim of making architects use low-cost technologies within the scope of Code '95 and the principles of performance standards, an arrangement was made with the Architectural Association of Kenya for their members to hold design clinics in Nakuru's unplanned settlements. AAK's response was enthusiastic, as the clinics would give their members in private practice the opportunity to interact with poor people and also help them to promote a more compassionate and caring image. The specific objectives of the clinics from ITDG Kenya's point of view were:

- to build awareness of revised by-laws, design principles and appropriate building technologies
- to share insights and perspectives of area-specific design preferences of community-based groups/housing agents
- to develop area-specific type plans based on affordable housing technologies
- to develop an action plan for building on partnerships in the design and implementation of affordable housing.

A pre-planning session was held on 11 March 1999 in the Stem Hotel on the outskirts of Nakuru between 8.30 p.m. and 9.30 p.m. Present at this session were:

MCN Team	Municipal Engineer
	Public Health Officer
	Works Officer
AAK Team	Architect
	Quantity Surveyor
	Engineer
ITDG Team	Co-ordinator
	Architect
	Three support staff

Introductions were carried out and the allocation of duties and tasks deliberated and confirmed. The second day of the programme was spent on plenary sessions held at the Genevieve Hotel. The sessions were organized so that the Community-Based Organizations (CBOs) presented their user needs first in order to set the clinic's agenda and also to establish the lingua franca of the deliberations. Pre-field working groups were also formed on the second day. The third day was devoted to field surveys and the preparation of urban design proposals, whose findings were then finally presented in a plenary session that marked the end of the deliberations.

Bondeni Working Group

Of all the scheduled areas for the application of the revised by-laws, Bondeni presents peculiar problems. It was established in 1902 by the colonial government with a leasehold title for 99 years. There are 97 plots in Bondeni, each measuring approximately 15m × 30m. The built environment of Bondeni, like any other settlement of a similar age, needs improving.

The Bondeni working group, including members of the CBO, carried out a survey on 13 March 1999 and held a meeting at Mama Fatuma's house. It was evident that they had a 'Mji Wa Kale Co-operative Housing Society' whose vice-chairman, Mr Mohamed Ali, was present. The current arrangement on any plot is that the landlord occupies some of the rooms and lets out the rest to tenants. The plot owners generally want to build their own houses with provision for lettable units. Mama Fatuma believed that they should build four self-contained bedsitters on the ground floor and four on the upper floor. The landlord could then occupy one or two of the units and let out the rest.

The residents thought that, in addition to providing water to each plot, there should be provision for a communal municipal water kiosk for selling water. The plots that have two road frontages could be designed to have commercial activities on the ground floor. Allowance should be made to accommodate 'Jua Kali' (i.e. informal business) activities. In general the whole settlement needs to be resurveyed and replanned. Through the co-operative society the members are willing to borrow funds for realizing this project.

Lanet/Lakeview Working Group

Mr John Mutio presented the views of the Lanet CBO. It was made clear that this organization started as the Lanet Cleaners' Group, with the aim of maintaining cleanliness in their neighbourhood with the support of MNC. The members clean every Tuesday between 9 a.m. and 12 noon. They would like to build a church, a chief's office, or improve the Lion-Hill Nursery School. There has previously been no initiative in the area of housing construction, although they are now beginning to focus on this area. Lanet adjoins the Lake Nakuru National Park, Kabacia Estate, Nairobi–Nakuru Highway. The plot sizes are generally 24.4m × 36.6m. Currently the buildings in Lanet are stone and mud-walled with iron sheet roofs. The CBO proposed that Mr Kanari's plot, which measures 24m × 36m, could be used to construct a demonstration house using stabilized soil blocks. The preferred unit was a residential house with rental rooms. The monthly rent for a 3.6m × 3.6m room whose walls are plastered is KSh600 or KSh800 if the walls are made of stone and KSh200 for mud wall construction. Dorcas Muthoni's plot, which measures 24m × 30m, could also be considered as a demonstration house, although she prefers to build rental houses. Generally the areas have piped water and have been surveyed – survey plans are easily available – but have poor security.

The Lakeview group was led by Mr Clement Njuguna. The Lakeview Environment Group was formed in 1993. Its members initially carried out cleaning exercises three times a week. MNC has given them a site for their operations, on which they are requesting ITDG to facilitate the construction of a physical structure. The group has in the past collaborated with Kenya Wildlife Services in the upgrading of their roads, and within their operational site they would like to build their environment office and market stalls for the women. The range of residential plot sizes is 0.4ha., 0.2ha., 0.1ha. and 5000 sq.m. The preferred unit type is a two-roomed flexible unit, which can be built as a demonstration house at their community ground. They also propose to build a nursery school, social hall and market stalls on the same site. The Lakeview group has a helping hand from WWF, KWS, MCN and Friends of Lake Nakuru.

Kwa Rhoda Working Group

Mr Daudi Kimemu presented the views of the Kwa Rhoda Neighbourhood Group. The main problem for this neighbourhood is disposing of rubbish, as they do not have any rubbish disposal chambers. There is also a problem with storm water from uphill. ITDG has facilitated the construction of four houses, a fifth house is under construction, while other two members are ready to start building their houses. The neighbourhood has its own block making machine and is networking with other groups, such as NACHU. Most of the plots in Kwa Rhoda measure approximately half an acre (35 × 60m), and the preferred design is the integrated type, which is a combination of shops and rental rooms. Solutions are also needed for solid and liquid waste, washing area and drying lines.

Based on the user needs analysis and the resultant area-based design briefs, some basic design types were created. Critical in these typologies is the plot layout, as the individual unit design is basically a combination of single or double rooms. In Kwa Rhoda the plots are generally large and three layout options have been proposed, including the corner plot solution. In Lanet a solution has been proposed for the typical 24.4m × 36.6m plot, while in Lakeview a proposal has been made for the smallest plot size, 15.24m × 30.48m. There has been no proposal for the layout of Bondeni as this particular settlement requires further discussion and clear strategies to upgrade it. Its historical background, culture and social fabric will all have to be taken into account in whatever strategy is proposed. It is important that these matters are resolved before work starts in order to avoid a situation that occurred in some projects in Nairobi, where the people are disillusioned with upgrading because plots are taken up by new immigrants, renters are displaced and infrastructure costs are generally unaffordable.

In general the proposals are that the built up area should not be more than 50 per cent of the plot size because all these areas are not sewered and are zoned as high-density areas. The current practice of most plot owners is to pack as many rooms as possible on each plot, some achieving as much as 90 rooms per plot in Kwa Rhoda. This practice is driven by greed, and does not take account of the user needs, apart from providing shelter from the elements. By restricting the built up area to 50 per cent of the plot size, it is possible to have ample space for sanitary facilities, landscaped gardens and children's play area. The soft landscaped gardens will enhance the concept of green cities.

At the unit design level, single occupancy rooms have been provided with a cooking and washing corner, including a patio at the entrance door. Although several members of the Kwa Rhoda neighbourhood group were opposed to the idea of a cooking/washing corner, this view was based on a reluctance to spend any more money on the construction of the room and ignored the needs of the end user (tenant). In terms of material use, most people in Kenya, and therefore CBOs, act by example. In fact, the popularity of SSBs and ferro-cement in Kwa Rhoda was because of the exchange visit to demonstration schemes in Nairobi and Kajiado. As this technology is now accepted in Nakuru, the proposal is that these materials should also be used in Lanet and Lakeview.

Results

The initiatives undertaken in Nakuru by community-based organizations with the support of ITDG Kenya, the Municipal Council and the Architectural Association of Kenya had a wide range of effects, as discussed in Chapter 3. The participatory design activities enhanced the opportunities offered by the revised code and appropriate building technologies. They also made it possible to experiment with new ways of creating partnerships between people, local government, the professions and NGOs. A basis was created for further collaboration in other neighbourhoods, while ITDG Kenya and AAK have negotiated a co-operation agreement that will enable them to work together in other parts of Kenya, where the type plans developed and ideas generated will also be useful.

Photo 10   A development in Kwa Rhoda, Nakuru, with shops at the front and rooms at the back.

Appendix 5

Comparison of pre-1992 and post-1992 low-income housing schemes in Harare, Zimbabwe

Aspect	Pre-1992	Post-1992
Building plans and designs	• 83 per cent provided by Harare City Council • No personal input into design • 50 per cent feel the need to reposition their houses on the plots • 55 per cent wanted to increase the number of rooms rather than the size of the rooms – to make it easier to accommodate lodgers • Building lines are largely 3m for the front and 1.5m at the back • Plinth size is about 70 square metres	• 4 per cent acquired plans from Harare City Council. Most were from building societies, or Ministry of Public Construction and National Housing • Very little personal contribution to the design of the houses • Building lines were about 1.5m at the front and minimum 1m at the back • 41 per cent of houses were below 51 square metres in plinth size • Smaller plots introduced in 1992 were improving access to low-income housing (28 per cent), though most people felt that smaller plots did not improve affordability
Construction materials	• 94 per cent of houses had polished cement floors • Walling material included common bricks, cement blocks • Asbestos main roofing material	• Floors of variable materials • Walling materials included steel frames, stabilized terra blocks • PVC used for piping as it is cheaper than steel
Construction process	• Hired builders • Plot owner purchased construction materials	• Contractors did most of the work (government or those engaged by building societies) • Small scale-contractors also used • Conventional approaches to construction increased costs • Need self-help approach in order to reduce costs

Cost of construction	• 72 per cent cost below Z$71 000 • 79 per cent of plots bought for less than Z$5 000 • Building materials – 70 per cent bought for less than Z$41 000 • Labour costs – 69 per cent for Z$10 000 and below	• 90 per cent of houses bought for Z$13 000–49 000. They are smaller in plinth size • Plots cost around Z$4 000. Plots are much smaller than pre-1992 • Labour costs were around Z$5 000 for the smaller houses
Housing finance	• Main sources were building societies (18 per cent) and own savings (59 per cent) and council loans • Monthly mortgage repayments were around Z$500 per month. Interest rates were high (16–20 per cent)	• 70 per cent was financed from own savings as a condition of the loan • Monthly mortgage rates were Z$224–673. The loans were relatively small
Regulations	• Majority aware of these regulations and their purpose	• Aware

Source: Field survey

References and Bibliography

Abdelhalim, Khaled (1999) 'Standards and Procedures of Housing for the Urban Poor in Egypt'. ITDG, Rugby

Acioly, Claudio C. Jr (1994) 'Incremental Land Development in Brasilia: Can the Urban Poor Escape from Suburbanisation?', *Third World Planning Review*, Vol. 16, No. 3. Liverpool University Press, Liverpool

Agevi, Elijah (1990) 'Statutory Building Regulations: A Situation Analysis and a Tentative Agenda for Action'. ITDG Kenya, Nairobi

Agevi, Elijah (1994) 'Building for Change: Low-cost Housing Regulations in Kenya', *Appropriate Technology*, Vol. 21, No. 2. IT Publications, London

Agevi, Elijah (1995) 'Building Standards and Planning Regulations: The Kenyan Experience', *Journal of the Network of African Countries on Local Building Materials and Technology*, Vol. 3, No. 3 (June). UNCHR Habitat

Agevi, Elijah (1998) 'Emerging Partnerships for Implementing Sustainable Building Standards', Report of the National Workshop on Housing Standards, ITDG Kenya, Nairobi

Agevi, Elijah, and J. Ngari (eds.) (1990) 'Proceedings of the Seminar on Building By-laws and Planning Regulations'. ITDG Kenya, Nairobi

Agevi, Elijah, J. Ngari and L. Muraguri (eds.) (1993) 'Proceedings of the Workshop on Implementation of Revised Building By-laws and Planning Regulations'. Department of Housing/ ITDG Kenya, Nairobi

Agevi, Elijah and Saad Yahya (1997) 'Seeking the Standard Bearer: A Study of Popular Knowledge of Shelter Standards in Kenya', Working Paper 2 on Enabling Housing Standards and Procedures Project. ITDG Kenya, Nairobi

Aka, Jean-Joseph (1996) 'La Normalisation du BTC en Côte d'Ivoire' (Standardization of Stabilized Earth Blocks in the Ivory Coast). CODINORM. Paper presented at Séminaire ACP-UE sur la Normalisation du Bloc de Terre Comprimée , 23–27 April 1996. CDI, Belgium

Amis Philip, and Peter Lloyd (1990) *Housing Africa's Urban Poor.* Manchester University Press

Anderson, Rae (1996) 'Integrating Residence and Work in Building Codes in Canada', *Open House International*, Vol. 21, No. 2. USA

ARSO/CSC/UNCHS (1987) 'Standards and Specifications for Local Building Materials', Report of the ARSO/CSC/UNCHS Workshop, Nairobi, 16–24 March 1987. IT Publications

ASCEND (1996) *Starter Standards Manual.* ASCEND, Office of the Prime Minister, Jamaica

Athman, Mungwe ABC (1992) 'Appropriate Dwelling Standards for Dodoma Low-income Groups in Tanzania'. PGCHS Catholic University, Tanzania

Atkinson, George (1995) *Construction Quality and Quality Standards: The European Perspective*. E&FN Spon, London

Banerjee, Banashree, and Gita Dewan Verma (1994) 'Three Indian Cases of Upgradeable Plots', *Third World Planning Review*, Vol. 16, No. 3. Liverpool University Press, Liverpool

Barama, Sarr (1996) 'Normalisation des matériaux locaux au Sénégal' (Standardization of Local Materials in Senegal). Institut sénégalais de normalisation, Dakar. Paper presented at Séminaire ACP-UE sur la Normalisation du Bloc de Terre Comprimée, 23–27 April 1996. CDI, Belgium

Baransaka, Daniel (1996) 'Le BTC, a-t-il une place dans le programme de reconstruction et de relance du développement du Burundi?' (The Stabilized Soil Block: Does it Have a Role in the Reconstruction and Enhanced Development of Burundi?). SIP (Société de Droit Public). Paper presented at Séminaire ACP-UE sur la Normalisation du Bloc de Terre Comprimée, 23–27 April 1996. CDI, Belgium

Barritt, C.M.H. (1995) *The Building Acts and Regulations Applied. Houses and Flats*, Longman Group, Harlow

Botswana, Republic of (1990) 'Impact of Design Standards on Costs of Urban Development on Botswana'. USAID, East and South Africa, PADCO, Washington, D. C.

BRE (1994) *Thermal Insulation: Avoiding Risks*. Building Research Establishment Report, HMSO, London

Briggs, A. (1990) *Victorian Cities*. Penguin Books, London

Burga, Jorge (1987) 'Las urbanizaciones populares', *Huaca*, No.1. Peru

Butcher, C. (1986) 'Low-income Housing in Zimbabwe: A Case Study of the Epworth Squatter Upgrading Scheme'. RUP Occasional Paper, University of Zimbabwe, Harare

Byaruhanga, E. (1998) 'The Current Review Process of the Building and Planning Regulations in Uy. ITDG, Rugby

Clauson-Kaas, Jes, Charles Surfadi, Niels Højlyng, Anton Baarl, Andre Dzikus, Henrik Jensen, Peter Aaby and Carolyn Stephens (1997) 'Crowding and Health in Low-income Settlements, Kali Anyar, Jakarta'. UNCHS (Habitat), Ashgate Publishing Ltd, Avebury

Chilowa, W. (1992) 'Socio-economic Survey of Ndirande Squatter Upgrading Area: Blantyre'. Centre for Social Research, University of Malawi

Cotton, A.P. (1998) 'Community Initiatives in Urban Infrastructure'. Water, Engineering and Development Centre (WEDC), Loughborough University

Crooke, P. (1981) 'Low-income Housing in Malawi: An Evaluation of British Aided Programmes'. Overseas Development Administration, London

De Soto, Hernando (1989) *The Other Path*. I.B. Tauris & Co., London

Diagne, Mamadou (1998) 'Building Codes and Planning Regulations in Senegal'. ITDG, Rugby

Díaz G., Anibal (1984) 'Normalización'. Instituto Nacional de Investigación y Normalización de la Vivienda (ININVI) promotional material

Djabbar, O.S. (1990) 'Basic Factors Determining Housing Standards in Tashkent', *IHS News*. Rotterdam

Dowall, David (1992) 'The Benefits of Minimal Land Development Regulation', *Habitat International*, Vol. 16, No. 4. Pergamon Press, London

Durand-Lasserve Alain (1996) 'Regularization and the Integration of Irregular Settlements: Lessons from Experience'. UMP/UNCHS, Working Paper, Series 6

Economic Commission for Africa (1990) 'Status of Building Codes in Some Countries of Africa. Addis Ababa'. Unpublished consultant's report. ECA, October 1990

El-Batran, Manal, and Christian Chandel (April 1998) 'A Shelter of Their Own: Informal Settlements Expansion in Greater Cairo and Government Responses', *Environment and Urbanisation*, Vol. 10, No. 1

ESCAP (1979) *'Guidelines for Human Settlements'*. Expert Group Meeting on Standards for Human Settlement, Bangkok 11–17 December 1979. UNCHS

Fattal, S.G. (1998) 'Use of Stabilized Adobe Block and Cane in Construction of Low-Cost Housing in Peru'. Center for Building Technology (IAT), Washington, D. C., USA

Fernandes, Edesio (1995) *Law and Urban Change in Brazil*. Ashgate Publishing, Aldershot

Fernandes, Edesio, and Ann Varley (1998) *Illegal Cities, Law and Urban Change in Developing Countries*. Zed Books, London

Gambia, the, Ministry for Local Government and Lands (1995) 'Laws and Regulations', Information leaflets, Banjul, The Gambia

Ganesan, S. (1979) *Growth of Housing and Construction Centres*. Pergamon Press, London

Goldberg, A. (1990) 'Building Codes versus Affordable Housing: The Silent Conflict', *Building Standards*, Vol. LIX, No. 3. International Conference of Building Officials, California, USA

Goodchild, Barry (1997) *Housing and the Urban Environment: A Guide to Housing Design, Renewal and Urban Planning*. Blackwell Science, Oxford

Gross, James G. (1991) 'Codes, Standards and Institutions: Pressures for Change', *Journal of Professional Issues in Engineering, Education and Practice*, Vol. 117, No. 2. ASCE Publications, Restoni, USA

Guasch, J. Luis, and Robert W. Hahn (1999) 'The Costs and Benefits of Regulation: Implications for Developing Countries', *The World Bank Research Observer*, Vol. 14, No.1, pp.137–58

Hahn, Peter (1997) 'Bricks: The Measure of All Things', *Ziegelindustrie International*, No. 8

Hakim, Besim Selim (1986) *Arabic Islamic Cities, Building and Planning Principles*. KPI, London. Reviewed by Brian Brace Taylor in *Mimar: Architecture in Development*

Home, R. (1993) *Transferring British Planning Law to the Colonies*. Liverpool University Press, Liverpool

Institute for Liberty and Democracy (1991) 'Property and Democracy', *Urban Perspectives*, Vol. 2, No. 1. Peru

International Federation of the Red Cross and the Red Crescent Societies (1996) *World Disaster Report 1996*. Oxford University Press, Oxford

International Legal Center (1972) *Law and Development: The Future of Law and Development Research*. Report of the International Legal Center, New York, USA

Jere, Natan M. (1999) 'The Case in Zambia'. Paper presented at the Enabling Housing Standards and Procedures Workshop, 14–17 June 1999. ITDG, Rugby

Jimenez, Emmanuel (1982) 'The Economics of Self-help Housing: Theory and Some Evidence from a Developing Country'. Reprint from the World Bank with permission from the *Journal of Urban Economics*, Vol.11, pp. 205–28. Washington, D. C.

Keare, D.H., and S. Parris (1982) 'Evaluation of Shelter Program for the Urban Poor: Principal Findings'. World Bank Staff Working Paper 547. Washington, D. C.

Kenya, Ministry of Works and Housing (1996) 'Kenyan National Plan of Action (NPA) for Shelter and Human Settlement' p. 118

Kenya, Republic of (1968) *What is a Drain? The Kenyan Building Code*. The Government Printer, Nairobi

Kenya, Republic of (1980) 'Kenya Low-cost Housing By-law Study'. Report, 2 vols. Ministry of Lands and Housing, Nairobi

Kenya, Republic of (1986) 'Kenya Low-income Housing By-laws Review', Nairobi

Kenya, Republic of (1993) 'Building By-laws and Planning Regulations Reviews'. Final Report, Interministerial Task Force, Nairobi

Kenya Workshop (1997) 'Seeking the Standard Bearer'. Report on Enabling Standards and Procedures Workshop in Kenya, 24–25 March, 1997, Lenana Conference Centre, Nairobi'. Building Materials and Shelter Programme, IT Kenya, Nairobi

Kingdom of Lesotho (1990) *Planning Standards for Lesotho*. Physical Planning Division, Department of Lands, Surveys and Physical Planning, Lesotho

Kioe-Sheng, Yap (1982) 'Leases, Land and Local Leaders: An Analysis of Squatter Settlements Upgrading Programmes in Karachi'. Vrije Universiteit Amsterdam, The Netherlands

Kioe-Sheng, Yap (November 1994) 'The Million Houses Programme in Sri Lanka', *RRA Notes*, No. 21. Special Issue on Participatory Tools and Methods in Urban Areas. IIED, London

Knowles C.C., and P.H. Pitt (1972) *The History of Building Regulation in London 1189–1972*. Architectural Press, London

Kraayenbrink, Elizabeth (1998) 'A South African Solution to Standards', *Basin News* No. 15. SKAT, St Gallen, Switzerland

Kraayenbrink, Elizabeth (1999) 'Standards Review in South Africa'. Paper presented at the Enabling Housing Standards and Procedures Workshop, 14–17 June 1999. ITDG, Rugby

Kuete Sonkoue, Maurice (1996) 'L'Expérience de Terkocam Face à la Normalisation du BTC'. (TERKOCAM's Experience Faced with the Standardization of Stabilized Earth Blocks). TERKOCAM. Paper presented at Séminaire ACP-UE sur la Normalisation du Bloc de Terre Comprimée, 23–27 April 1996. CDI, Belgium

Lall Stuti (1999) 'Housing Standards for the Poor'. Paper presented at the Enabling Housing Standards and Procedures Workshop, 14–17 June 1999. ITDG, Rugby

Laquian, Aprodicio (1983) 'Building Codes and Housing Standards' in *Basic Housing: Policies for Urban Sites*. International Development Research Center, Ottawa, Canada.

Lowe, Lucky (1995) 'Building Standards and Housing Provision in Less Developed Countries'. Cranfield University

Lowe, Lucky (1998a) 'Earth Building Standards in Africa'. Case study No. 1 prepared for the ITDG Enabling Housing Standards and Procedures Project, ITDG, Rugby

Lowe, Lucky (1998b) 'Jamaica: A case study on regulation and review', *Basin News* No. 15. SKAT, St Gallen, Switzerland

Lowe, Lucky (1999a) Interview with Mr N'gunjiri, Engineer, Nakuru Municipal Council, Kenya

Lowe, Lucky (1999b) Telephone interview with Mr R. Holdsworth, Building Control Officer, Cherwell District Council

Lowe, Lucky (1999c) 'Literature Review'. Enabling Housing Standards and Procedures Project, ITDG. ITDG, Rugby

Mabogunje, Akin, R.P. Misra and J.E. Hardoy (1976) 'Shelter Provision in Developing Countries: The Influence of Standards and Criteria'. Scope 11, International Council of Scientific Unions (ICSU). John Wiley & Sons, London

Mafico, C.J.C. (1989) 'An Evaluation of Urban Planning Standards for Low-income Housing in Zimbabwe'. RUP Occasional Paper, University of Zimbabwe, Harare

Mafico, C.J.C. (1991) *Urban Low-income Housing in Zimbabwe.* Avebury

Mapedza, E. (1998) 'A Comparative Analysis of the pre- and post- 1992 Housing Schemes'. ITDG, Zimbabwe

Martin, Richard (1980) 'Standards: Can They Be Made Relevant?'. Paper presented at the Conference towards a National Housing Policy, 3–8 March 1980, Arusha International Conference Centre, Centre for Housing Studies, Tanzania

Matthews Glenn, Jane and Jeanne M. Wolfe (1996) 'The Growth of the Informal Sector and Regularization of Spontaneous Development', *Third World Planning Review*, Vol. 18, No. 1. Liverpool University Press, Liverpool

Matthews Glenn, Jane, Ronald P. Labossiere and Jeanne M. Wolfe (1993) 'Squatter Regularization: Problems and Prospects. A Case Study from Trinidad', *Third World Planning Review*,Vol. 15, No. 3. Liverpool University Press, Liverpool

Mbiriri, P.I. (1990) 'Costs and Standards: Whose Costs and Whose Standards? A Glance at the Future'. ZIRUP, Harare

McHardy, Pauline (1998) 'Revising Development Standards in Jamaica'. Case study No. 7 prepared for the ITDG Enabling Housing Standards and Procedures Project. ITDG, Rugby

Mehta, Banjor, Banashree C. Mitra and Peter Nientied (1989) *Building Regulations and Low-income Housing: A Case Study from India.* Butterworth & Co., London

Mercado, Rodolfo and Ricardo Uzín (1996) 'Regularization of Spontaneous Settlements', *Building Issues*, Vol. 8, No. 2. Lund Centre for Habitat Studies, Sweden

Messick, Richard E. (1999) 'Judicial Reform and Economic Development: A Survey of Issues', *The World Bank Research Observer*, Vol. 14, pp. 117–36

Mitra, Banashree C. (1990) 'Impact of Tenure Regularization and Environmental Upgrading Programmes on Shelter Consolidation in Squatter Settlements in Bhopal', *Open House International*, Vol. 15, No. 4

Mohammed, Asad (1997) *Problems in Translating NGO Successes into Government Settlement Policy: Illustrations from Trinidad and Tobago and Jamaica.* IIED, London

Moudzingoula, Joseph (1996) 'Situation de la Réglementation des Normes des Blocs de Terre Comprimée au Congo' (The Position of Regularization of Stabilized Earth Blocks Standards in Congo). Ministry of Industrial Development of Energy, Congo. Paper presented at Séminaire ACP-UE sur la Normalisation du Bloc de Terre Comprimée, 23–27 April 1996. CDI, Belgium

Mshila, D.L. (1997) 'Community Land Trust Project Upgrading of Tanzania Bondeni Settlement in Voi'. Ministry of Local Government and GTZ, Nairobi

Mubvami, Takawira (1999) 'Evaluation of the ITDG Project on Enabling Housing Standards and Procedures'. ITDG Zimbabwe

Mugova, Alex, and Oscar Musandu-Nyamayaro (1997) 'Housing Standards Review Processes and Procedures in Zimbabwe'. ITDG Working Paper No. 1 on Enabling Housing Standards and Procedures Project. ITDG Zimbabwe, Harare

Mugova, Alex and Oscar Musandu-Nyamayaro (1998) 'Housing Urban People in Zimbabwe – a Handbook of Housing Application Procedures and Building Processes'. ITDG Zimbabwe, Harare

Mugova, Alex and Oscar Musandu-Nyamayaro (1999) 'A Case Study based on Project Experience', ITDG Case Study No.13 on Enabling Housing Standards and Procedures Project. ITDG Zimbabwe, Harare

Musandu-Nyamayaro, O. (1993) 'Housing Design Standards for Low-income Housing Delivery in Zimbabwe', *Third World Planning Review*, Vol.15. Liverpool University, Liverpool

Musandu-Nyamayaro, O. (1994) 'Procedural Impediments to Low-income Housing Delivery in Zimbabwe'. Paper presented at European Network on Housing Research, Birmingham

Mutizwa-Mangiza, N.D. (1985) 'An Analysis of Low-income Housing Strategies in Harare, Zimbabwe'. Paper presented at UWIST, Cardiff, Wales

Nagarajan, R. (1976) *Standards in Building*. Pitman Publishing, London

Nzinahora, Gervais (1996) ' La Problématique de l'Élaboration de Normes: cas du BBN' (The Problems of Developing Standards; the Case of Burundi Standards Bureau). BBN, Burundi. Paper presented at Séminaire ACP-UE sur la Normalisation du Bloc de Terre Comprimée, 23–27 April 1996. CDI, Belgium

Okonkwo, Osita (1999) 'Building Codes and Planning Regulations Review in Malawi'. Case study No.5 prepared for the ITDG Enabling Housing Standards and Procedures Project, ITDG, Rugby

Patel, D. (1985) 'Evaluation of Kuwadzana Low-income Shelter Project Phase 1'. Report for USAID, Harare

Pennant, Thomas (1990) 'The Growth of Small-scale Renting in Low-income urban Housing in Malawi' in Philip Amis and Peter Lloyd (eds.) *Housing Africa's Urban Poor*. Manchester University Press, Manchester

Peru, Ministerio de Vivienda y Construcción (1977) 'Normas de Diseño Sismo Resistente: Construcciones de Adobe'. Ministerio de Vivienda y Construcción, Peru

Phillipe, Jonathan (1986) 'Beijing', *Mimar: Architecture in Development* January–March 1986, Special supplement

Potts, Deborah (1994) 'Urban Environmental Controls and Low-income Housing in Southern Africa' in H. Main and S.W. Williams (eds.) *Environment and Housing in Third World Cities*. John Wiley & Sons, London

Potts, Deborah and C.C. Mutambirwa (1991) *High-density Housing in Harare: Commodification and Overcrowding*. Liverpool University Press, Liverpool

Rakodi, Carole (undated) 'Housing Production and Housing Policy in Harare, Zimbabwe'

Rakodi, Carole and P. Withers (1986) 'Sites and Services: Home Ownership for the Poor? Issues for Evaluation and the Zimbabwean Experience', *Habitat International*, Vol. 19, No. 3, pp. 317–89

Reimers, Carlos, and Maria Portela (1995) 'Progressive Development in Housing: Planned vs Unplanned Settlements', *Open House International*, Vol. 20, No. 4

Rezende, Marisa B.G.M. (1993) 'Decentralized Popular Planning: A Strategy for Change', *Habitat International*, Vol. 17, No. 3. Pergamon Press, London

Romangnolo, Philippe (1996) 'Normalisation et formation: un tandem nécessaire à la diffusion du BTC'. (Standardization and Training: a Necessary Tandem in the Dissemination of Stabilized Earth Blocks). Art'Terre. Paper presented at Séminaire ACP-UE sur la Normalisation du Bloc de Terre Comprimée, 23–27 April 1996. CDI, Belgium

Rotters, H. (1994) 'Manual on Development Control Regulations'. The Dwelling House in the Gambia

Royal Institute of British Architects (1983) *Homes for the Future*. RIBA, London

Rwelamilla, P.M.D. (1996) 'Quality Management in the Public Building Construction Process'. Ph.D. Thesis, University of Cape Town.

Saad, Hamman Tukur (1991) 'Between Myth and Reality: The Aesthetics of Architecture in Hausaland'. Dissertation work, Doctoral Program in Architecture, College of Architecture and Urban Planning, University of Michigan, Ann Arbor

Salama, Rafik (1998) 'Understanding Public Housing Transformation in Egypt', *Open House International*

Schilderman, Theo (1992) 'Housing Standards: Can They be Appropriate?', *Appropriate Technology Journal*. IT Publications, London

Schilderman, Theo (1998) *Standards and Procedures*. IT Publications, London

Schilderman, Theo (1999) Minutes of the End of Project of the Enabling Housing Standards and Procedures Workshop, 14–17 June 1999. ITDG, Rugby

Senegal, Ministry of Urban Planning and Housing (1996) *Urban Upgrading and Land Legalization in Senegal*. Dakar

Sherer, S.A. (1987) *Legal and Administrative Issues Regarding Land and Housing Development in Bangkok*. PADCO, Bangkok

Shirong, Li, and Wei Ming (1999) 'A Brief Induction to the Administration System of Housing in China'. Case study No. 8 prepared for the ITDG Enabling Housing Standards and Procedures Project, ITDG, Rugby

Shove, Elizabeth (1998) 'Constructing Regulation and Regulating for Energy Efficient Construction'. End of Award Report, CSEC, Lancaster University

Siddiqui, Tasneem A., and M. Azhar Khan (1994) 'The Incremental Development Scheme', *Third World Planning Review*, Vol. 16, No. 3. Liverpool University, Liverpool

Siebolds, Peter and Florian Steinberg (1982) 'Tanzania: Sites and Service', *Habitat International*, Vol. 6, No. 1/2. Pergamon Press, London

Sirivardana, Susil (1999) 'Sri Lanka Housing Standards Study (1984–94)'. Case study No.9 prepared for the ITDG Enabling Housing Standards and Procedures Project. ITDG, Rugby

South Africa, Republic of (RSA) (1997) *Urban Development Framework*. Department of Housing, Pretoria

Swazuri, M. (1999) 'ESHP project evaluation'. ITDG Kenya, Nairobi

Syagga, P.M., and J.M. Malombe (1995) 'Development of Informal Housing in Kenya'. Case Studies of Kisumu and Nakuru Towns. University of Nairobi

Tanzania Housing Bank (1978) *House Type Designs for Site and Services Project in Tanzania*. Tanzania Housing Bank, Tanzania

Tanzania, Ministry of Works (1977) *Regulations, Standards, Research and Information*. Ministry of Works, Dar es Salaam, Tanzania

Tiemoko, Yamba (1996) 'La Construction en Terre au Burkina Faso' (Earth Construction in Burkina Faso). LOCOMAT. Paper presented at Séminaire ACP–UE sur la Normalisation du Bloc de Terre Comprimée, 23–27 April 1996. CDI, Belgium

Tipple, A. Graham (1999) 'Urban Poverty Alleviation and Housing Creation' in S. Jones and N. Nelson (eds.) *Urban Poverty in Africa*. IT Publications, London

Tipple, A. Graham, and Shahidul Ameen Md., (1999) 'User Initiated Extension Activity in Bangladesh: "Building Slums" or Area Improvement?', *Environment and Urbanisation* Vol. 11, No.1

Turner, J. (1976) *Housing by People: Towards Autonomy in Building Environment.* Marion Boyars, London

Uganda, Ministry of Lands (1992) 'A National Shelter Strategy for Uganda: Vol. 1 & 2'. Department of Housing and Urban Development, Kampala, Uganda

UK (1961) *Home for Today and Tomorrow.* HMSO, London

UNCHS (undated) 'The Social Impact of Housing Goals Standards and Housing Indicators and Popular Participation'. UNCHS (Habitat), Nairobi

UNCHS *Co-operation in the African Region on Technologies and Standards for Local Building Materials.* UNCHS (Habitat),Nairobi, Kenya

UNCHS (1976) 'A New Agenda for Human Settlements', Global Conference, Vancouver, Canada

UNCHS (1980) 'UN Seminar of Experts on Building Codes and Regulation in Developing Countries: How Building Codes and Regulations can be Adapted to meet the Basic Needs of the Poor', 17–24 March 1980. UNCHS (Habitat), Sweden

UNCHS (1981) *Building Codes and Regulation in Developing Countries.* UNCHS (Habitat), Nairobi

UNCHS (1985) *The Reformulation of Building Acts, Regulations and Codes in African Countries.* UNCHS (Habitat), Nairobi

UNCHS (1986) 'The Land Sharing Projects in Bangkok' in *Rehabilitation of Inner City Areas: Feasible Strategies.* UNCHS (Habitat), Nairobi

UNCHS (1996) *The Habitat Agenda, Goals and Principles, Commitments and Global Plan of Action.* UNCHS (Habitat), Nairobi

UNCHS (1997) 'The Istanbul Declaration and The Habitat Agenda. United Nations Conference on Human Settlements (Habitat II)'. Istanbul, Turkey 3–14 June 1996, UNCHS (Habitat), Nairobi

UNECA and Shelter Afrique (1996) *Continental Shelter Atlas for Africa. Nairobi.* Economic Commission for Africa, Ethiopia

United Kingdom Department of the Environment and the Welsh Office (1992) *The Building Regulations 1991; Materials and Workmanship.* HMSO, London

United Kingdom Department of the Environment and the Welsh Office (1992) *The Building Standards 1991 M, Access and Facilities for Disabled People.* HMSO, London

United Nations Economic Commission for Africa (1985) 'Indicators for Revised Building Codes and Regulations in Africa'. A paper presented at the third meeting of the Joint Intergovernmental Regional Committee on Human Settlements and Environment, Addis Ababa, 22–26 July 1985

US Department of Housing and Urban Development (1996) *State of the Nation's Cities.* Washington, D. C.

Van Nostrand, John (1982) *Old Naledi: The Village Becomes Town.* James Lorimer and Co., Canada

Walker, P.J. (1995) 'Standard Performance Criteria for Stabilized Soil Blocks'. University of New England, Australia. Paper presented at the fourth Australian Masonry Conference, 23–24 November 1995

Wanjohi, Patrick (1997) ' The Health Impacts of Improved Maasai Housing'. ITDG Kenya, Nairobi

Williams, S.W. in H. Main (1994) *Environment and Housing in Third World Cities.* John Wiley & Sons, London

Wodobode, Jean-Prosper (1996) Speech by J.-P. Wodobode (Ministère des Travaux Publics, Bangui, Rep. Centrafricaine) made at the Séminaire ACP-UE sur la Normalisation du Bloc de Terre Comprimée, 23–27 April 1996. CDI, Belgium

World Bank (1993) *Housing: Enabling Markets to Work.* A World Bank Policy Paper. The International Bank for Reconstruction and Development, World Bank, Washington, D. C.

World Bank (1995) *Better Urban Services: Finding the Right Incentives.* World Bank, Washington, D. C.

World Bank (1995) *Urban Policy and Economic Development: An Agenda for the 1990s.* World Bank, Washington, D. C.

World Bank (1999) *World Development Indicators.* World Bank, Washington, D. C.

World Health Organization (1989) *Health Principles of Housing.* WHO, Geneva

Yahya, Saad (1980) 'Building Codes and Regulations in Kenya'. UNCHS, Sweden. Paper presented at UNCHS Seminar on 'Building Codes and Regulations in Developing Countries', March 1980

Yahya, Saad (1987) 'Review of Building Codes and Regulations – a Manual Based on Kenya's Experience'. HRDU, Nairobi

Yahya, Saad (1998a) 'Enabling Development Control Procedures – An African Overview'. Emerging Partnerships for Implementing Sustainable Building Standards. Elijah Agevi (ed.) 'Report on the National Workshop on Housing Standards', March 1998. ITDG, Nairobi

Yahya, Saad (1998b) 'Enabling Housing Standards for Botswana'. Case study No. 4 prepared for the ITDG Enabling Housing Standards and Procedures Project. ITDG, Rugby

Yahya, Saad and Elijah Agevi (1997) 'Report on Workshop on Enabling Standards and Procedures in Kenya', 24–25 March, 1997, Lenana Conference Centre, Nairobi'. Building Materials and Shelter Programme, ITDG Kenya

Yahya, Saad and Associates (1988) 'Simplified Building Regulations for Somalia'. A UNCHS/SDR project

Yahya, Saad, Elijah Agevi and Josiah Omotto (1999) 'Deemed Satisfaction: Lessons from Housing Standards Revision in Kenya', Case Study No. 11 on Enabling Housing Standards and Procedures Project. ITDG Kenya, Nairobi

Yitna, W.B. (1994) 'Towards Appropriate Design Standards and Planning Regulations for Basic Housing in Ethiopia'. Post-graduate Centre Human Settlements, Leuven

Zambia, Republic of (1996) *National Housing Policy.* Ministry of Local Government and Housing, Lusaka

Zambia, Republic of (1996) *Zambia National Plan of Action Report to Habitat II.* The National Steering Committee, Lusaka

Zimbabwe (1977) *Model Building By-laws.* Government Printers, Harare

Zimbabwe, Ministry of Local Government and National Housing (1981). *Design Approach to Roads and Storm Water Problems Relative to High Density Developments in Zimbabwe Guidelines.* Harare, Zimbabwe

Zimbabwe, Ministry of Public Construction and National Housing (1991) 'Report of Development of Human Settlements in Zimbabwe'. Paper presented at the Thirteenth Session of the United Nations Commission on Human Settlements (Habitat), 29 April–8 May 1991, Harare, Zimbabwe

www.ingramcontent.com/pod-product-compliance
Lightning Source LLC
Chambersburg PA
CBHW052011030426

42334CB00029BA/3175